THE ORIGINALISM TRAP

...e People... of...

...nquility provide for the common defence, promot...
...f ordain and establish this Constitution for the Un...

Article. I.

...legislative Powers herein granted shall be vested i...

...House of Representatives shall be composed of Me...
...have the Qualifications requisite for Electors of the most num...
...shall be a Representative who shall not have attain...
...when elected, be an Inhabitant of that State in which...
...atives and direct Taxes shall be apportioned among the...
...shall be determined by adding to the whole Number of f...
...ljths of all other Persons. The actual Enumeration...
...ry subsequent Term of ten Years, in such Manner as...
...d, but each State shall have at Least one Representa...
...e three; Massachusetts eight; Rhode Island and P...
...vacancies happen in the Representation from any...
...Maryland six; Virginia ten; North Carolin...
...House of Representatives shall chuse their Speaker a...
...The Senate of the United States shall be composed...
...all have one Vote....
...mediately after they shall be assembled in Conseque...
...ators of the first Class shall be vacated at the Expirat...
...l Expiration of the sixth Year, so that one third may b...
...any State, the Executive thereof may m...
...ll not have att...

THE ORIGINALISM TRAP

HOW EXTREMISTS STOLE THE CONSTITUTION AND HOW **WE THE PEOPLE** CAN TAKE IT BACK

MADIBA K. DENNIE

RANDOM HOUSE

NEW YORK

Published in the United States by Random House,
an imprint and division of Penguin Random House LLC, New York.

RANDOM HOUSE and the HOUSE colophon are registered
trademarks of Penguin Random House LLC.

Library of Congress Cataloging-in-Publication Data
Names: Dennie, Madiba K., author.
Title: The originalism trap: how extremists stole the Constitution and how
we the people can take it back / Madiba K. Dennie.
Description: New York: Random House, 2024. | Includes index.
Identifiers: LCCN 2023059052 (print) | LCCN 2023059053 (ebook) |
ISBN 9780593729250 (hardcover) | ISBN 9780593729267 (ebook)
Subjects: LCSH: Constitutional law—United States—Interpretation and
construction. | Originalism (Law)—United States. | United States.
Supreme Court—Cases—History. | Reproductive rights—United States—History.
Classification: LCC KF4552 .D46 2024 (print) | LCC KF4552 (ebook) |
DDC 342.73001—dc23/eng/20240129
LC record available at https://lccn.loc.gov/2023059052
LC ebook record available at https://lccn.loc.gov/2023059053

Printed in the United States of America on acid-free paper

randomhousebooks.com

2 4 6 8 9 7 5 3 1

First Edition

Book design by Jo Anne Metsch

To my mother, who knew I would write a book long before I did.

"We, the people—not we, the white people—not we, the citizens, or the legal voters—not we, the privileged class, and excluding all other classes but we, the people . . . the men and women, the human inhabitants of the United States, do ordain and establish this Constitution."

—FREDERICK DOUGLASS, speech on the
Dred Scott decision, May 14, 1857

CONTENTS

PREFACE

When I entered law school as a fresh-faced twenty-year-old, I was convinced that law was the principal avenue through which rights were protected. But in both the classroom and from the world around me, I quickly learned that wasn't quite right. I spent long hours learning how the law works in theory, and then I would go home and grieve how the law works in practice. My academic career coincided with the evisceration of the Voting Rights Act, the acquittal of the man who killed Trayvon Martin, and the failure to indict the police officer who killed Michael Brown—a particularly astonishing departure from the course material's suggestion that indictments are so easy to come by, a prosecutor could basically get a grand jury to indict a ham sandwich.

I wanted to learn how to use the law to fight for marginalized people, but I watched the law repeatedly fail people like me. So I had to refine and clarify my optimism: law *can* be a critical avenue for protecting rights *if* we make it so.

This philosophy—requiring the use of the laws we have, fighting for better ones, and empowering other people to do the same—has guided me through my work as an attorney, columnist, and professor. Shaping legal thought and providing sharp, accessible analysis attuned to the needs of marginalized people is literally my job. And I don't pretend to be dispassionate about it. When you're a Black immigrant woman and a lawyer, and when you understand how the law is weaponized against Black people, immigrants, and women (among others), you feel a unique pain—and a unique power. I'm both professionally and personally invested in radically reforming our sociopolitical and legal systems, and I can treat the Supreme Court's embrace of oppressive legal theories with the rigor and rage it deserves.

I wrote this book because I believe that innovative legal analysis and public education are both necessary in order to achieve a multiracial democracy. People who are harmed by what the Court is doing should be able to understand what the Court is doing. People with and without access to the halls of power should be able to challenge those who would abuse that power and dress up plain old oppression in legal garb. Everyone should be able to make and defend the claim that rights and equal justice under law are for all of us. And so, *The Originalism Trap* is for all of us, too.

I sometimes asked myself, in frustrated moments a decade or so ago, what the point of my legal education was. You're reading my answer.

THE ORIGINALISM TRAP

CHAPTER 1

HEIST

Lawyers don't often admit this in mixed company, but I'll let you in on a secret about interpreting the Constitution: there is no one objective way to interpret the Constitution. If there were, what would be the point of judges? We could resolve legal disputes by simply inputting our claims and evidence into a computer that would output uniform rulings. We don't do that, though, because judging calls for . . . well, judgment. A classic hypothetical law can show you what I mean: imagine a statute reading, "Vehicles are banned in the park."[1] One would have no trouble discerning that such a law would be broken by an adult wantonly driving a sports car over the public's flowerbeds. But what about a child driving a toy convertible? Or a tourist riding a motorized scooter? Or a first responder driving an ambulance to an injured park-goer? Whether those are "vehicles" within the meaning of the law's prohibition is debatable, so legal arbiters make judgment calls. Judgment is generally exercised in the American legal system through methods of constitutional interpretation. These methods tell us what should or shouldn't be considered in order to figure out a law's meaning. Judges need a fair and consistent way to determine what constitutional provisions mean and how to apply them in new and different cases. And "legal interpretative method" is a fancy way of saying "There's a method to the madness."

There's been considerable debate historically over what sources and analytical approaches form the best basis for judicial decision-making. Indeed, courts may and often do consider more than just one interpretative method in isolation; they call upon a variety of factors including judicial precedent (what courts have done), historical practices (what people have done), and of course, the text of the Constitution itself.[2] But over the last forty years or so, the conservative legal movement has been wildly successful at promoting the idea that "originalism" is the only legitimate way to interpret the Constitution.[3] The originalist method ostensibly determines constitutionality by relying on the original public meaning of the Constitution at the time it was drafted. Circumstances may evolve, but the Constitution's meaning does not—or as former Supreme Court justice and fierce originalist Antonin Scalia famously put it, "It's not a living document. It's dead, dead, dead."[4]

The sales pitch for originalism goes a little like this: originalism is objective.[5] We can know authoritatively what the Constitution means, its supporters argue, by discovering what it meant to the public when it was adopted.[6] And, some say, this is what the Constitution's ratifiers wanted—former solicitor general and one-time Supreme Court nominee Robert Bork once wrote that "only the approach of original understanding meets the criteria that any theory of constitutional adjudication must meet in order to possess democratic legitimacy. Only that approach is consonant with the design of the American republic."[7] So, if you want to know what rights you have, originalism commands you to consult a time capsule. Its proponents contend that to do otherwise is to lawlessly substitute your own policy preferences for the wisdom of the Founding

Fathers. However, ironically enough, historical evidence suggests the Framers themselves did not want generations of Americans to be bound to their view of the document.[8] Thomas Jefferson explicitly cautioned against excessive reverence of constitutions at the expense of societal progress, and further illuminated the absurdity by way of analogy. "We might as well require a man to wear still the coat which fitted him when a boy," he wrote, "as civilised society to remain ever under the regimen of their barbarous ancestors."*

Despite originalism's reputation as a serious intellectual theory, it's more like dream logic: it seems reasonable at first, but when you wake up, you can recognize it as nonsense. Originalism deliberately overemphasizes a particular version of history that treats the civil-rights gains won over time as categorically suspect. The consequences of its embrace have been intentionally catastrophic for practically anyone who isn't a wealthy white man, aka the class of people with exclusive possession of political power at the time the Constitution's drafters originally put pen to paper (or quill to parchment). By treating the Constitution as "dead," originalism deliberately entombs historically marginalized groups' legal claims to liberation.

WHICH HISTORY MATTERS?

There are levels to the intellectual dishonesty. Sometimes history surprises us. Yes, there's a lot of bad, but it's not actually *all* bad *all*

---

* An eyebrow-raising suggestion that he was aware of his own barbarity, to be sure. "Proposals to Revise the Virginia Constitution: I. Thomas Jefferson to 'Henry Tompkinson' (Samuel Kercheval), 12 July 1816," *Founders Online*, National Archives, https://founders.archives.gov/documents/Jefferson/03 -10-02-0128-0002. Original source: Thomas Jefferson, *The Papers of Thomas Jefferson: Retirement Series, Volume 10, 1 May 1816 to 18 January 1817*, ed. J. Jefferson Looney (Princeton: Princeton University Press, 2013), 222–28.

the time. The period of radical reform following the Civil War is particularly noteworthy here. During Reconstruction, as this time is called, the country constitutionalized the emancipation of enslaved people and created federal safeguards to both protect their newly recognized freedom and affirmatively foster legal equality nationwide. Mention this to originalists, though, and they're suddenly stricken with memory loss.

The Thirteenth, Fourteenth, and Fifteenth Amendments to the Constitution fundamentally changed the document for the better by dramatically expanding the sociopolitical community and—for the first time—seeking to build a multiracial democracy with equal membership for Black people and other marginalized persons.* The Thirteenth Amendment formally abolished slavery, except as punishment for a crime.[9] The Fourteenth Amendment created birthright citizenship, forbade states from violating certain rights of citizens and noncitizens alike (more on this later) and prohibited states from denying any person equal protection of law, limited the political power of insurrectionists, empowered Congress to legislatively enforce these provisions, and more.[10] The Fifteenth Amendment established a nationwide prohibition on race-based denial or abridgment of the right to vote, and again gave Congress the power to legislatively enforce this command.[11] These provisions, collectively known as the Reconstruction Amendments, embody a constitutional renunciation of the government-mandated political, economic, and social inferiority of Black people that had existed for the entire history of the United States. Contemporary thinkers and activists used these antislavery ideals to challenge oppressive conditions throughout society and pushed the country to reassess what it meant by "freedom."[12] Professor

---

*Obviously they did not succeed, but never before had the government deigned to even try.

Eric Foner, the preeminent historian of the Reconstruction era, tells us that the post–Civil War Amendments "transformed the Constitution from a document primarily concerned with federal-state relations and the rights of property into a vehicle through which members of vulnerable minorities could stake a claim to substantive freedom and seek protection against misconduct by all levels of government."[13]

The Reconstruction vision has revolutionary potential.[14] This part of history is powerful. It is also not the part of history originalists care about. An academic analysis of how Congress members discuss the Constitution shows that originalism's chief advocates (Republicans) frequently invoke the Founding Fathers and the Framers' Constitution but remain practically silent on the Reconstruction Amendments and their ratifiers.[15]

Instead, when originalists want to do a bad thing and the history isn't on their side, they choose their favorite tidbits of the past and rewrite history until it is. Actual historians have decried this practice sometimes conducted by us attorneys as "law office history— a results-oriented methodology in which evidence is selectively gathered and interpreted to produce a preordained conclusion."[16] More simply, it's cherry-picking.

The formalizing of women's second-class citizenship provides the most notorious illustration: when Justice Samuel Alito justified the decision to overturn *Roe v. Wade,* he did so in part by citing a famous seventeenth-century witch hunter and spousal-abuse apologist as a proper authority on women's rights.[17] You might hope that the prospect of curbing the rights of women based on the say-so of Sir Matthew Hale, whose contributions to the legal system include sentencing women to death as "witches" and establishing that men couldn't be prosecuted if they raped their wives, would prompt some self-reflection. Unfortunately for millions of Americans of reproductive age, it did not. The Supreme Court ruled in *Dobbs v. Jackson*

Women's Health Organization that pregnant people do not have a constitutional right to end their pregnancies—and as a result can be legally forced by the government to carry a pregnancy to term—in large part because some misogynists of yore regarded abortion as a criminal act.[18]

This was not the only view in centuries past, or even the dominant view, and prominent historical organizations submitted an amicus brief in *Dobbs* in an effort to set the record straight. (Amicus is shorthand for amicus curiae, which is Latin for "friend of the court," meaning groups who file briefs to help courts make decisions even though they aren't parties to a case. Lawyers love Latin.) Actual experts said there was no evidence to support the claim that abortion was criminalized throughout pregnancy in early America. Rather, early Americans relied on a body of English precedents called "common law" that didn't even recognize an abortion as occurring until a pregnant person could feel a fetus move, which could occur as late as the twenty-fifth week of pregnancy. Historians confirmed *Roe*'s conclusion that "American history and traditions from the founding to the post–Civil War years included a woman's ability to make decisions regarding abortion, as far as allowed by the common law."[19] Justice Alito ignored the brief and asserted that there was an "unbroken tradition" of criminalizing abortion "from the earliest days of the common law to 1973."[20] This can be generously described as historical fan fiction.

Thirty organizations signed on to a statement jointly released by the American Historical Association and the Organization of American Historians after the *Dobbs* ruling which expressed dismay that the Court referred to "history" dozens of times while refusing to take their expert historical claims seriously. The historians further observed that the Court robbed people of their fundamental rights by enshrining "misrepresentations . . . in a text that becomes authoritative for legal reference and citation in the future."[21] The alarming takeaway from *Dobbs* is that you do not have a constitutionally protected right if enough Supreme Court justices think, rightly or wrongly, that the right was contested when the country was founded. As Professor Khiara Bridges has explained, "The existence of other perfectly plausible histories of abortion suggests that the *Dobbs* majority's decision to elevate as right and true the historical account that it provides in its opinion is not the apolitical exercise that the majority pretends it to be. Instead, it is an exercise that is fraught with values, convictions, preferences, and, perhaps most of all, power."[22] Originalism gives the judiciary extraordinary power to put historically marginalized people "back in their place" and buttress the country's long-standing stratification of power and wealth.

Judicial reliance on shoddy history lessons threatens myriad areas of law and the people who are subject to those laws. The Supreme Court's 2022 decision in *New York State Rifle & Pistol Association v. Bruen*—and lower courts' subsequent struggle to apply the high court's ruling—provides a glaring example. In *Bruen,* the Court was asked to determine the constitutionality of a New York State law that made it a crime to possess a firearm without a license, and that limited licenses for concealed carry of handguns outside the home to individuals who could demonstrate a special need for self-protection distinguishable from that of the general community. To assess the legality of this gun-licensing regime, the Court's conservative supermajority announced a brand-new originalist test, which (surprise, surprise) the law failed.

Since the Court's 2008 decision in *District of Columbia v. Heller,* the early originalist victory that first recognized an individual right to bear arms, courts have assessed the constitutionality of gun regulations by using a two-step framework.* The first step looked at

---

*Yes, you read that correctly. The idea that the Second Amendment protects individual gun ownership is a modern invention that former chief justice Warren Burger, a Republican appointed by President Richard Nixon, described in 1991 as "one of the greatest pieces of fraud—I repeat the word 'fraud'—on the

whether the conduct being regulated fell within the scope of the Second Amendment as historically understood, which means asking, "Would citizens in the founding generation have thought the Second Amendment protected the conduct being regulated by this law?" If the Second Amendment was implicated, the courts would move to a second step and evaluate the strength of the government's justification for that regulation and how proportionate it was to the burden on the Second Amendment right. The second step is essentially judging whether a law has a small enough impact on the right at issue, for a good enough reason. Analysis of a law's means and ends like this can be a good thing to consider when you live in a society with hundreds of millions of people whose rights and interests are sometimes in competition with one another; means–end scrutiny can help ensure that the needs of the public are not unreasonably subordinated to a maximalist interpretation of an individual right or freedom.*

But in *Bruen,* the Court decided this two-step test was—and I'm quoting here—"one step too many."[23] Instead, Justice Clarence Thomas wrote for the majority, courts can only look at the history.† More specifically, they can only look at whatever historical snapshot the Court's conservatives prefer; the gun law that the Court ruled

---

American public by special interest groups that I have ever seen in my lifetime." See, e.g., Jay Willis, "Heartbreaking: Chief Justice Warren Burger Just Made a Great Point," Balls and Strikes, July 4, 2022, ballsandstrikes.org/newsletter /balls-and-strikes-newsletter-july-8-warren-burger-fraud/.

* For example, the Court once upheld a law criminalizing the promotion of sexual performances by children under the age of sixteen against a First Amendment challenge, in part because "the evil to be restricted so overwhelmingly outweighs the expressive interests, if any, at stake." *New York, Petitioner v. Paul Ira Ferber,* 458 U.S. 747, 763–64 (1982).

† Justice Thomas's Scalia-on-steroids approach is not entirely surprising; Scalia was once asked to compare his legal philosophy to Thomas's and said "I'm an originalist, I'm not a nut." Joe Patrice, "Scalia Calls Thomas 'A Nut,'" *Above the Law,* July 11, 2014, abovethelaw.com/2014/07/scalia-calls-thomas-a-nut/.

unconstitutional was enacted by New York in 1911, making it over a hundred years old when it was struck down. One would assume a century on the books might pass historical muster. But Thomas wrote (seriously), "Not all history is created equal."[24] Some history that supported the regulation was ignored because it was before the Founding, which made it too early. Other history was too late. Some historical laws were too different from the New York statute. Other historical laws were similar but were outliers, and unrepresentative of the historical period. Basically, any history that supported the gun regulation didn't count. But the history that allowed the Court's conservatives to do what they wanted to in the first place? *Just* right. Prominent legal historians have criticized *Bruen*'s law-office history as "embarrassing" and chastised the Court for applying not "history, text, and tradition" but "fiction, fantasy, and mythology."[25]

Bruen's à la carte approach to history is also stunning in juxtaposition to *Dobbs,* which was decided the very next day. In *Bruen,* the Court's originalists said if a gun regulation did not exist in the past, it was because the regulation was constitutionally impermissible, and today's laws can go no further.* In *Dobbs,* the Court's originalists said that the fact that an abortion regulation did not exist in the past has no bearing on whether the regulation is constitutionally permissible, and today's lawmakers can prohibit abortion in any way they want.† In these cases, the Court used the nonexistence of a law to

---

* *New York State Rifle & Pistol Association v. Bruen,* 142 S. Ct. 2111, 2131 (2022). ("When a challenged regulation addresses a general societal problem that has persisted since the 18th century, the lack of a distinctly similar historical regulation addressing that problem is relevant evidence that the challenged regulation is inconsistent with the Second Amendment. Likewise, if earlier generations addressed the societal problem, but did so through materially different means, that also could be evidence that a modern regulation is unconstitutional.")

† *Dobbs v. Jackson Women's Health Organization,* 142 S. Ct. 2228, 2255 (2022). ("Regardless, the fact that many States in the late 18th and early 19th

support directly conflicting inferences about Congress's power to legislate. It's outrageous that, when it comes to regulating guns, the Supreme Court says, "If it was legal it would have been done by now," but when it comes to regulating abortion, a lack of past regulation is no barrier to a legislative free-for-all in my uterus. Judicial bodies that don't respect human bodies aren't worthy of respect to begin with, but the least they could do is be internally consistent.

The Goldilocks-esque reasoning in *Bruen* and *Dobbs* takes its cues from the policy preferences of the conservative legal movement rather than the principles of the Constitution. No constitutional clause says future would-be interpreters of the document must first walk a mile in a plantation owner's shoes. There's nothing that requires the Supreme Court to limit its inquiry to the Founding. The Court could just as easily consider how the law was interpreted over time, or—stick with me here—not lock themselves into a strictly historical analysis at all. It's of the utmost importance that we recognize this, because right-wing legal elites act as though Moses himself descended from a mountaintop and hand-delivered a tablet to the Supreme Court onto which the fundamental originalist precept had been carved: "Things shall not be if they have not already been." But constitutional interpretation is not set in stone. We are not bound to originalism's selectively historical maneuvers and the abhorrent results they necessarily produce.[26]

Post-*Bruen* decisions have made it all too clear that the consequence of originalism's makeshift historical standards is the endangerment of historically marginalized people. In *United States v. Perez-Gallan,* for instance, a Texas federal district court had to determine the legality of a gun regulation. The law makes it a federal crime for a person to possess a firearm if a court imposed a restrain-

---

century did not criminalize pre-quickening abortions does not mean that anyone thought the States lacked the authority to do so.")

ing order against them in protection of an intimate partner or child. The court heeded *Bruen* and reasoned that the constitutionality of the statute depended on "whether regulations prohibiting those subject to a protective order from possessing a firearm align with the Nation's historical tradition of firearm regulation."[27] It's painfully obvious that they do not: government intervention of any kind in response to domestic violence is largely a modern invention. For much of American history, husbands had a legal right to beat their wives.[28] The legal system did not move away from actively supporting spousal abuse until the late nineteenth century.[29] And even then, family violence was often treated as an insufficiently serious harm to warrant government intrusion into the home for white families, and little more than an opportunity for the criminal legal system to inflict violence on communities of color.[30] The *Perez-Gallan* court observed that "consistent examples of the government removing firearms from someone accused (or even convicted) of domestic violence" were "glaringly absent from the historical record—from colonial times until 1994."[31] As a result, the law was found unconstitutional. Women are five times more likely to be killed by an abusive partner when their abuser has access to a gun.[32] But according to originalism, the state didn't try to stop people from hurting women in the past, so it can't try to stop people from hurting women in the present.

The Fifth Circuit Court of Appeals exacerbated this ludicrous state of affairs in *United States v. Rahimi*.[33] The Fifth Circuit is one of the thirteen federal appellate courts that sit below the Supreme Court and above the country's district courts.[34] Its jurisdiction covers Mississippi, Louisiana, and Texas, and it is often the last word on the law for the roughly thirty-seven million people who live in those states.[35] Like the district court in *Perez-Gallan,* the circuit court in *Rahimi* had to rule on the constitutionality of a federal statute that bans gun possession for people who have protective orders against them.[36] The Fifth Circuit had heard and rejected this exact challenge multiple times, concluding that the statute was reasonably adapted to the compelling government interest of reducing domestic gun violence.[37] But the court was asked to reconsider its jurisprudence in light of *Bruen*. The court accepted the invitation to reevaluate its precedent and concluded that there was no sufficiently analogous law when the country was founded, so it struck the statute down. Even though there were historical statutes that prohibited gun possession for certain people, the court distinguished those laws away by highlighting that the Founding-era laws disarmed classes of people—specifically, Native Americans and enslaved Black people—in order to protect the discriminatory social order and prevent armed rebellion, while the statute in question disarmed people after individualized findings of credible threats to their partner or child.[38] This rationale encapsulates the intellectual and moral bankruptcy of the originalist ideology. *Rahimi* concluded that intimate partner violence was not a constitutionally acceptable reason to place limits on gun possession and instead lifted up rank bigotry as the standard to which today's gun laws must be held. Originalism observes that white supremacy dominated the country's past and reasons that it must also dominate the country's future.[39] The Department of Justice petitioned the Supreme Court to review the Fifth Circuit's decision, and the Court heard oral argument in *United States v. Rahimi* in November 2023. Soon it will have the opportunity to clarify how *Bruen* applies to statutes disarming people subject to orders of protection. Perhaps the Court will twist itself into an originalist pretzel to avoid further damaging its reputation by affirming the Fifth Circuit's horrific reasoning. Perhaps not.

The ominous implications of the district court's decision in *Perez-Gallan* and the Fifth Circuit's decision in *Rahimi* should make even the most ardent gun lovers nervous. Taking the Supreme Court's jurisprudence seriously empowers lower courts to strip us of innumerable freedoms if they have any reason to think that we would have been unfree in early America. Originalism is regressive by nature: an outsized focus on the alleged original meaning of the Constitution at the time of drafting means the rights of modern-day individuals—and the ability of legislatures to protect those rights—must be constrained by the outdated concerns of the Framers, like keeping British soldiers out of their living rooms. Former justice Stephen Breyer's dissenting opinion in *Bruen* spotlighted how originalism binds lawmakers from meeting the present needs of their constituents. Even if the justices were trained historians (which, remember, they aren't), Breyer argued that "laws addressing repeating crossbows, launcegays, dirks, dagges, skeines, stilladers, and other ancient weapons will be of little help to courts confronting modern problems."[40] This, to be sure, was the plan all along. The originalist ideology declares that random historical windows of conservatives' choosing are society's high-water marks, and we are constitutionally powerless to surpass them without formal amendment. The core function of originalism is providing aesthetically pleasing legal flourishes around the uglier idea that things shouldn't get better than they've been. And if originalism is left unchecked, things will keep getting worse.

LOWERING THE BAR AND RAISING THE STAKES

The conservative legal movement is not and will not be satiated with the fall of *Roe* (or, for that matter, the rise of guns). The Court was clear in *Dobbs* that rights are entitled to constitutional protections only if they are explicitly enumerated in the Constitution or deeply rooted in American history and tradition. This understandably set off alarm bells for historically underprotected groups.[41] With all the credibility of the Wizard of Oz crying out, "Pay no attention to that man behind the curtain," Justice Alito has advised us not to worry: "Nothing in this opinion should be understood to cast doubt on precedents that do not concern abortion."[42] But last time I checked, one plus one equals two, and Alito's statements don't add up.

Justice Thomas, however, did the math. In his separate concurring opinion, he urged the Court to take the next logical step and overrule a slew of cases including *Griswold v. Connecticut,* which decriminalized the use of contraception for married couples, *Lawrence v. Texas,* which decriminalized private, consensual intimacy between people of the same sex, and *Obergefell v. Hodges,* which recognized the legality of marriage between people of the same sex.[43] Justice Thomas's omission of *Loving v. Virginia,* which recognized the legality of interracial marriages like his own, is not subtle, but *Loving* may be vulnerable to the same reasoning threatening other landmark rights-protecting cases. Congress has responded to this threat by passing the Respect for Marriage Act. Signed into law in December 2022, the law does give some statutory protections to gay and interracial marriages by ensuring that the marriage is still valid if the couple crosses state lines, but it leaves human dignity an open constitutional question. Even with the law's passage, states would still be free to deny marriage licenses to same-sex and interracial couples if *Obergefell* and *Loving* were to go the way of *Roe*.[44] And the Court is already pushing legal boundaries toward bigotry. In 2023, an extremist conservative Christian advocacy organization widely recognized as a hate group successfully represented a website designer before the Supreme Court.[45] The website designer claimed that she wanted to start selling wedding websites and advertise that she would not sell them for use in gay marriages, but feared that doing so would violate her state's antidiscrimination law. The Supreme Court ruled—for the first time in history—that businesses presenting themselves as open to the public have a constitutional right to deny some goods and services to same-sex couples.[46]

Without the Constitution as a safeguard, fundamental rights are quite literally up for debate. The Court's misbehavior has encouraged political actors to push legal limits to determine what the Court will allow, like the raptors in *Jurassic Park* systematically testing the fences for weaknesses. More than two hundred members of Congress observed in their *Dobbs* amicus brief that "the trend of state legislatures passing patently unconstitutional laws has accelerated in recent years with changes in the composition of the Court," as legislators count on the Court to overturn its established precedents like *Roe*.[47] I call this phenomenon trickle-down lawlessness. The Supreme Court's demonstrated willingness to bend the law to protect and further the interests of racial capitalism and patriarchy emboldens the conservative legal movement to aggressively pursue legislation and litigation crafted to remold law and society in originalism's image—meaning, to enact the causes célèbres of the Republican Party and target its perceived enemies.[48] Between 2021 and 2022, for instance, scholars observed a 250 percent increase in proposed legislation restricting teaching about topics such as race, gender, and sexual identity.[49] In 2023 alone, dozens of states proposed hundreds of laws targeting trans people's right to exist; these proposals borrow heavily from ready-made legislation crafted by conservative special interest groups and supplied to lawmakers across the country, allowing an unrepresentative fringe to impose its will.[50] At the time of writing, seventy-two anti-trans bills have been signed into law, and arguments about whether basic protections for trans youth in schools should be ruled unconstitutional are coursing their way through federal courts across the country.[51] Lower courts, too, are susceptible to the trickle-down effect: some reporters have critiqued federal district and appellate courts for following the Supreme Court's example of indifference to pesky things like facts and precedent and their "embrace of slipshod 'originalist' history," resulting in opinions that "match the right-wing agenda but not well-established law."[52] Originalism encourages far-right agitators throughout the government to let their reactionary freak flags fly.

The originalist ideology's claim to singular objectivity and legal legitimacy is fascinating, because the Venn diagram between the results originalism produces and conservative policy preferences is a circle—they completely overlap. The ascendance of originalism has yielded nationwide policy wins that the conservative legal movement arguably would not have achieved if it had to gain majority support through the political process. Among them are the elimination of pregnant people's right to end their pregnancies,[53] the protection of public-school officials leading students in prayer,[54] the novel curtailment of legislatures' ability to regulate the concealed carrying of guns outside the home,[55] the prohibition of race-conscious admissions policies in higher education,[56] and more. Originalists' goals are, by and large, too odious to successfully pursue democratically, so they use the courts. The alignment of unpopular conservative policy aims and "correct" constitutional interpretation would be a lovely coincidence for the far right if it were at all coincidental. In reality, it's exactly what was planned. Originalism in its present form emerged in earnest not out of some deeply held belief in fidelity to the Constitution, but as a backlash to the successes of the civil rights era.[57]

EVERY VILLAIN HAS AN ORIGIN STORY

Most stories about originalism's rise begin with Robert Bork—the aforementioned failed Supreme Court nominee widely regarded as the intellectual father of the legal theory—but I prefer to start a bit earlier with *Brown*. In *Brown v. Board of Education,* the Supreme Court held that state-sanctioned racial segregation was unconstitutional, thereby overruling *Plessy v. Ferguson* and the abominable fiction of "separate but equal." The *Plessy* Court had reasoned that the Constitution permitted racial segregation because the Fourteenth Amendment's reach was limited to questions of legal and political equality rather than social standing. This conceptualization of the Fourteenth Amendment would prevent the government from explicitly disadvantaging a racial group, but not disrupt broader societal inequality. The Court also contested whether segregation really constituted a stamp of inferiority anyway and suggested that Black people simply hurt their own feelings by "choos[ing] to put that construction upon it."[58] *Brown* abandoned this conclusion and determined that separate was inherently unequal and a deprivation of the Fourteenth Amendment's guarantee of equal protection of the laws. There should be no question that this was the correct decision.* The interesting question, for our purposes, is *how* the Court came to that decision. And the answer is this: the Supreme Court requested, received, and rejected originalist arguments.

Prior to making its ruling, the Court solicited additional arguments about the drafting and ratification of the Fourteenth Amendment and how the lawmakers viewed its applicability to segregation. The Topeka Board of Education opted not to provide such arguments because it had agreed by that point to end segregation in elementary schools, but the state of Kansas intervened to defend the policy's constitutionality. Stakeholders on either side dug deep and scoured the history of the Reconstruction era. Unsurprisingly, there

---

* It was a hard question, though, for dozens of Donald Trump's federal judicial nominees, who declined to say whether they believed that the Supreme Court's unanimous and landmark ruling in *Brown v. Board* was correctly decided. See "Oppose the Confirmation of Judicial Nominees Who Decline to State Brown v. Board of Education Decision Was Correctly Decided," letter from the Leadership Conference on Civil and Human Rights, May 13, 2019, civilrights .org/resource/oppose-the-confirmation-of-judicial-nominees-who-decline-to -state-brown-v-board-of-education-decision-was-correctly-decided/.

was no singular view of the historical record. The NAACP Legal Defense and Educational Fund (LDF) argued on behalf of the excluded Black children that state enforcement of racial segregation in schools was incompatible with the intent of the Reconstruction Amendments' drafters to protect Black people from racial discrimination.[59] They contended that congressional debates, reports, and other records clearly evidenced radical abolitionists' efforts to destroy America's racial caste system, root and branch, by translating the principle of absolute equality into broad constitutional language.[60] They further claimed that a purely historical approach to legal decision-making risked leaving the country stuck in discriminatory stagnancy: "Even if there be some situations in which custom, usage and tradition may be considered in testing the reasonableness of governmental action," the attorneys warned, "customs, traditions and usages rooted in slavery cannot be worthy of the constitutional sanction of this Court."[61]

Kansas's attorney general argued that the Fourteenth Amendment was concerned with "the fundamental rights of life, liberty, and property" as opposed to "the right to mingle with other races in the public schools."[62] Kansas further argued that the courts don't have the authority to construe the Fourteenth Amendment differently than the Framers did at the time of adoption without a showing of some substantial change in conditions that created a new situation, thereby calling for a new interpretation. Otherwise, they suggested, there would have been no point in Congress writing the Constitution down; a new understanding would require a new act of Congress.[63] The attorney general of the United States also submitted an amicus brief. The brief concluded that there was ample evidence that the Fourteenth Amendment was contemporarily understood as establishing a broad constitutional principle of equality under law, but insufficient evidence to conclude one way or the other whether the Fourteenth Amendment was understood at the time of adoption to permit or prohibit segregated schools.[64] Still, the government acknowledged that "the essence" of the Fourteenth Amendment's provisions is "their vitality and adaptability to the progressive changes and needs of the nation."[65]

"Originalist" did not yet exist in 1953 as a term describing a theory of legal interpretation focused on how a provision was understood when enacted, but it's plainly the best way to describe the arguments made to the Court in *Brown*. Kansas's claim about judicial authority in particular bears the hallmark of originalism. While LDF, Kansas, and the United States all made arguments informed by the history of the Fourteenth Amendment's adoption, only Kansas put forth the view that our understanding of what a law means today *must* be constrained by the law's alleged original meaning at the time it was written. The arguments in *Brown* also showcase some of originalism's flaws.

For starters, determining the original intent of a provision can be a Herculean task. A group of drafters may have varied desires and expectations, leading to at least as many original intentions as there are individuals who wrote and ratified the Constitution. Originalists eventually recognized that and gradually shifted to the allegedly more objective "original public meaning" standard, which focuses its inquiry on how common people would have understood the provision at the time of enactment (sometimes consulting contemporary dictionaries, grammar books, and newspapers) instead of focusing on a legislator's subjective intent. But that always seemed to me like splitting centuries-old hairs. The "original public meaning" of a right does not account for the diversity of the public and its viewpoints—not to mention *whose* viewpoints have been most valued and centered in our constitutional memory. When originalists ask, "What did the post–Civil War Amendments mean?" they're not asking, "What did the post–Civil War Amendments mean to the formerly enslaved?"[66] The views of Indigenous people forcibly removed from their land aren't consulted to determine the original understanding of the Fifth Amendment's prohibition on government taking of private property without just compensation. The originalist standard privileges the historic voices of the already powerful, when it's the marginalized who most need to be heard.[67]

Furthermore, originalism encourages lawyers to go spelunking through archives for whatever they want to find. We can see this tension play out in the proto-originalism of *Brown v. Board*. LDF and Kansas each conducted a historical search, the results of which turned on how they defined the right they were looking for—seeking evidence of a right to be free from racial subordination is very different from seeking evidence of a right to socialize with white children. Originalism does little to constrain that search, nor does it adequately justify why we should principally subject ourselves to such dubious constraints. The ideology makes promises of fairness, objectivity, and limited discretion, and it delivers on none of them.

Thankfully, the *Brown* Court recognized that. And promptly after inviting originalism into the judicial chambers, the Supreme Court showed the theory the door. The Court reasoned that history could be helpful, sure, but it could not—and should not—be determinative. Writing for a unanimous Court, Chief Justice Earl Warren laid out a different methodology:

> In approaching this problem, we cannot turn the clock back to 1868 when the Amendment was adopted, or even to 1896 when *Plessy v. Ferguson* was written. We must consider public education in the light of its full development and its present place in American life throughout the Nation. Only in this way can it be determined if segregation in public schools deprives these plaintiffs of the equal protection of the laws.[68]

The Supreme Court's rebuke of racial segregation in *Brown* reflects a critical understanding that originalism aims to obscure.

Brown's reasoning vindicates the wisdom of applying inclusive democratic principles like antiracism and equal educational opportunity to the present and the folly of limiting our understanding of rights to the most narrow version of the Framers' imaginations.[69]

Prominent political conservatives spoke out against *Brown*'s methodology and outcome as illegitimate. Nearly one hundred members of the United States Congress, all representing former Confederate states, signed on to a document formally titled the Declaration of Constitutional Principles. This document came to be known as the Southern Manifesto.[70] In it, the congresspeople advocated resistance to integration and marshaled a breadth of legal arguments to cast *Brown* as constitutionally unsound. Chief among them was the claim that the ratifiers of the Fourteenth Amendment did not intend for it to prohibit states from maintaining segregated schools.[71] This is the crucial backdrop against which originalism began to formalize and flourish as an intellectual theory.[72] It sounds much more polite and intelligent to couch opposition to *Brown* in terms of constitutional fidelity, Framers' intent, and states' rights rather than saying honestly and outright, "I support the use of state power to ensure my white children don't learn next to those Black children." And legal elites picked up what their counterparts in Congress were putting down.[73]

Robert Bork published a seminal paper in 1971 that advocated judicial reliance on the Framers' intent. Additionally, he denounced the main legal hooks on which the judiciary hangs marginalized people's rights, criticizing the Court's substantive due process and substantive equal protection rulings as "improper" and contending that "broad areas of constitutional law ought to be reformulated."[74] (We'll dig into substantive due process with more nuance and detail in chapter 2, but the CliffsNotes version of how these provisions work is "the Due Process Clause demands a reasonable process and basis for state action that hurts my interests, while the Equal Protection Clause demands a reasonable basis for state action that hurts my interests but not yours."[75]) Bork reasoned that it is "always a mistake for the Court to try to construct substantive individual rights under the due process or the equal protection clause" because there is insufficient constitutional guidance to prevent judges from importing their personal values rather than applying neutral principles.[76] While Bork did seek to rationalize *Brown v. Board* as somehow consistent with originalism, he maintained during his ill-fated confirmation hearing that *Brown*'s companion case outlawing segregation in D.C. public schools, *Bolling v. Sharpe,* had no constitutional basis.[77] (That argument hasn't entirely fallen out of favor; Justice Clarence Thomas voiced agreement with it in 2022.[78]) In 1977, prominent Harvard Law professor Raoul Berger railed against racially integrated schools as incompatible with the Framers' original intent. Berger stopped short of calling for the overruling of *Brown v. Board* only because he believed the ruling had spurred "expectations" among Black Americans that made it too impractical to do right by the Constitution (which, for him, meant doing wrong by Black people).[79] It is not by accident that these legal arguments reinforce opposition to equal rights: the development of originalism as a legal theory is inextricable from the development of a palatable cover story for reactionary politics.

The reversal of civil rights was and remains a key originalist target. Still, both then and now, it was not the sole concern of the conservative legal movement. Bork's paper also took direct aim at a Supreme Court decision that struck down a law criminalizing the use of contraception, criticizing the ruling as "unprincipled."[80] That same year, former American Bar Association president Lewis Powell published an influential memorandum directing conservative business elites to fight back against a perceived sweeping attack on capitalism, and identifying the judiciary as potentially "the most important instrument for social, economic and political change."[81]

Powell would go on to be confirmed as an associate justice of the Supreme Court a few months later.[82] In 1985, Attorney General Edwin Meese III gave a speech before the American Bar Association in which he promoted originalism in direct contrast to the "threat," as he viewed it, of "the radical egalitarianism and expansive libertarianism of the Warren Court."[83] Meese later articulated that the policy of the Ronald Reagan Administration was to "endeavor to resurrect the original meaning of constitutional provisions and statutes as the only reliable guide for judgment."[84] Under Meese's leadership, the Department of Justice functioned as an "academy in exile" working to expound on originalism and mobilize legal elites and the public around the ideology as a serious school of constitutional interpretation.[85] In 1988, Reagan addressed the Federalist Society—an extremely well-funded and powerful conservative legal organization that promotes originalist decision-making—and called for "an end to the fanciful readings of the Constitution that produce such decisions as *Roe v. Wade*."[86] The Federalist Society and Reagan's Justice Department pushed back against advancements made by people's movements for racial justice, women's liberation, organized labor, and more by consciously developing a pipeline of young originalists to be steered into judgeships.[87] Simultaneously, conservatives propagandized liberal victories in the courts on issues like affirmative action, abortion, gay rights, the social safety net, and the rights of defendants as ahistorical and lawlessly activist departures from the true meaning of the Constitution.[88] It's not an exaggeration to say that Reagan Republicans looked at landmark rights-protecting Supreme Court decisions during Chief Justice Warren's tenure such as *Brown v. Board of Education* (desegregating schools), *Griswold v. Connecticut* (allowing married couples to buy birth control), and *Miranda v. Arizona* (if you've seen *Law and Order,* you know the speech), and thought, "Hmm, the Supreme Court actually seems to be recognizing that people other than us have rights, too. We ought to do something about this."[89]

Enter originalism, stage right.

The professionalization of white patriarchal grievance politics, coupled with the right wing's laser focus on the judiciary, drove us to our regrettable present position where, for the first time in history, self-described originalists dominate the Supreme Court.* Conservatives locked in a supermajority on the high court in late 2020, composed of Chief Justice John Roberts and Associate Justices Clarence Thomas, Samuel Alito, Neil Gorsuch, Brett Kavanaugh, and Amy Coney Barrett.

With that said, please don't interpret this to mean that the Court's jurisprudence prior to 2020 was strictly or even mostly laudable.[90] Harvard Law professor Niko Bowie submitted testimony to the Presidential Commission on the Supreme Court referencing dozens of federal laws designed to expand political equality that the Court had invalidated *before* Donald Trump's appointees joined its ranks.[91] Professor Erwin Chemerinsky, a titan of constitutional law, argues that the Court has "largely failed" throughout its history to protect the rights of disadvantaged minorities and to uphold the Constitution in defiance of repressive political majorities, falling short when it is needed most.[92] A growing chorus of academics and activists alike are making the case that the judiciary has always been a fickle friend at best to marginalized groups.[93] I don't disagree; I simply wish to point out how the new lopsidedness makes the liber-

---

*Justice Alito has referred to himself as a "practical originalist." Justices Thomas, Gorsuch, and Barrett use no such qualifiers. And all six conservative justices frequently use originalist language in the opinions they write, and sign on to the expressly originalist opinions of their fellow conservatives. See, e.g., Erwin Chemerinsky, "Originalism Has Taken Over the Supreme Court," *ABA Journal,* September 6, 2022, abajournal.com/columns/article/chemerinsky-originalism-has-taken-over-the-supreme-court.

als on the bench particularly unable to exercise any viable check and makes the conservatives on the bench particularly cavalier. The late justice William Brennan, Jr., famously used to tell his law clerks that the most important constitutional rule was the "rule of five," because with five votes, you could accomplish anything.[94] Conservative extremists have six.* And in just a few short years, the supermajority has repeatedly relied on flimsy reasoning and procedural shortcuts to upend decades' worth of previously settled law and trample the rights of disfavored groups.[95] This "restless and newly constituted court," to borrow a withering turn of phrase from Justice Sonia Sotomayor, has the numbers to do whatever it wants—and it knows it.[96]

Shunning the Warren Court's admonition in *Brown,* the supermajority is very clearly on a mission to "turn back the clock" through its reliance on originalism at the expense of centuries of progress, precedent, and the public interest.[97] This produces a tragic irony: originalism pretends to facilitate faithfulness to the Constitution and constrain judicial discretion, but in reality, it has freed the Court to undermine core constitutional values and democratic principles for which the country claims to strive. The Constitution's preamble states that it is ordained by a collective "we the people" for purposes including establishing justice, promoting the general welfare, and striving to become a more perfect union.[98] Article IV of the Constitution requires the federal government to guarantee to every state a republican form of government ("republican" as in representative democracy, not "Republican" as in MAGA hats and tax cuts for billionaires).[99] And the Declaration of Independence proclaims that all men are created equal, and the people have the right to abol-

---

* Yes, John Roberts, I'm counting you. You don't get to systematically dismantle voting rights, hollow out reproductive rights into nothingness, emphasize your opposition to marriage equality by reading your dissenting opinion from the bench for the very first time, halt school integration, and more, and still hold yourself out as anything less than extreme.

ish tyranny and institute a new government in order to secure our lives, liberty, and pursuit of happiness.[100] If our founding documents are to be believed, the whole point of the great American experiment is the creation of a society with equal membership, in which people are not simply ruled but participate in making and interpreting the rules that govern our lives. Relying on wealthy, white, colonial-era men as the sole arbiters of constitutionality denies us that democratic inheritance, entrenches the rampant inequality of that era, and reduces our capacity for self-governance.

Those who weaponize the law recast their wrongdoing as impartial legal interpretation. But nothing about this is neutral, objective, or harmless. For all their talk about the need for limiting principles, originalists don't really care about judicial restraint. We need to complete the thought: they care about restraining judges *from doing good things*—like recognizing the rights of groups that originalists prefer to marginalize and preventing the concentration of power by oligarchs. The behavior originalism is intended to rein in is fostering a more equitable democratic society. It's an outcome-oriented ploy to disguise oppressive choices as constitutional requirements. Justice Brennan called out this phenomenon in his time. Brennan argued that originalism, far from having a singular claim to judicial legitimacy, is a political choice against minority rights, and "those who would restrict claims of right to the values of 1789 specifically articulated in the Constitution turn a blind eye to social progress and eschew adaptation of overarching principles to changes of social circumstance."[101]

This approach creates foreseeable danger. Senator Ted Kennedy gave an incendiary speech in 1987 focusing on the harms that originalist ideology would yield if Robert Bork were elevated to the Supreme Court:

> Robert Bork's America is a land in which women would be forced into back-alley abortions, blacks would sit at segregated

lunch counters, rogue police could break down citizens' doors in midnight raids, schoolchildren could not be taught about evolution, writers and artists would be censored at the whim of government, and the doors of the federal courts would be shut on the fingers of millions of citizens for whom the judiciary is—and is often the only—protector of the individual rights that are the heart of our democracy.[102]

Many considered the speech exaggerated and improper at the time. And although the nomination was defeated on a bipartisan basis, 58–42 (including six Republicans voting Bork down), prominent conservatives continue to openly harbor a grudge about what they deem to be partisan and unfair treatment of Bork's ideological "bias against those rights not listed in the Bill of Rights."[103] But in hindsight, Kennedy's denunciation seems not just fair but eerily prescient. Bork did not make it onto the Supreme Court, but his ideology did. And as predicted, the Supreme Court's originalist jurisprudence has been rife with intellectually indefensible reasoning and results.

In short, conservative extremists stole the Constitution, and we need to take it back.

ROOM FOR REDEMPTION?

Originalism is clearly an object of scorn for much of the legal left—and correctly so, I would argue. But this is not a universal view. A growing cadre of liberals argue that originalism can and should be used to achieve liberal outcomes. These "progressive originalists" share my recognition that the dominance of originalism as applied by the right wing is dangerous. Where we part ways is that they accept the legitimacy of relying principally on the purported original public meaning of the Constitution to interpret laws today. These scholars locate the problem in originalism's use rather than originalism itself, and believe that the theory can do some good in the right hands. (To put it another way: originalism is like a ne'er-do-well love interest; progressive originalists are saying, "I can fix him," and I'm the friend saying, "Girl, dump him.")

There are a few factors that explain how some liberals learned to stop worrying and love originalism. One is the belief that originalism is the only game in town. Conservatives have so successfully dictated the terms of acceptable constitutional interpretation in both the courtroom and the court of public opinion for decades that then–solicitor general Elena Kagan told the Senate during her Supreme Court confirmation hearing that "we are all originalists." Her testimony was a testament to originalism's ascendancy.[104] Legal decision-makers and commentators who don't claim the originalist mantle have been maligned as unfaithful to the Constitution.[105] And a 2016 report conducted by the Pew Research Center showed that the American population was evenly divided at 46 percent each on the question of whether the Supreme Court should base its rulings on what the Constitution means in current times or what it meant when originally written. (I'll note that these winds are changing, though: the Pew Research Center produced a new report in 2018 which showed that the share of Americans who believed the Court should base its rulings on what the Constitution means in the present had increased to 55 percent.[106]) Recognizing that originalism has significant legal and political capital, some liberals believe that they must adopt originalism in order to bolster their arguments' legitimacy among both lawyers and laypeople.[107]

Progressive originalists may also find the theory valuable because they see an opportunity to focus the law's historical inquiry on the bright spots scattered throughout the country's dark past.[108] Conservative originalists, for instance, are suspiciously preoccupied with the Constitution as it existed before the Civil War.[109] Their liberal counterparts often aim to lift up original understandings of the Fourteenth Amendment.[110] For some, Justice Ketanji Brown Jackson's jurisprudence provides a model of what a new and improved originalism could be.

Justice Jackson is the newest member of the Supreme Court (and the first Black woman ever to serve in that role). Jackson was sworn in as a justice in the summer of 2022 and began participating in cases when the Court began its term that October. In her first week on the job, the Court heard *Allen v. Milligan*—a case that threatened what's left of the Voting Rights Act after the Supreme Court bulldozed through the landmark legislation in *Shelby County v. Holder* a decade earlier.[111] The issue in *Milligan* centered on electoral-district maps drawn by Alabama Republicans. A three-judge federal district court including two Donald Trump appointees found that Alabama's maps violated the Voting Rights Act by unlawfully diluting the voting power of the state's Black residents. But Alabama claimed the maps could not be fixed. Even though Black voters were illegally disempowered, Alabama argued that re-empowering them would violate the Fourteenth Amendment's guarantee of equal protection of laws by taking race into account. It's a disingenuous and dangerous argument—they effectively claimed that protecting Black voters from discrimination is equivalent to discriminating against Black voters—and it's also an ahistorical one. Justice Jackson explained as much at great length during oral argument, providing contemporaneous record after record showing that the Reconstruction Amendments' drafters unambiguously adopted them in a race-conscious way in order to secure the rights of freed former slaves.[112] The whole point, she made clear, was "trying to ensure that people who had been discriminated against, the freedman, during the Reconstruction period, were actually brought equal to everyone else in society."[113] Commentators observed that Justice Jackson "brilliantly turned the tables" on the right-wing justices by using originalism to defend the rights of Black people rather than dismantle them.[114]

Justice Jackson again put on a master class on the history of race in America later that month when the Supreme Court heard oral argument about the constitutionality of race-conscious admissions programs in *Students for Fair Admissions* [SFFA] *v. University of North Carolina* [UNC]. SFFA brought a challenge to UNC's holistic review process of student applicants, which evaluated whole individuals and acknowledged race as one characteristic among many in order to produce a diverse student body and obtain the educational benefits that flow from it. Here, too, self-proclaimed originalists insisted that this practice ran afoul of the Fourteenth Amendment's originally understood commitment to "colorblindness" above all. So, once again, Justice Jackson and others set the record straight and questioned the attorneys about the lawmakers' use of explicitly race-conscious remedies, including the Constitution itself.[115]

Credit where credit is due: progressive originalism is a step above the originalism that we're used to. Eric Foner captured my feelings on Justice Jackson's refreshing analysis exactly when he said, "Originalism is intellectually indefensible. But if you are going to talk about history you had better get it right."[116] I wholeheartedly agree that the Reconstruction Amendments are underutilized, and I understand working within the confines that exist. But, as with original-recipe originalism, the progressive flavor still leaves a bad taste in my mouth.

Originalism for liberals comes up short on both intellectual and strategic grounds. By conceding that constitutional interpretation ought to be linked to the original understanding of a provision at the time it was written, it legitimizes originalism as the one correct legal

decision-making model and still constrains our constitutional imagination to an era where much of America was much worse off. All ver-
sions of originalism definitionally put some perception of the past
on a pedestal and inherently privilege an existing legal order. Our
constitutional beacon should not be a point in time; it should be the
principles of antisubordination, equal freedom, and justice for all.
And to the extent that an objective public meaning at the time of
ratification can be discovered, the original meaning of the Fourteenth Amendment would be a poor substitute for its meaning today.
The Fourteenth Amendment is currently understood to protect
people across multiple axes of discrimination such as race, gender,
and national origin. That may not remain true if we were to start
turning back the clock.[117]

Consider the case of Myra Bradwell: Myra attended law school,
graduated with honors, and passed the Illinois bar exam in 1869, but
was denied a license to practice law because she was a woman.[118]
Myra brought a legal challenge under the Fourteenth Amendment
within a few years of its ratification. The Supreme Court ruled
against her 8–1.[119] The majority of justices in 1872 did not consider
women's equality to be a Fourteenth Amendment issue. And three
justices added in a concurring opinion that "the paramount destiny
and mission of woman are to fulfill the noble and benign offices of
wife and mother."[120] It would take another century for the Supreme
Court to finally recognize that the Fourteenth Amendment prohibited discrimination because of sex.[121]

The Court has repeatedly reaffirmed this sex-discrimination
principle since identifying it in *Reed v. Reed* (1971). But, disturbingly, as recently as 2011, Justice Scalia argued that the Fourteenth
Amendment's protections didn't extend to women.[122] "Certainly the
Constitution does not require discrimination on the basis of sex," he
said in an interview. "The only issue is whether it prohibits it. It

doesn't. Nobody ever thought that that's what it meant." Scalia and his supporters suggested that didn't necessarily mean discrimination against women and others in want of equality couldn't be *made* unlawful under the Constitution, but that it would have to go up for a vote.[123] (Yes, ladies, the recognition of our rights under law is so suspect that we may need a show of hands on whether women are people.*) There may be little to nothing for liberals to gain as a matter of law from playing by originalists' rules. Conversely, there's nothing to lose by dreaming bigger.

Further weakening the case for liberal originalism is the reality that it will probably not make many friends on either side of the aisle. Progressives are (with good reason) deeply distrustful of originalism and may be disinclined to rally around it.[124] And I wouldn't expect any conservative converts either. Justice Jackson conducted a thorough analysis of the explicitly and deliberately race-conscious remedies of the Reconstruction era in *Students for Fair Admissions*—a history that should be central to any fair originalist reading of the Fourteenth Amendment—and this did not prevent the Court from striking down race-conscious admissions as unconstitutional in July 2023. Scholars like Professor Eric Segall have catalogued how famed self-

---

* The Equal Rights Amendment has not (yet) been widely recognized as part of the Constitution, but the movement for its ratification influenced how courts and the public came to understand and interpret the Fourteenth Amendment. That the Fourteenth Amendment now protects against some forms of sex discrimination shows that originalism doesn't accurately describe how constitutional meaning is determined—and it wouldn't be desirable if it did. See, e.g., Melissa Murray, "The Equal Rights Amendment: A Century in the Making Symposium Foreword," *The Harbinger* 43 (2019): 91, 96–97; Reva B. Siegel, "Constitutional Culture, Social Movement Conflict and Constitutional Change: The Case of the De Facto Era, 2005–06 Brennan Center Symposium Lecture, 94," *California Law Review* 94, no. 5 (October 2006): 1323, 1390.

identified originalists have repeatedly carved out and cast aside historical evidence that is inconsistent with Republican priorities.[125] Take Scalia, who Professor Rick Hasen described as an originalist except when it came to race and the Equal Protection Clause.[126] Or Thomas, who Constitutional Accountability Center founder Doug Kendall and Professor Jim Ryan observed "will use originalism where it provides support for a politically conservative result, even if that support is weak . . . But where history provides no support, he's likely to ignore it altogether."[127] Or Alito, who I'm pretty sure wouldn't revise his views on the Fourteenth Amendment even if the provision's drafters appeared to him like the Ghost of Christmas Past to scare him into changing his ways.* Yale Law professor Reva Siegel has also documented instances of the originalist justices going beyond mere avoidance of inconvenient facts to actively reject history and tradition that doesn't entrench their preferred hierarchies.[128] Committed conservative originalists will not be convinced by originalist evidence that furthers progressive goals because originalism itself was never the point. Originalism's authority comes from its utility as a vehicle to mobilize conservatives and achieve their policy goals.[129] Instead of courting unwinnable people with an insufficiently protective model of constitutional interpretation, progressives could articulate and advocate for an affirmative vision that allows and encourages growth in service of an equitable democracy. Developing and promoting a positive alternative method free from originalism's artificial constraints can shift what lawyers and the general public come to expect and demand from the law. Originalism cannot be saved, and even if it could be, it wouldn't be worth it.

When defending the mode of thought, Justice Scalia waved off originalism's perceived flaws. "My burden is not to show that origi-

---

* "Equality? Bah, humbug!"

nalism is perfect," he once stated at a lecture, "but that it beats the other alternatives, and that, believe me, is not difficult."[130] But how can that be? What degree of pessimism is required to believe that *this* is the best we're capable of mustering up? You've seen throughout this chapter (and will continue to see throughout this book) that originalism condemns the rights of oppressed people to stagnate, stuck in amber like the mosquito in *Jurassic Park,* except here the preservation reanimates racism instead of raptors. Are our intellectual abilities so meager that we must resign ourselves to obvious ploys to subordinate racial, gender, and sexual minorities? Does interpreting laws in a discriminatory way honestly beat the alternative of *not doing that*? I say no. We must reject this sort of cynical laziness. Antonin Scalia is dead; the Constitution is not.

A FAIRER FUTURE UNDER LAW

The opposite of a "dead" Constitution, so to speak, is a living one. Supporters of the living Constitution theory dismiss originalist claims about frozen freedoms and argue instead that the Constitution's meaning does—and should—change over time.[131] For living constitutionalists, the idea that originalism's unexamined acceptance of the Constitution's purported (or cherry-picked) original meaning should bind contemporary Americans is a critical failure in a democratic society.[132] Originalists often link their interpretive theory's democratic legitimacy to the idea that they are uncovering what the people who were authorized to draft and ratify the Constitution sought to communicate.[133] But even if we were confident that there is an objective discoverable meaning, what of those of us who were denied a stake in authorization for lack of whiteness, manhood, wealth, or some combination thereof?[134] Living constitutionalists typically find it difficult to justify centuries of subservience to discriminatory constitutional interpretations that we had no part in making.[135] Rather than relinquish self-rule to the antidemocratic, dead hand of the past, the living Constitution idea seeks to vindicate popular sovereignty and, at its best, the egalitarian ideals embodied in the Constitution.[136]

These concerns motivated Justice Thurgood Marshall's explicit embrace of a living Constitution. In a 1987 speech commemorating the two hundredth anniversary of the Constitution, Justice Marshall emphasized that he was celebrating the life of the document as opposed to its underwhelming birth. Marshall was better positioned than most to speak about the evolution of constitutional interpretation, and the shortcomings of originalism and the Founding Fathers alike: he was the attorney who successfully argued *Brown v. Board* before the Court, and roughly a dozen years later, he was the first Black person to become a Supreme Court justice. His speech reflected on the role law played in shaping the conditions of Black America (for better and for worse) as well as the emergence of new constitutional principles over time. He praised the Fourteenth Amendment as a basis for justice that people have built upon and can continue to build upon. Justice Marshall recognized that the hard-won progress made by oppressed people and allies and the continuing fight for equality would surely be anathema to the Framers— men who he said "could not have imagined, nor would they have accepted, that the document they were drafting would one day be construed by a Supreme Court to which had been appointed a woman and the descendent of an African slave."[137] Yet Marshall made a crucial observation. He was capable of acknowledging both the Constitution's failures and its promise. For all its flaws (of which there are many*), the Constitution articulated the same principles

---

*See, e.g., Elie Mystal's incisive debut book *Allow Me to Retort: A Black Guy's Guide to the Constitution* (2022), the opening line of which is "Our Constitution is not good." (He elaborates.)

that social justice movements are built on: equality, liberty, and justice for all. And these movements in turn have forged those principles into recognized canons of constitutional law.[138]

Historically, the ivory tower has undervalued the role of social movements in constructing constitutional meaning. But that's changing. Reva Siegel is a leading scholar in this area who contends that the meaning of the Constitution cannot be fixed, as originalism claims, because mobilized citizens can be and have been instrumental in shaping legal understandings "that we now venerate as core features of our constitutional order," like integration and women's suffrage.[139] Other scholars have similarly suggested that the framers of the Fourteenth Amendment are less responsible for the modern meaning of the amendment's Equal Protection Clause than the movements for racial and gender justice that built power and reshaped norms.[140] Originalists would deem this improper, but it's not necessarily a bad thing for living constitutionalists. Adherents don't view interpretive evolution as a departure from the founding document. Rather, they contend that continuing to develop and refine our understanding of the Constitution is more consistent with its spirit. Professor Charles Reich cautioned in an early *Harvard Law Review* article on the subject that stagnating jurisprudence in the face of societal change causes constitutional atrophy, with the terms losing their meaning and utility. Reich argued that "a constitutional provision can maintain its integrity only by moving in the same direction and at the same rate as the rest of society. In constitutions, constancy requires change."[141]

The idea that our legal interpretation could be in a state of boundless flux has made the living Constitution concept vulnerable to attack. Critics fear that it reduces jurisprudence to the whims of a few elites and enables judges to independently impose their own values outside the democratic process.[142] I'm sympathetic to this concern, but I believe it is misguided. The critique points to two main issues—undemocratic rule and lack of judicial constraint—neither of which is unique to the idea of a living Constitution.

The risk of undemocratic rule is more connected to our existing legal structures than to any singular model of legal interpretation. This is another one of those things lawyers are often reluctant to admit in public. But scholars like Niko Bowie have made compelling arguments that the consequence of giving nine unelected, unaccountable, life-tenured, elite attorneys the ability to strike down federal law is that "the political choices available to us as a democracy depend not on our collective will but on the will of people who hold power until they resign or die."[143] Ryan Doerfler and Samuel Moyn have supported their similarly thought-provoking arguments for reforms to disempower the Supreme Court with a meticulous examination of the institution as an obstacle to democracy.[144] Admittedly, the legislature and the presidency aren't consistently meeting democratic standards either—other scholars have suggested that court rulings aren't necessarily so undemocratic after all because "sometimes in a representative democracy, the representative branches *aren't*."[145] But even so, systemic change is needed to address the ways the Court is both a product and a source of antidemocracy in the United States. That includes reforming the way people get on the Court, the way they stay on the Court, what powers they can exercise once on the Court and for how long, and how they are permitted to use that power.[146] But, until these institutional changes occur, the adoption of new theories would tangibly reduce harm for a society that cannot wait. Both laypeople and lawpeople should refuse to accept originalism as a legitimate means of interpreting the Constitution, and instead interpret the Constitution in alignment with democratic values.

Importantly, a mass movement for non-originalist legal interpretation would inherently undercut the idea that the Supreme Court alone is responsible for constructing constitutional meaning. This in turn would build support for structural reform because, as the authors of *The Anti-Oligarchy Constitution* have argued, "to confront a hostile Supreme Court, the people and their elected leaders need to be confident that they, too, have the power and the obligation to interpret the Constitution. . . . To persuade Americans that stern court-curbing measures are necessary, progressives must first convince enough Americans that the court is dead wrong about the Constitution."[147]

The risk of an unconstrained judiciary is a stronger but still flawed critique of the living Constitution idea. A living Constitution is no more prone to manipulation and the substitution of individual preferences in lieu of law than originalism, as the Supreme Court's originalist cohort has amply demonstrated. There's even a case to be made that the two theories are, or at least can be, one and the same; Reva Siegel has argued that the originalism on display in *Dobbs* was really just living constitutionalism in service of antidemocratic goals.[148] (This critique may scandalize originalists, but it's actually paying them a courtesy—famed constitutional law scholar Erwin Chemerinsky rejects the idea that originalism is "a theory of judging at all" and regards it as "only a rhetorical ploy to make it appear that decisions are based on something other than political ideology."[149]) The point is well taken, though, that a living Constitution in and of itself can disorient the legal system; granting that constitutional meaning changes with society implies that the Constitution can mean anything, and if society changes for the worse, so too can the Constitution. The biggest flaw with the living Constitution idea, then, is that it is more descriptive than prescriptive. By this I mean, it describes its acceptance of things changing without necessarily prescribing how they should change. The Constitution can go on living to steer us toward collective justice or jeopardy.

Providing a principled answer to this question of how our legal interpretation should evolve is where *The Originalism Trap* comes in. Originalists often claim that there is no real alternative to their methodology.[150] Fortunately, I'm here to present you with another option. The Supreme Court's ongoing assault on rights and intellectually indefensible justifications of democratic backsliding call for a new mode of legal thought that bolsters an inclusive, participatory democracy rather than marginalizing huge swaths of the country. Wherever possible, legal interpretation should fulfill America's promises rather than surrender to its shortcomings. An inclusive alternative to originalism does not cabin its analysis to whether a right is "deeply rooted in this Nation's history and tradition," as emphasized by Justice Samuel Alito in the opinion ruling that there is no federal right to abortion.[151] To be frank, much of this nation's history and tradition leaves much to be desired. I'm a Black woman who emigrated to this country as an infant, and my very humanity is still not a matter of national consensus. The *fight* over my humanity, though, has existed for as long as those in power have tried to deny it, and my humanity persists all the same. Justice for all may not be a deeply rooted tradition, but fighting for it is. The Constitution should be understood as a powerful ally in the people's fight for freedom.

A frequently overlooked reason why America's promises remain unfulfilled is because of the fraud perpetuated by originalism. The Constitution has never been a dead letter, as originalism claims. It has always been up to the people to breathe life into it. The American tradition of constitutional interpretation is one in which fugitive slave and abolitionist Frederick Douglass made his case to the nation that a document widely understood at the time to condone enslavement would be more accurately interpreted as commanding emancipation—even before the Civil War.[152] Douglass had no doubt as to what he termed "the wicked intentions of our Constitution makers" with respect to slavery, but he considered and ultimately rejected the idea that his interpretation of legal doctrine should be bound by the Constitution's original understanding.[153] In the Constitution, Douglass saw justice, liberty, welfare, and peace. "Shall we condemn the righteous law because wicked men twist it to the support of wickedness?" he asked. His answer was no. "Where a law is susceptible of two meanings, the one making it accomplish an innocent purpose, and the other making it accomplish a wicked purpose, we must in all cases adopt that which makes it accomplish an innocent purpose."[154]

Justice Marshall and Justice Brennan were right—the core directive the amended Constitution gives to us is to cast off the yoke of subordination. Originalism is inconsistent with the Constitution's rejection of exploitation and dominance, made explicit in the nineteenth century by the Reconstruction Amendments. Uncritical acceptance of amateur history that ignores the realities of oppression and the breadth of the country's diversity does not make the courts and their application of law impartial. It makes them impoverished.[155] I propose a new method of legal interpretation that is guided by the country's purported principles and not its failure to live up to them. I call it "inclusive constitutionalism."

INCLUSIVE CONSTITUTIONALISM

Inclusive constitutionalism is an interpretive framework that disentangles the Constitution's ideals from originalist ideology and instead emphasizes the transformative goals of the Reconstruction Amendments.[156] The Constitution as originally drafted was a compromise with chattel slavery (quite literally, as you'll see in chapter 4). But the Reconstruction Amendments remade the Constitution with the aim of freeing the nation as a whole from the shackles of white supremacy—both literal and metaphorical. As articulated nearly two hundred years ago in an antislavery political party's platform, abolitionists organized not "merely for the overthrow of slavery" but to "carry out the principle of equal rights into all its practical consequences and applications, and support every just measure conducive to individual and social freedom."[157] Abolitionist legal theory has a long and rich history that is foundational to the Reconstruction Amendments, and that the legal field has sometimes preferred to ignore.[158] Scholars like Professor Dorothy Roberts have sought to uncover the contemporary relevance of this intellectual tradition, particularly with respect to American policing and prisons, the death penalty, and the exploitation of incarcerated workers.[159] But the potential implications go far beyond prison walls and touch every aspect of our democratic society. Inclusive constitutionalism means what it says: the Constitution includes everyone, so our legal interpretation must serve to make the promise of inclusive democracy real. When the judiciary is called upon to resolve a legal ambiguity or when there are broad principles at issue, the application of which must be made specific, it is proper for courts to consider how cases may relate to systemic injustices and how different legal analyses would impact marginalized people's ability to participate in the country's political, economic, and social life.[160] We can't fulfill the Reconstruction Amendments' radical vision of full equality and freedom if we can't be attentive to the ways in which we have been made unequal and unfree.

To be very clear, inclusive constitutionalism does not mean any law can mean anything; it provides an avenue through which a law's meaning can be better understood if its meaning is not already plain. Some constitutional provisions are transparent, while others are more opaque. The constitutional requirements for the presidency provide a helpful example of both. Among the qualifications specified in Article II of the Constitution are that the president must be a natural-born citizen of the United States and at least thirty-five years old. No one can reasonably question what thirty-five years old means.* But "natural-born citizen" is less clear. At one end of the spectrum, it seems obvious that a child would be a natural-born citizen if they were born in the United States to two parents who were U.S. citizens. At the other end of the spectrum, it seems obvious that I am not a natural-born citizen because I was born in Saint Vincent and the Grenadines to two Vincentian parents. While I resent the implication that naturalized citizens who chose this country are less American than those who happened to be born here, I accept that a plain reading renders me categorically ineligible.[161] (Feel free to breathe a sigh of relief, Federalist Society.) But what about the cases that fall somewhere in between?

For example, a 2008 law review article by Professor Gabriel Chin contended that the late senator John McCain was not a natural-born citizen because he was born in the Panama Canal Zone.[162] The Canal Zone was an unincorporated territory of the United States that Representative John Sparkman described on the House floor in 1937 as a "no-man's land" with respect to citizenship status, covered by neither the Constitution nor immigration law.[163] And John McCain was born there in 1936. In 1937, Congress passed a statute that granted citizenship to people who were born in the Canal Zone from 1904 onward and had at least one citizen parent. So, the argument goes, McCain could not be a natural-born citizen, because he was not actually a citizen at the moment of birth; rather, an act of Congress conferred him citizenship when he was eleven months old.[164] There's a reasonable counterargument to be made that McCain should have been considered a natural-born citizen even without that statute, because both of his parents were American citizens who were only in the Canal Zone because of his father's military service. There is also

*To any fellow nerd wondering, "Well, what about time dilation?" I think we're a ways off from that being a meaningful concern.

some historical evidence that children of public officials serving abroad were recognized as natural-born citizens, in exception to the general rule. (The Senate recognized as much and unanimously passed a resolution in 2008 stating that McCain was a natural-born citizen under the Constitution.)[165] Chin acknowledged that some legal theories are more protective of rights and would consider McCain a citizen by birth for those reasons, but that would require the law to "abandon a century of restrictive doctrines developed by conservative justices."[166] Chin later remarked, "It's preposterous that a technicality like this can make a difference in an advanced democracy, but this is the constitutional text that we have."[167]

Several legal scholars have similarly argued that an originalist reading of the Constitution would disqualify Senator Ted Cruz for the presidency. Cruz has a harder case to make than McCain did.[168] Unlike McCain, he was born in an indisputably foreign country (Canada) to an indisputably foreign father (Cuban) and an American civilian mother.[169] Some scholars argue that Cruz is a natural-born citizen nonetheless because the immigration law in place when Cruz was born provided that a person automatically becomes a U.S. citizen at birth if one of their parents is a U.S. citizen who established residency in the United States before the child was born. But different methods of interpretation reach different conclusions.[170] Ironically, Cruz has long been adamant that the Supreme Court must enforce the original understanding of the Constitution. "If he's right," Eric Posner writes, "then he's not eligible for the presidency."[171] Professor Laurence Tribe (who, fun fact, taught Cruz constitutional law at Harvard) also argued that Cruz's own logic made him ineligible because eighteenth-century understandings of natural-born citizenship required birth on U.S. soil, and having an American mother alone was insufficient.[172] Professor Mary Brigid McManamon found the matter quite simple, too, concluding that the Framers clearly required the president of the United States to be born in the United States.[173]

It will come as no surprise that I opposed the presidential candi-dacies of John McCain and Ted Cruz. But I did so because of their policies, not because of their parentage or the landmass on which they happened to take their first breaths. It's nonsensical and offen-sive to the idea of an inclusive democratic society that "natural-born citizen" should be interpreted to prevent an American citizen who was born to an American citizen from seeking to represent America. In debatable cases like those of McCain and Cruz, inclusive consti-tutionalism would err on the side of recognizing people's member-ship in the community rather than cutting them out, allowing them to participate in the political process, and letting the voters cast their ballots as they wish—thereby bolstering the democratic value of inclusion and minimizing the impact of a biological caste system repugnant to democracy.

This is not beyond judicial capabilities. Judges make these kinds of judgment calls all the time; I'm merely calling on them to better exercise that judgment. The Supreme Court famously recognized that the judiciary has a responsibility to democracy nearly a century ago. Somewhat comically, this foundational component of the Court's rights-protecting jurisprudence was tucked away in a foot-note of a case about a product of yesteryear called "filled milk." Car-olene Products Company was indicted for violating the Filled Milk Act—a statute enacted in 1923 that prohibited the shipment of skimmed milk compounded with any fat or oil other than milk fat (so as to resemble milk or cream) in interstate commerce.[174] The company challenged the statute's legality in *United States v. Car-olene Products Co.* and lost. In upholding the act as constitutional, the Court explained that Congress has the authority to regulate or-dinary commercial transactions so long as it has a rational basis for doing so. This is a very deferential standard, meaning the govern-ment only has to clear a low bar for courts to uphold a law as constitutional. But the Court explained in a footnote that, while such a deferential standard makes sense for regular commerce laws, it didn't make sense for *all* laws. Some cases call for stricter and more exacting scrutiny. The Court wrote this footnote to clarify that the deferential standard it was using applied to a narrow scope of cases, and to identify some cases it might not apply to. Specifically, the Supreme Court stated that judicial intervention may be needed when prejudice against minority groups limits "the operation of those political processes ordinarily to be relied upon to protect minorities."[175] The paradigmatic example here is denying Black people the right to vote.

The fourth footnote of *United States v. Carolene Products Co.* suggests that courts have a duty to ensure that the democratic process is actually functional and accessible to marginalized groups. Renowned constitutional law scholar John Hart Ely built on this idea in his influential text *Democracy and Distrust,* which for decades was the premier liberal justification of the courts' authority to strike down laws. Ely argued that procedural fairness is the focal point of the Constitution, that judicial intervention is warranted when the government excludes groups from the political process. *Carolene* and Ely provide a helpful starting point for thinking about the role of the judiciary in protecting democracy—and just how far astray the Supreme Court is today.[176]

The trail of tattered rights and democracy protections left in the wake of the Supreme Court as helmed by Chief Justice Roberts show that the current Court couldn't care less about *Carolene*'s or Ely's guidance.[177] Harvard Law professor Nicholas Stephanopoulos has characterized it as an "anti-*Carolene* Court" that not only declines to intervene to ensure that democracy works but actually intervenes to ensure that it doesn't. He explains that the Court's perpetuation of the "pathologies of modern American democracy" like "gerrymandering, voter suppression, the enormous influence of the wealthy, and so on" is linked to partisan advantage more than any consistently applied legal interpretative theory.[178] Stephanopoulos has also called attention to a particularly dangerous perversion of *Carolene:* not only is the Court unwilling to curb undemocratic abuses and promote democratic values itself, it is simultaneously unwilling to allow other actors outside the courts, like legislators or voters, from doing so, either.[179] (We'll talk more about the lengths the Court goes to in order to insulate voter suppression and gerrymandering from democracy-enhancing interventions in chapter 3.)

Such rulings and the reasoning that undergirds them should be regarded as legally, intellectually, and morally unacceptable. Ely was right to contend that the judiciary should "unblock stoppages" in the democratic process. Where Ely fell short, however, is that he conflated democracy with simple majoritarianism, while paying insufficient attention to what underlying conditions must be met for people to be able to participate equally in the political process. Although he regarded voting and speech as essential democratic rights that courts should protect, he considered anything not explicitly guaranteed in the text as "constitutionally gratuitous" and discouraged courts from protecting it.[180] This is a serious error that discounts many forms of democratic exclusion and takes people's movements to articulate and advance their rights for granted.

For a specific example, Ely strongly disagreed with *Roe v. Wade* despite supporting abortion as a policy matter; the *Dobbs* opinion actually quotes Ely's assessment that *Roe* was "not constitutional law" and gave "almost no sense of an obligation to try to be" in two separate places.* Abortion fell outside the Constitution's scope for

---

* Whether the repetition was for emphasis or simply indicative of sloppy writing is unclear, but the point remains. *Dobbs v. Jackson Women's Health Organization*, 597 U.S. __ (2022).

Ely for two main reasons. First, he didn't see abortion as related to political participation, failing to understand that your ability to participate in the political process is vastly diminished if the government can coerce you into motherhood. Second, he believed that the right to abortion could not be inferred from the Constitution's text or principles, the Framers' intent, or the structure of government.[181] In contrast, I believe the right is squarely grounded in the principles and history of the Reconstruction Amendments, I'm not especially preoccupied with what the Framers would have thought, and I contend that a person's legal rights and liberties cannot be dependent on their reproductive status in a democratic society. (I have much more to say about this in chapter 2.) For these reasons, inclusive constitutionalism extends beyond Ely's narrow focus. Democracy—and the Court's facilitation of democracy—requires honoring the Constitution's substantive commitments to liberty and equality and fostering practical access to citizenship.

Real consideration for the lives of real people—especially the people who have historically been overlooked and underserved by American institutions—should be a part of our legal interpretation. As *New York Times* columnist Jamelle Bouie writes, "Democracy is more than just a set of rules, institutions and procedures . . . And at its most robust—much to the chagrin of the keepers and defenders of wealth and privilege—democracy holds the promise of a more egalitarian world."[182] That is the world inclusive constitutionalism is fighting for.

The Constitution gives us the tools we need to build that better world. Whether and how those tools are used is a question of interpretation. Similar to how a federal trial judge described the Trump campaign's effort to overturn a democratic presidential election as "a coup in search of a legal theory," originalism is injustice in search of a legal interpretative method.[183] We should instead adopt a theory of interpretation in active pursuit of justice.

Justice Alito would say that the Constitution means only what people would have understood it to mean at the time it was written.[184] He is wrong. But hundreds of millions of dollars have been spent over the course of decades to convince us that legitimate constitutional interpretation is primarily the province of white men in robes who graduated from Yale Law School and use Ouija boards to communicate with the spirits of dead slaveholders.* I decline to be bullied by ghosts any longer. And I invite you to do the same. The hypocrisies of the Framers need not be our own. By being honest about the law—both its shortcomings and its possibilities—we can discard the harmful originalist model of legal interpretation in favor of a new approach tied to underused constitutional principles like freedom from oppression, due process, and equal protection under law.

Dispensing with originalism's artifice of legitimacy is our first step toward reclaiming the Constitution. The Supreme Court seeks to quell public revolt—even while vindicating the interests of the powerful over the rights of the marginalized with alarming regularity—by presenting its chosen outcomes as eminently reasonable. Such decisions are rational and objective, they assure us, because originalism says our rights and liberties are frozen in the 1800s. But our country's founding documents are aspirational, and we can reject the originalist command to stop striving. In the next few chapters, I interrogate how originalism tries to limit what control we have over our lives (in due

---

*The co-chair of the Federalist Society, a powerful conservative legal non-profit that has influenced and advised multiple Republican presidential administrations, helped raise over $250 million in dark-money donations between 2014 and 2017 alone in order to fund campaigns supporting the confirmation of conservative judges. Robert O'Hara, Jr., and Shawn Boburg, "Federalist Society's Leonard Leo Is Helping Trump Make Courts More Conservative," *The Washington Post,* May 19, 2019, washingtonpost.com/graphics/2019/investigations/leonard-leo-federalists-society-courts/.

process and equal protection law), what say we have in our communities (in election law), and who deserves to have a say (in the census, an underappreciated but absolutely essential part of understanding how our democracy works—or doesn't). And through inclusive constitutionalism, I show how we can demand better for our democracy and for ourselves.

CHAPTER 2

STEALING OUR LIBERTIES

There are a number of things in my personal life I neither want nor need the government's opinion on. The conservative legal movement has nevertheless made it its business to decide personal matters like who people can love, what people can wear, where people can use the bathroom, and when people must give birth. These impositions on autonomy and dignity add up: the conservative conception of law denies us basic control over our own identities and futures. Extremists like Federalist Society co-chair Leonard Leo regard the small victories for human decency eked out over the last few decades as an unacceptable departure from "the natural order of things."[1] For them, laws that cement social hierarchies are only validating the societal conditions that are supposed to exist anyway. And wouldn't you know it, those conditions typically privilege a narrow version of Christianity that's bound up with wealth, whiteness, and stereotypical gender roles, and subordinate people who are unable or unwilling to fit into those boxes.

It's a good thing, then, that the Constitution does not share the conservative movement's disdain for laws that let people live with equal dignity. The central purposes of the Second Founding—the term popularized by historian Eric Foner to describe the remaking of the country and the Constitution after the Civil War—were to end the all-encompassing exploitation and domination of slavery and to imbue the Constitution with a commitment to freedom and equality (for real this time). This required Congress to "readjust the foundations of political power," as Senator Charles Sumner of Massachusetts articulated it in 1866.[2]

One of the major vehicles designed to drive this wide-scale transformation of society is the Fourteenth Amendment of the Constitution, which redefined political and social membership in the wake of the Civil War. Here's how the amendment begins:

All persons born or naturalized in the United States, and subject to the jurisdiction thereof, are citizens of the United States and of the State wherein they reside. No State shall make or enforce any law which shall abridge the privileges or immunities of citizens of the United States; nor shall any State deprive any person of life, liberty, or property, without due process of law; nor deny to any person within its jurisdiction the equal protection of the laws.

This language clearly puts limits on the ability of states to oppress the people within their borders. But, as you may have noticed, the text does not specifically say what those limits are—only that there are some lines that shouldn't be crossed, or at least, only crossed with a proper exercise of caution. The second sentence's clause about due process of law (called, inventively, the Due Process Clause) has historically stood out for its room for interpretation. Activists have fought many legal and political battles over the meaning of the Fourteenth Amendment's command that no person shall be deprived of "life, liberty, or property, without due process of law" in efforts to protect people from infringements of their individual rights.* For example, does liberty merely mean freedom from confinement, or does it mean something grander? If life, liberty, and property interests are so fundamental that there are constitutional protections against state deprivation, is the state obligated to ensure that people have a minimum level of necessities like food, water, and shelter to protect in the first place? What is the process that is due under the Due Process Clause? How much of it? And are there some circumstances where no amount of process is sufficient to justify the curtailment of a right?

To help answer those questions, courts and other legal actors have interpreted the Due Process Clause as having two parts: procedural and substantive. These legal concepts are inferred from the Clause so that its abstract terms can be put into practice. Procedural due process ensures that we receive adequate notice and the opportunity to be heard when our rights are being impacted by the government. It's the reason why, for example, states can't just assume unmarried fathers are unsuitable parents and take their kids away without even having a hearing to determine their fitness as parents first. (Yes, that really was legal until the Supreme Court said otherwise about fifty years ago.)[3] Substantive due process, in contrast, ensures that the government doesn't intrude on our constitutional rights for no good reason—regardless of whether the government checked all the right boxes along the way. It's the reason why you can't be jailed for teaching a kid how to speak a foreign language.

---

*This command actually appears in both the Fifth and Fourteenth Amendments. Like the rest of the Bill of Rights, the Due Process Clause of the Fifth Amendment applies directly to the federal government. The Fourteenth Amendment, however, applies to the states. The Fourteenth Amendment has been read to "incorporate" the Bill of Rights, though, so states don't get a free pass on violating the first several amendments. (U.S. Constitution, Amendments V, XIV.)

(Yes, this, too, was a real law!)[4] While procedural due process is concerned with the question of how a deprivation of life, liberty, or property is occurring, substantive due process is concerned with why that deprivation is occurring at all, meaning: Does the government have a sufficient substantive reason to justify its action?[5] As the Supreme Court once explained, "By requiring the government to follow appropriate procedures when its agents decide to 'deprive any person of life, liberty, or property,' the Due Process Clause promotes fairness in such decisions. And by barring certain government actions regardless of the fairness of the procedures used to implement them, it serves to prevent governmental power from being 'used for purposes of oppression.'"[6]

Our understanding of oppression has, thankfully, developed over time. So the reach of substantive due process has shifted, too. Like Justice Anthony Kennedy wrote for the Supreme Court when it ruled that a law criminalizing gay intimacy between consenting adults in their homes was unconstitutional, "As the Constitution endures, persons in every generation can invoke its principles in their own search for greater freedom."[7] When not unduly restrained, substantive due process offers an empowering rebuke of injustice.

So naturally, originalists want it gone.

THE CASE AGAINST SUBSTANTIVE DUE PROCESS

In fairness, originalists aren't the only ones who have a problem with substantive due process. The concept sometimes gets a bad rap among conservative and liberal legal minds alike, notwithstanding its frequent use in the protection of fundamental rights.[8]

On the right, Justice Thomas has derided the "'substantive' 'due process' 'doctrine'" (scare quotes his) as an oxymoron with no legal basis that lets the Court invent rights without constitutional constraint.[9] Robert Bork called it a "momentous sham" used by judges to "write their personal beliefs into" the Constitution.[10] For them, the only function of the Due Process Clause is to guarantee that some procedures are followed before a person is deprived of rights, and the Clause says nothing about what those rights could be or what deprivations, if any, are simply off limits. Substantive due process is problematic, then, because it identifies and protects rights that fall under the scope of "life, liberty, and property" and are not explicitly stated in the Constitution. Conservatives start from the premise that a procedural requirement cannot have a substantive meaning, so they arrive at the conclusion that any judge recognizing substantive due process rights is just making stuff up.

On the left, Professor Samuel Moyn has chastised liberals for using raw judicial power to achieve their policy preferences in what he termed "so-called 'substantive due process'" decisions. Moyn considers the doctrine risky because it elevates rationales, such as freedom from unwelcome government intrusions, which often serve the interests of corporations (ever eager for deregulation) rather than regular people.* And even John Hart Ely's foundational text making the case for democracy-reinforcing judicial review treated substantive due process as contradictory and an object of rebuke, again reading "process" as necessarily limited to steps and regarding the terms "substance" and "process" as inherently in conflict. He notably analogized the phrase "substantive due process" to "green pastel redness." Ely, you'll remember, was the liberal legal scholar who argued that courts' main responsibility is to keep political channels open for legislative decision-making. For him, substantive due pro-

---

* Moyn's broader point was not just dunking on substantive due process but calling on progressives to focus more on mass politics and winning the people rather than winning in courts—and that point is very well taken. Samuel Moyn, "Resisting the Juristocracy," *Boston Review,* October 5, 2018, bostonreview .net/law-justice/samuel-moyn-resisting-juristocracy.

cess issues like abortion were distinct from people's ability to participate in the political process, and therefore an improper use of judicial power. Spoken like someone who never had to think seriously about the impacts of unplanned pregnancy, childbirth, and motherhood.[11]

Columbia Law School professor Jamal Greene has observed that the criticism of substantive due process as oxymoronic gained popularity concurrently with "the rise of a certain kind of originalism" deliberately manufactured by conservative activists in Reagan's Justice Department and elsewhere.[12] Nevertheless, substantive due process now has naysayers across the political spectrum. A common theme in both the left and the right's critiques is that substantive due process allows judges to give their idiosyncratic values the force of law without regard for democratic preferences and the political process.* The concept is therefore linked in the American legal imagination to the Supreme Court's much-maligned ruling in *Lochner v. New York* (1905).

Lochner is very high on most lawyers' list of Things Not to Do. Joseph Lochner was the owner of Lochner's Home Bakery in Utica, New York, and on at least two occasions, he violated a state law regulating the number of hours bakeries could have their employees work.[13] Bakery owners violated the law if they required or permitted their employees to work more than sixty hours in one week, or more than ten hours in any one day.[14] Passed unanimously by the New York legislature, the law's aims included limiting employees' exposure to health and safety issues common among bakers slaving away in dank tenement basements, and strengthening workers' ability to collectively bargain for better workplace conditions. Workers had

---

* Here's a particularly absurd (and offensive) example: Justice Scalia argued in his dissent in *Lawrence v. Texas* that if courts could strike down laws criminalizing gay sex on substantive due process grounds, they could strike down laws criminalizing bestiality for the same reason.

limited power to negotiate for fair and equitable employment, and the American labor movement believed that the government needed to intervene to shorten work hours.[15]

Lochner was convicted under the law and appealed the decision to the Supreme Court. The Court's 5–4 majority framed the bakery law as unfair and patronizing to workers who voluntarily entered contracts and therefore had no need for state protection, and who may want to earn more money by working longer hours.[16] It reasoned that the provision necessarily interfered with the right of employers and employees to contract. And for the first time, the Court said the right to contract to purchase and sell labor was part of the liberty interest protected by the Fourteenth Amendment. Sidenote to any sex worker who just raised an eyebrow: the Court conceded that this right was not a trump card, and certain kinds of contracts could still be lawfully prohibited. Such laws would pass constitutional muster if the Court found them sufficiently related to the protection of the health, safety, morals, and general welfare of the public. But unlike mining underground or smelting ore—occupations for which the Court had previously upheld work-hour restrictions—baking does not endanger workers' health and safety, the Court reasoned. So, limiting the working hours of bakers failed to meet its standard. The Court ruled that the regulation was unconstitutional, rejecting New York's justification of the law as a reasonable effort to safeguard public health and welfare, and intimating that the state was trying to disguise a labor law as a health law.

The word "labor" summoned the specter of socialism—a scary word to some in 1905—which was left unmentioned in the opinion but is a salient background condition giving context to the Court's ruling.[17] Socialism is attuned to just how much power employers have over their employees, including power to keep hours long and wages low to increase bosses' profits while workers literally can't afford to push back without putting their livelihoods at risk. But the Court's conclusion that the legislature "interfered" with "the freedom of master and employee to contract with each other" presupposed that employees and their "masters" are equally free to negotiate the conditions of their employment (despite the very word choice suggesting otherwise) or at least that any power differential was not a cause for concern. Justice Oliver Wendell Holmes wrote a stand-alone dissent which recognized that the New York legislature may have been influenced in part by a belief that employees and employers were "not upon equal footing," but rejected the idea that such a belief would make the law unconstitutional. Holmes further criticized the decision as reliant on an economic theory not supported by the Constitution or the people.[18] "A Constitution is not intended to embody a particular economic theory," he wrote, and "the Fourteenth Amendment does not enact Mr. Herbert Spencer's *Social Statics,*" referring to the 1851 classic libertarian text.[19] The other three dissenters strongly rebuffed the majority's characterization of the law as unconnected to legitimate health concerns by pointing to contemporary research on the physical toll bakers suffered from their work, including damaged lungs due to flour inhalation ("white lung disease," the bakers called it), overheating in poorly ventilated buildings, and exhaustion from long hours.[20]

There's disagreement on what exactly *Lochner*'s fatal flaw was— some critics focus on its embrace of rights not explicitly listed in the Constitution (here, the right to contract), others on its protection of rights related to economics specifically, still others on judicial activism and ideological bias more broadly, and so on—but *Lochner*'s place in the constitutional anticanon is basically a consensus opinion.[21] Most scholars pinpoint *Lochner* as the origin of substantive due process, since the Court contended that the government infringed on an unenumerated right where it had no business doing so.[22] The concept has been branded with a scarlet *L* as a result.

This unshakeable association is a bit unfair to modern substantive due process decisions. Some scholars contest the doctrine's standard origin story and link its beginnings not to the *Lochner* era but to the World War II era. Strong individual rights emerged, the argument goes, as a form of resistance to the clear dangers of fascist persecution. If that's the case, due process has long been slandered based on a faulty premise.[23]

Even if substantive due process was born from *Lochner,* though, the doctrine formed over time repudiates *Lochner*'s sins—it does not perpetuate them. Professors Douglas NeJaime and Reva Siegel explain that, in modern substantive due process cases, "the Court has invalidated laws that *harmed* vulnerable individuals and *entrenched* dominant power relations."[24] But "when the *Lochner* Court struck down the wage-and-hour law protecting employees, it invalidated laws that sought to *empower* vulnerable individuals and *unsettle* dominant power relations in the workplace." The big problem with *Lochner,* from an inclusive constitutionalist perspective, is not its determination that there are substantive liberties to be protected within the Due Process Clause or that some of those liberties are economic in nature. The problem is that it ignored the reality of the bakers' lives—both by dismissing documented health issues as insignificant and by failing to take stock of the power imbalance between owner and employee—and blessed the exploitation of the working class. Using the law to protect marginalized people and diffuse power is different from using the law to keep power concentrated in the hands of a few. Inclusive constitutionalism understands the former as encouraged by the democratizing mission of the Reconstruction Amendments and the latter as prohibited by it.

The Supreme Court backed away from *Lochner* in 1937 when it decided *West Coast Hotel Company v. Parrish*. Elsie Parrish was a maid at a hotel in Wenatchee, Washington. Washington had a state law establishing a minimum wage for women of $14.50 per forty-eight-hour workweek. But Elsie's boss was underpaying her, amounting to $216 of stolen wages over the course of a year—equal to nearly $5,000 today.[25] Elsie sued for her back pay, and after she won before the state's highest court, the hotel owner appealed to the U.S. Supreme Court. The owner argued that he and Elsie had entered into an agreement that she would be paid less than the law required, so the minimum-wage law violated the Fourteenth Amendment by impairing the freedom of contract.[26] But the Supreme Court wasn't having it, asking rhetorically in its decision, "What is this freedom? The Constitution does not speak of freedom of contract."[27] Substantive due process, it seemed, was over.

Justice Charles Evans Hughes authored the opinion for a 5–4 majority and clarified that liberty is not unfettered—especially when community welfare is at stake. The Court further made reference to the Great Depression and identified the "exploitation of a class of workers who are in an unequal position with respect to bargaining power and are thus relatively defenseless against the denial of a living wage" as an injury to the whole community, which legislatures are "clearly entitled" to address.[28] The dissent argued that the majority made a serious error by considering lessons learned from the Depression in its analysis, writing that "the meaning of the Constitution does not change with the ebb and flow of economic events." The dissenters also criticized the majority at length for ditching precedent and allowing "the words of the Constitution" to "mean today what they did not mean when written" without an intervening constitutional amendment.[29] Although none of the justices used the words "originalism" or "living Constitution," acclaimed legal historian G. Edward White described this as "one of the first illustrations in American constitutional history of those clashing approaches."[30] The majority and dissenting opinions foreshadowed conflicts to come over the correct way to determine the Constitution's meaning, unenumerated rights, and the role of the judiciary.

SUBSTANTIVE DUE PROCESS IS DEAD;
LONG LIVE SUBSTANTIVE DUE PROCESS

The Court's jurisprudence in later decades proved that the rumors of substantive due process's death had been greatly exaggerated. As early as 1949, in a decision about how the Fourteenth Amendment may apply to criminal cases in state courts, the Supreme Court described due process as a "living principle" that develops along with the public. "It is of the very nature of a free society to advance in its standards of what is deemed reasonable and right," Justice Felix Frankfurter observed. "To rely on a tidy formula for the easy determination of what is a fundamental right for purposes of legal enforcement may satisfy a longing for certainty but ignores the movements of a free society. It belittles the scale of the conception of due process."[31]

Substantive due process really began to blossom in the 1960s, when the Supreme Court heard multiple challenges to the legality of anticontraception laws.[32] The first case, *Poe v. Ullman* (1961), centered on a married couple using the aliases of Paul and Pauline Poe and an anonymous Mrs. Jane Doe. Mrs. Poe had three consecutive pregnancies. Three times in a row, her pregnancies ended with infants who had multiple congenital abnormalities and died moments after birth. Mrs. Doe had also recently been pregnant, and her pregnancy made her critically ill; she experienced partial paralysis, speech impairment, and weeks of unconsciousness, among other symptoms. Mr. and Mrs. Poe and Mrs. Jane Doe both consulted Dr. C. Lee Buxton, who believed the best and safest treatment for their physical and psychological distress would be advice on preventing conception, but Connecticut law prohibited the use of contraception and the giving of medical advice on how to use it.[33]

Banning the use of contraception may strike you as impractical. Rightly so. But that's where the part of the law that treats a doctor like an accessory to a crime comes in. Some lucky women had private physicians willing to break the law, but poor women and women of color had to rely on free or low-cost clinics—clinics that were forced to close their doors in Connecticut because the law banning contraception advice didn't allow them to operate openly. Dr. Buxton saw too many women suffer severe medical complications when they were unable to obtain birth control, so he teamed up with Planned Parenthood attorneys to find a way to provide necessary medical services and bring down the law.[34] Dr. Buxton, Mr. and Mrs. Poe, and Mrs. Jane Doe asked the Court to declare that the anti-birth-control law violated the Fourteenth Amendment by depriving them of liberty without due process of law. Their brief described a bevy of harms:

> Spouses are prohibited from planning their families in accordance with their economic conditions and consistent with their physical, psychological and emotional welfare; women are subjected to the hazard of loss of life and health; physicians are prevented from practicing their profession in accordance with approved scientific principles; and clergymen are prohibited from the free practice of their religion. Surely this is an arbitrary curtailment of "those liberties of the individual now enshrined in the due process clause of the Fourteenth Amendment."[35]

The divided Court declined to decide the question, though, reasoning that judicial intervention wasn't necessary because the state didn't rigorously enforce the law, and so the plaintiffs didn't have a reasonable fear of imminent prosecution—totally ignoring that clinics weren't being prosecuted because the clinics had ceased to exist.[36] Willfully ignorant, the Court declared there was no harm, no foul, case dismissed.

The dissenters vigorously opposed the Court leaving carceral consequences for reproductive healthcare up to prosecutorial whims. Importantly, the absence of the words "birth control," "marriage," or "privacy" in the Constitution was no bar to the dissenting justices' conclusion that the law was an intolerable intrusion into married people's bedrooms. They argued that the Fourteenth Amendment implicitly protects substantive rights (meaning rights beyond mere guarantees of procedural fairness) that are indispensable to a free society—and a free society could not permit police to investigate and criminally punish marital intimacy. Justice Harlan's dissent recognized that the Due Process Clause must have a substantive component, because laws could have "the fairest possible procedure" and "nevertheless destroy" people's life, liberty, or property.[37] Harlan further emphasized that due process could not be reduced to a formula, but he did not think that meant judges had boundless discretion. He argued instead that judges should be guided by reason and the purposes behind the Constitution and should pay attention to how the country has evolved outside the courtroom. Harlan determined that the liberty protected by the Due Process Clause is "a rational continuum which . . . includes a freedom from all substantial arbitrary impositions and purposeless restraints" and, in the spirit of that famous footnote in *Carolene,* recognizes that some interests call for heightened scrutiny of states' justifications for abridging those rights and freedoms.[38] Harlan's influential dissent in particular is now viewed as an early weathervane indicating the shifting winds regarding substantive due process.*

---

* I should clarify who I mean by Harlan: the dissent in *Poe v. Ullman* was written by Justice John Marshall Harlan, who served on the Court from 1955 to 1971 and was the grandson of another Justice John Marshall Harlan, who served on the Court from 1877 to 1911. Yes, for most of the Supreme Court's history, there were more family members of previous justices than people of color or women of any race on the highest court.

A few months after the Court's ruling in *Ullman,* Planned Parenthood set out to determine if they could publicly provide services after all, opening a center in New Haven, Connecticut, and employing Dr. Buxton as medical director. A local busybody promptly contacted the state police, city police, city mayor, and local prosecutor to complain about the open violation of state law and, according to him, "natural law which says marital relations are for procreation and not entertainment."[39] The center was open for ten days, at which point Dr. Buxton and Planned Parenthood League of Connecticut executive director Estelle Griswold were arrested for advising married couples on how to prevent conception. Griswold and Buxton were fined $100 each—equivalent to about $1,000 each today—and alleged that the statute violated their Fourteenth Amendment rights. Their criminal conviction was an indisputable harm which foreclosed the avoidance maneuvers of *Poe v. Ullman*. By 1965, Connecticut's anti-birth-control law was back before the Supreme Court.

The Court ruled in *Griswold v. Connecticut* that Connecticut's anti-birth-control law violated the constitutional rights of Griswold and Buxton's married patients. *Which* constitutional right was violated is less clear. The Court expressly rejected the Fourteenth Amendment's Due Process Clause as its source of constitutional authority and took great pains to disclaim any relationship to *Lochner*. Unlike the *Lochner* Court, the majority swore, it would not use the Due Process Clause to "sit as a super-legislature to determine the wisdom, need, and propriety of laws that touch economic problems, business affairs, or social conditions."[40] But this law is different, the Court said, because it "operates directly on an intimate relation of husband and wife and their physician's role in one aspect of that relation."[41]

From there on, parts of the opinion read like a Mad Libs where the phrasal template is "any amendment that isn't the Fourteenth."

The Court concluded that the combined powers of the First Amendment right of association, the Third Amendment prohibition against quartering soldiers in the home, the Fourth Amendment protection against unreasonable searches and seizures, and the Fifth Amendment right against self-incrimination link up with the Ninth Amendment's acknowledgment of unenumerated rights to "create zones of privacy" that protect the use of contraception.[42] The majority correctly recognized that the Bill of Rights has been construed to protect conduct that's not literally stated in the text of the amendments, and its incorporation of other amendments into its analysis would be fine if it were fully supported. But the opinion's defense of the invocations was lackluster and strangely worded: the Court declared that its precedents "suggest that specific guarantees in the Bill of Rights have penumbras, formed by emanations from those guarantees that help give them life and substance." If that sentence strikes you as kind of absurd, you are far from the only one. In its desperation to beat the *Lochner* allegations, the Court seemed like it was just throwing things at the wall to see what stuck. This passage gave generations of conservative lawyers fodder for bullying their liberal colleagues, and made liberal lawyers cringe with secondhand embarrassment.

The haphazard rationale compelled Justice Harlan to concur only in the judgment, which means he believed the Court came to the right decision for the wrong reasons. Harlan's concurrence is an elevated version of saying "the Due Process Clause is right there." For him (and for me), Connecticut's statute criminalizing birth control violated basic values underlying society such as privacy, bodily autonomy, and freedom from arbitrary police intrusions. And while other provisions in the Bill of Rights could be brought into such a discussion, the inquiry doesn't depend on them. "The Due Process Clause of the Fourteenth Amendment stands, in my opinion, on its own bottom."[43] Justice Byron White also concurred in the judgment on the grounds that Connecticut's ban on using contraception violated the Fourteenth Amendment's protections against deprivations of liberty without due process of law. White further argued that a state's substantial intrusion on a right should have a similarly substantial justification.[44]

Despite the majority's efforts to distinguish itself from *Lochner,* the two dissenters were not convinced. Justice Hugo Black argued that *Griswold* and *Lochner* both relied on personal formulations of justice—a method for decision-making he "had thought that we had laid . . . to rest once and for all in cases like *West Coast Hotel Co. v. Parrish.*"[45] Justice Potter Stewart agreed, and confessed that he believed the Connecticut statute was an "uncommonly silly law," but that didn't mean it was an unconstitutional one.[46] The dissenters feared that the Court was supplanting the role of the people and their elected representatives by empowering itself to strike down any law they deem "irrational, unreasonable, or offensive" based on malleable standards.[47]

This concern about a judicial power grab calls for two clarifications. First, as a concurring opinion in *Griswold* authored by Justice Arthur Goldberg reminds us, it does not follow that recognizing fundamental rights not explicitly stated in the Constitution improperly broadens judicial authority—not when the Ninth Amendment clearly says that the Bill of Rights is not an exhaustive list of rights to be protected from government abridgment. Second, we should remember that seemingly rigid standards do not prevent the Court from striking down duly enacted statutes based more on vibes than law. (The rule set forth in *Bruen* that gun laws violate the Second Amendment unless there's a historical analogue that Clarence Thomas deems close enough comes to mind.) It is for this reason that Justice Harlan expressed deep skepticism about the majority's aversion to the Due Process Clause in his concurring opinion: "While I could not more heartily agree that judicial 'self restraint' is an indispensable ingredient of sound constitutional adjudication, I do submit that the formula suggested for achieving it is more hollow than real. 'Specific' provisions of the Constitution, no less than 'due process,' lend themselves as readily to 'personal' interpretations."[48] What Harlan is saying here is that the Due Process Clause is not uniquely vulnerable to judges' personal preferences. Clamping down on substantive due process wouldn't make judges any more likely to stay in their lane, but it would deprive them (and, by extension, us) of an important tool for protecting unenumerated constitutional rights.

Let's be real: judicial decision-making regularly calls for the exercise of discretion and the issuance of value judgments. If judges have the power to assess constitutionality, and if we know that value considerations are inherent to constitutional adjudication, then the question for us should be which values are established and accepted as proper, legitimate considerations. Justice Goldberg's concurrence points us in that direction, telling us, "The inquiry is whether a right involved is of such a character that it cannot be denied without violating those fundamental principles of liberty and justice which lie at the base of all our civil and political institutions."[49] Inclusive constitutionalism seeks to identify and align our jurisprudence with those fundamental liberatory principles. In this way, inclusive constitutionalism is both a practice and a purpose—it's a method for us to think about and interpret the law so that we fulfill the Constitution's democratic ideals and so that we may all be free.

The identification of core values inherent to a multiracial free society factored into the Supreme Court's decision in *Loving v. Virginia*, a foundational Fourteenth Amendment case decided two years after *Griswold*.[50] Richard and Mildred Loving were a husband and wife residing in Virginia. Richard was a white man. Mildred was a Black woman. On the basis of these facts alone, Richard and Mildred had committed a crime. Virginia was one of more than a dozen states that still outlawed interracial marriage at that time; fourteen other states had repealed their bans on interracial marriages during the preceding fifteen years. The newlyweds were arrested in their bedroom. The Lovings pled guilty to violating Virginia law and were sentenced to one year in jail. The trial judge suspended the sentence for twenty-five years, though, on the condition that the Lovings leave Virginia at once and not return to the state together until the twenty-five years were up. "Almighty God created the races white, black, yellow, malay and red, and he placed them on separate continents," the judge stated. "And but for the interference with his arrangement there would be no cause for such marriages. The fact that he separated the races shows that he did not intend for the races to mix."[51] The Lovings left their home and moved to D.C. Wanting to return, they filed a motion to vacate the judgment and set the sentence aside, arguing that the laws they were convicted of violating were themselves violative of the Fourteenth Amendment. By 1967, the Lovings' case had worked its way up to the Supreme Court.

Virginia defended the legality of its anti-miscegenation law on originalist grounds. The o-word was still not in common usage, but the analysis is unmistakable: the state argued at length that the meaning of the Constitution is fixed at the time of adoption and courts must give effect to the intent of the Framers and the people who adopted it. If one accepts that premise, they continued, there's no constitutional problem with criminalizing interracial marriage. The congressional record showed that the legislators who framed and adopted the Fourteenth Amendment explicitly considered whether it would prohibit states from enacting anti-miscegenation laws and concluded that it would not and should not. Contemporary legislators reasoned that marriage was not a right covered by the amendment's protections, and interracial marriage bans were not discriminatory because they were equally applicable—white people couldn't marry Black people, Black people couldn't marry white people, and the punishments were the same.[52] (For what it's worth, Virginia's law worked a bit differently.*) Virginia also highlighted the fact that many state legislatures ratified the Fourteenth Amendment and maintained their prohibitions on interracial marriage for nearly a century, showing that they did not believe them to be in conflict.† Further, anti-miscegenation laws survived previous constitutional challenges in state and federal court.

North Carolina submitted an amicus brief that echoed Virginia's claim that courts cannot deviate from the Constitution's original understanding and expressed skepticism about the Court's authority to disrupt historical legal bigotry: "Unless, therefore, the Fourteenth Amendment is construed as a grand commission which constitutes the federal courts as a species of judicial privateers to sink every state ship in sight if they do not like the cut of its sails, then the historic position asserted by Virginia is clearly sound."[53] We should pay no attention, apparently, to the fact that the "sail" in question was a giant, billowing Confederate flag.

The American Civil Liberties Union (ACLU), which represented the Lovings, did not entertain Virginia's argument that the Constitution's meaning was fixed. "If such legislative history—whatever its real meaning assuming one could read the minds of the legislators from the historical record—were determinative of the scope of the

---

* Virginia's law prohibited marriage between white people and all nonwhite people. Because the central concern of the law was maintaining white supremacy, intermarriage between nonwhite races did not constitute a threat to the "Act to preserve racial integrity." The law also made a specific exception in order "to recognize as an integral and honored part of the white race the descendants of John Rolfe and Pocahontas." Persons "who have one-sixteenth or less of the blood of the American Indian and no other non-Caucasic blood" were considered to be white persons and could legally marry white people. *Loving v. Virginia,* 388 U.S. 1 (1967).

† The unstated alternative explanation is that the states were flagrantly violating the Constitution for a hundred years.

Fourteenth Amendment," the ACLU remarked, "then it might not have been applicable to school segregation, jury service and other forms of segregation."[54] It instead argued that a "correct appraisal of the legislative history of the Fourteenth Amendment" revealed that its "guarantees were open-ended and meant to be expounded in light of changing times and circumstances to prohibit racial discrimination."[55] This value of broadly confronting oppression and racial hierarchies was at the heart of the ACLU's argument. The majority of its brief was devoted to explaining in stomach-wrenching detail how interracial marriage bans, first, arose to protect the economic and social structures slavery depended on; and second, persisted in furtherance of modern racism manifested in spurious claims of white superiority, unreasonable fears about racial mixing and rising immigration leading to white genocide, and maintaining white men's sexual access to Black women without conferring upon Black women the dignity and socioeconomic benefits of marriage.[56] The ACLU made painfully clear that the purpose of anti-miscegenation laws was "to express the subordinate status of the Negro people and the exalted position of the whites" and function "chiefly as the State's official symbol of a caste system." Such laws, the ACLU reasoned, "must be dealt with accordingly."[57] And the tools to deal with them were the Equal Protection Clause and the Due Process Clause of the Fourteenth Amendment.

The ACLU argued that the Lovings' Equal Protection rights were violated because their marriage would have been valid but for their races. Guided by *Brown v. Board,* which struck down school segregation on Equal Protection grounds, the ACLU claimed that states could not intentionally disadvantage Black people via segregation or deny Black people's freedom of association, and there was no rational explanation for a law that singles out Black people and stamps them as inferior.[58] The ACLU supported their Due Process claim by pointing to *Griswold* and *Bolling v. Sharpe,* the other desegregation case mentioned in chapter 1. *Griswold* justified its decision about contraception by focusing on the right to marital privacy, and the lawyers took that as evidence that the right to marry is a constitutionally protected liberty. *Bolling v. Sharpe* held that segregated schools violated Black children's due process rights by arbitrarily depriving them of liberty for an illegitimate governmental purpose. And the ACLU argued that the same principle applied here: Virginia's anti-miscegenation law deprived people of liberty for no good reason.[59]

The Lovings won—much like love itself.* As in *Brown,* Chief Justice Earl Warren authored the opinion for a unanimous Court that treated evidence as to the Framers' intent as inconclusive at best. The Court observed that "proponents of the post-War Amendments undoubtedly intended them to remove all legal distinctions among 'all persons born or naturalized in the United States,'" while their opponents "were antagonistic to both the letter and the spirit of the Amendments and wished them to have the most limited effect."[60] The Supreme Court didn't accept Virginia's argument that the statute's "equal application" to white and nonwhite participants of a marriage immunized its use of racial classifications, either; formal equality as advocated by Virginia was actually a trap that perpetuated oppression. The Court recognized that the interracial marriage ban was "designed to maintain White Supremacy" and, as such, had "no legitimate overriding purpose independent of invidious racial

---

* On the eve of the Massachusetts legislature's vote for marriage equality, Mildred Loving remarked, "I am still not a political person, but I am proud that Richard's and my name is on a court case that can help reinforce the love, the commitment, the fairness, and the family that so many people, black or white, young or old, gay or straight seek in life. I support the freedom to marry for all. That's what Loving, and loving, are all about." "Private: Mildred Loving Endorses Marriage Equality for Same-Sex Couples," American Constitution Society, *Expert Forum* (blog), June 15, 2007, acslaw.org/?post_type=acsblog&p=3747.

discrimination."[61] Ultimately, the Court concluded that the law ran afoul of the Equal Protection Clause by restricting the freedom to marry solely based on race and for solely racist reasons. The Court similarly reasoned that the law deprived all Virginians of liberty without due process of law by restricting the fundamental freedom to marry on the basis of invidious racial discrimination—racial classifications the Court described as "directly subversive of the principle of equality at the heart of the Fourteenth Amendment."[62]

The Supreme Court's decision in *Loving* should be read as clear and compelling guidance for constitutional interpretation: the substance of due process is bound up with the values of equality and antisubordination, and the originalist notion that a case could or should be resolved based on an identifiable original understanding is infinitely less instructive than the Fourteenth Amendment's command to the government to confront America's caste systems— chiefly, white supremacy.[63]

Quick sidenote—a couple of modern originalists have made a valiant, though verbose, effort to argue that the Fourteenth Amendment can be properly understood to prohibit bans on interracial marriage on originalist grounds. They reason that the Fourteenth Amendment constitutionalized the Civil Rights Act of 1866; the Civil Rights Act of 1866 recognized that Black people have the same right as white people to make and enforce contracts; dictionaries commonly in use in the 1860s confirm that "same" was understood to mean identical rather than different but equivalent; and marriage contracts are contracts. Thus, "if a white citizen could enter into a marriage contract with another white citizen in 1866, then so could citizens of all other races and colors."[64] Personally, I'm not entirely convinced. If you consider that nineteenth-century white people did not have a legal right to marry outside their race, constitutionalizing white people's contractual rights in 1866 could arguably still exclude interracial marriage. And while I appreciate that these originalists

reached the correct destination, I simply don't believe that the con-
voluted, over-the-river-and-through-the-woods path they took to
get to the right side of history is any more principled than letting
democratic values like antisubordination be your guide. It's low-key
insulting as a Black person and embarrassing as an attorney to think
my legal equality depends on tortured analysis of mid-nineteenth-
century contract law rather than a simple recognition of our shared
human dignity.

In the years following *Griswold* and *Loving,* the Court continued to shape the contours of substantive due process. *Eisenstadt v.
Baird* (1972) expanded *Griswold*'s principle by striking down a Massachusetts law that made it a crime to provide an unmarried person
with contraception. The law failed on Equal Protection grounds because the Court reasoned that there was no rational basis for the
state's different treatment of single and married people. "If the right
of privacy means anything," wrote Justice Brennan for the six-justice
majority, "it is the right of the individual, married or single, to be free
from unwarranted governmental intrusion into matters so fundamentally affecting a person as the decision whether to bear or beget
a child."[65] *Griswold, Loving, Eisenstadt,* and others led, in turn, to
Roe v. Wade (1973). The Court's precedents made it clear that the
"liberty" protected by the Fourteenth Amendment includes a fundamental right to personal privacy, which extends to matters like
marriage, procreation, family relationships, and childrearing. *Roe*
recognized that a person's decision whether to end a pregnancy is
encompassed by that privacy right.[66] Central to all these cases is the
recognition that constitutional protections against deprivations of
liberty without due process of law would be hollow if we did not
identify and give substance to those liberties themselves.

Griswold, Loving, Roe, and other cases built an interpretive
foundation that encouraged and helped facilitate marginalized communities' push for legal recognition of other rights pertaining to pri-

vacy and intimate associations. And as the public fought for their rights, the justices on the Court fought over the best method to determine which rights fall under the Fourteenth Amendment's protections and which don't. The tension between the competing analytical approaches—one focusing on history and tradition and the other focusing on dignity and equality—is particularly exemplified by the evolution of the Court's gay rights jurisprudence.

In a significant 1986 decision, the Supreme Court ruled that there was no Fourteenth Amendment problem with making it a crime for adults to engage in consensual, noncommercial oral sex or anal sex. Georgia's law against "sodomy," as the state called it, made those sex acts punishable by incarceration for up to twenty years. Michael Hardwick, a then-twenty-nine-year-old gay man, was arrested in his bedroom while violating the statute with another man. While the text of the law was ostensibly gender-neutral, criminalizing oral and anal sex regardless of the parties' identities, Georgia was clear that same-sex relations were the law's exclusive target. Hardwick challenged the statute as unconstitutional, and the trial court dismissed his claim. But the Eleventh Circuit reversed the dismissal and remanded the case for trial, understanding cases like *Griswold, Eisenstadt, Loving,* and *Roe* to mean the Ninth and Fourteenth Amendments protect intimate associations and individual decisions critical to personal autonomy against state interference.[67] The case reached the Supreme Court in *Bowers v. Hardwick,* where the majority did not disguise its animosity to gay rights. Five justices—four of whom you can blame on Richard Nixon and Ronald Reagan—framed the issue as determining "whether the Federal Constitution confers a fundamental right upon homosexuals to engage in sodomy and hence invalidates the laws of the many States that still make such conduct illegal and have done so for a very long time."[68]

To answer that question, the majority referred to two earlier ways the Court characterized unenumerated rights worthy of protection under the Fourteenth Amendment. The first focused on fundamental liberties that are "implicit in the concept of ordered liberty." Ordered liberty isn't actually defined by the Court, but the term broadly describes the idea that freedom can be reasonably regulated to maintain a stable society. Something is implicit in ordered liberty if you can't have a free and just society without it. The second characterization of unenumerated rights described liberties as worth protecting if they are "deeply rooted in this Nation's history and tradition."[69] The Court concluded that it was "obvious" that "neither of these formulations would extend a fundamental right to homosexuals to engage in acts of consensual sodomy" because same-sex conduct had been condemned under law for hundreds of years. The majority's reasoning boiled down to little more than asking, "How can criminalizing homosexuality be unconstitutional when we've always criminalized homosexuality?" Chief Justice Warren Burger wrote a separate concurrence that doubled down on the argument that proscriptions against homosexuality have "ancient roots" and emphasized that courts would "cast aside millennia of moral teaching" if they decided the Constitution "somehow protected" same-sex conduct.[70] Not once did the Court consider that "a free and just society" and "a society that incarcerates people for being gay" are mutually exclusive categories.

The dissenters, in contrast, regarded it as "revolting to have no better reason for a rule of law than that so it was laid down in the time of Henry IV."[71] Pointing to *Brown v. Board, Loving v. Virginia,* and *Roe v. Wade,* they rejected the idea that legislation can avoid the Court's scrutiny simply because it has been a law for a long time or people feel strongly about it. Dissenting justices reminded the majority that interracial relationships, like same-sex relationships, were also long treated as a crime, immoral, and against some people's gods; yet history and tradition did not save antimiscegenation laws from the Constitution in *Loving*. And *Griswold* and *Eisenstadt* showed that individuals' decisions about intimate relationships are protected by the Due Process Clause, including nonreproductive sexual conduct that others may find immoral or offensive. These cases reflect America's growth over time, but originalism denies everything we've learned and calls that principled wisdom.

Just a few months after the *Bowers* decision came down, Justice Scalia joined the Court, and conservatives continued to aggressively push backward-looking tests for due process rights. In *Michael H. v. Gerald D.* (1989), Scalia wrote a plurality opinion that advanced a substance-skeptical approach to the Fourteenth Amendment and claimed that only an assiduous focus on history and tradition could keep judges from arbitrarily enforcing their personal preferences—a standard that was itself an arbitrary choice. *Michael H. v. Gerald D.*—full names redacted for discretion's sake—was a case about parental rights over a child born of an affair. An oil executive named Gerald married a model named Carole in Las Vegas. The couple moved to Los Angeles, where Carole became romantically entangled with their neighbor, Michael. A child was born, and a blood test showed a 98.07 percent probability that Michael was the father. Michael, Carole, and the child resided together for several months, but Carole later reconciled with Gerald. Gerald, Carole, and the child moved to New York, and Michael sought visitation rights as the child's father. The lower courts ruled against Michael because of a century-old California law that stated that the child of a wife who lives with her husband is "conclusively presumed to be a child of the marriage," so long as the husband is not impotent or sterile. Michael appealed up to the Supreme Court on substantive due process grounds, arguing that the California law deprived him of his liberty in maintaining a parental relationship with his child.[72]

As in *Bowers v. Hardwick,* the Court in *Michael H. v. Gerald D.*

engaged in a historical survey for proof of an oddly stated right; Scalia wrote that the Court "found nothing in the older sources, nor in the older cases, addressing specifically the power of the natural father to assert parental rights over a child born into a woman's existing marriage with another man."[73] He elaborated in an important footnote, arguing that judges should only protect liberties under the Due Process Clause if there is evidence of a historical tradition protecting the asserted right, articulated at the most specific level of generality. This meant it wouldn't be enough for Michael to show that courts had previously protected parents' rights or the rights of fathers. Scalia specifically searched for evidence of courts protecting "the rights of the natural father of a child adulterously conceived." Unsurprisingly, he found none. Michael therefore had no legal right to establish that he was the child's father and seek visitation rights, even though he literally was the child's father, and Scalia was able to protect what he saw as the sanctity of the marital unit.

Scalia is basically the patron saint of originalism, but in *Michael H. v. Gerald D.,* he curiously dispensed with the trappings we associate with originalist interpretation. He did not explicitly discuss how the public originally understood a given legal provision, or even the Framers' intent. Skipping all the artifice, he cut straight to the point: to be an originalist is to treat the Constitution as a vehicle to preserve a version of the past that aligns with conservative preferences. Scalia wrote for a plurality of the Court that the purpose of the Due Process Clause "is to prevent future generations from lightly casting aside important traditional values—not to enable this Court to invent new ones."[74]

The Court's ruling was badly fractured: while a majority of justices agreed with Scalia's conclusion, a majority disagreed with his explanation. Only one other justice signed on to the opinion in full. Two justices signed on to all but the footnote in which Scalia outlined his recommended historical method for identifying what liberties are protected by the Due Process Clause—namely, define a right as narrowly as possible, go on a historical scavenger hunt, then act surprised when you come back empty-handed. Another justice concurred only in the judgment. Dissenting and concurring justices alike expressed concern that the proposed standard for analyzing due process claims—relying on a deeply rooted history of protecting a specific right articulated at the most granular level—was incompatible with the Court's decisions in cases like *Griswold, Eisenstadt,* and *Loving*. Yet, as we saw when the Court rescinded constitutional protection for abortion in 2022, this aversion did not prevent the proposed standard from sticking around like gum on the bottom of America's shoe.[75]

Scalia's focus on a specifically articulated historical right was "embraced with a vengeance" in *Washington v. Glucksberg* (1997).[76] The plaintiffs in that case were three terminally ill patients who died before the Supreme Court issued its decision, four Washington physicians who sometimes treated terminally ill patients, and a non-profit organization called Compassion in Dying, which provided counsel to people seeking physician-assisted suicide. The state of Washington made it a crime to knowingly cause or aid another person to attempt suicide. Plaintiffs successfully argued at the district court and at the Ninth Circuit that the statute was unconstitutional because the Fourteenth Amendment protects the liberty of mentally competent, terminally ill adults who wish to hasten their deaths with medication prescribed by their physicians. The Supreme Court rejected this argument.

Chief Justice William Rehnquist wrote for the majority that the Court had an "established" two-step methodology in due process cases. That was a warning: when discussing this case in a recent book about substantive due process, legal scholar James E. Fleming astutely observed that "whenever the Court says something like 'our established method is' or 'it is well settled that,' it is likely about to put forward a new method and to utter something controversial."[77] Rehnquist claimed that, first, the Due Process Clause "specially protects those fundamental rights and liberties which are, objectively, deeply rooted in this Nation's history and tradition . . . and implicit in the concept of ordered liberty, such that neither his liberty nor justice would exist if they were sacrificed"; and second, substantive due process cases require "a careful description of the asserted fundamental liberty interest."[78] While the groups challenging the law asserted the right at issue in various ways, including a "right to choose a humane, dignified death," "liberty to choose how to die," and "right to control one's final days," Rehnquist phrased the inquiry as whether the liberty protected by the Due Process Clause includes a "right to commit suicide which itself includes a right to assistance in doing so."[79] Rehnquist concluded that the right as he defined it had been consistently and almost universally rejected throughout history and was therefore not entitled to the Due Process Clause's protections.

Significantly, *Glucksberg* leaned into the standard Scalia advocated for in his *Michael H. v. Gerald D.* footnote and stacked the jurisprudential deck against substantive due process. The "established" approach it described was dramatically far removed from the approach seen in cases like *Griswold, Loving,* and *Roe,* and diametrically opposed to Justice Harlan's foundational argument in *Poe v. Ullman* that substantive due process has not been and cannot be reduced to a formula.[80] Those cases did not treat history as an inherent bar to recognizing and protecting rights, and they acknowledged there wasn't some kind of mathematical equation that would definitively produce the limits of liberty. Society, and our understanding of it, changes. Progress happens. So we have to use our brains and make reasoned judgments.

Entering the twenty-first century, the Court began to course correct. The Supreme Court again heard a constitutional challenge to a law criminalizing same-sex intimacy in *Lawrence v. Texas* (2003). Unlike the facially neutral law at issue in *Bowers v. Hardwick,* which ostensibly made all oral and anal sex a crime and didn't explicitly single out any group, the Texas statute specifically applied only to individuals of the same sex. Tyron Garner and John Geddes Lawrence were arrested in Lawrence's apartment and convicted for allegedly engaging in the prohibited conduct.* Lawrence and Garner were represented by Lambda Legal, a civil rights organization that focuses on lesbian, gay, bisexual, and transgender communities. Lambda Legal challenged the statute on both Equal Protection and Due Process grounds. With respect to Equal Protection, they argued that the law discriminated against gay men and lesbians without a rational and legitimate purpose. They further argued that the state violated the Due Process Clause by improperly intruding on same-sex couples' fundamental interests in intimate relationships, bodily integrity, and the home.[81]

Texas responded by arguing that criminalizing homosexual conduct was rationally related to their legitimate goal of promoting public morality and family values. Texas also contended that *Wash-*

---

* I say "allegedly" because conflicting statements made by the police, and interviews with the two men, suggest they were not actually having sex. Tyron Garner's offense may have simply been existing as a Black and gay man—a jealous partner of his made a false 911 call claiming that a Black man was "going crazy with a gun," and the response to that 911 call ultimately resulted in Garner and Lawrence's arrests. See, e.g., Dahlia Lithwick, "Extreme Makeover," *The New Yorker,* March 4, 2012, https://www.newyorker.com/magazine/2012/03/12/extreme-makeover-dahlia-lithwick. ("That's the punch line: the case that affirmed the right of gay couples to have consensual sex in private spaces seems to have involved two men who were neither a couple nor having sex. In order to appeal to the conservative Justices on the high court, the story of a booze-soaked quarrel was repackaged as a love story. Nobody had to know that the gay-rights case of the century was actually about three or four men getting drunk in front of a television in a Harris County apartment decorated with bad James Dean erotica.")

ington v. Glucksberg—the case where the Supreme Court rejected terminally ill patients' request to die with dignity—provided the definitive test for substantive due process rights, namely, there must be a history of a specifically defined right. "Our nation's history has not been rewritten in the seventeen years since *Bowers* was decided," wrote Texas's attorneys, "and that history contradicts any assertion that a right to engage in homosexual anal intercourse has been a valued and protected right of American citizens. The fact that the states have traditionally prohibited the act as a crime is utterly inconsistent with any claim that our legal tradition has treated the choice to engage in that act as a 'fundamental' right." Going a step further, Texas suggested that a right cannot be "truly fundamental" if "its public acceptance and societal value" are "the subject of vehement and widespread disagreement."[82] This standard should terrify anyone with even a passing awareness of the country's continuous struggles for freedom. If vocal or even sustained opposition renders a right nonfundamental, every group that has had to fight for the recognition of its rights is at risk.

The Supreme Court's decision in *Lawrence v. Texas* rejected the idea that the recognition of fundamental rights turns on history alone. Justice Anthony Kennedy clarified for the majority that "history and tradition are the starting point but not in all cases the ending point of the substantive due process inquiry."[83] The Court also contested the *Bowers* Court's version of history, determining that the truth was "more complex" than *Bowers* made it seem and describing *Bowers*'s historical premises as doubtful and, at minimum, overstated.[84] In contrast to originalists' focus on the Founding era and Chief Justice Burger's reference to "ancient roots" in *Bowers,* the Court believed that the most relevant laws and traditions were those of the past fifty years that "show[ed] an emerging awareness that liberty gives substantial protection to adult persons in deciding how to conduct their private lives in matters pertaining to sex."[85]

The majority viewed this analysis as wholly consistent with the terms of the Constitution as bestowed to us to interpret:

> Had those who drew and ratified the Due Process Clauses of the Fifth Amendment or the Fourteenth Amendment known the components of liberty in its manifold possibilities, they might have been more specific. They did not presume to have this insight. They knew times can blind us to certain truths and later generations can see that laws once thought necessary and proper in fact serve only to oppress.[86]

The Court recognized that the criminalization of gay conduct is effectively the criminalization of gay people and, as such, functions as an open invitation for public and private discrimination—an astonishing assessment, from my 2024 vantage point, for a majority-Republican Court to make twenty years ago. The majority in *Lawrence v. Texas* was expressly concerned with equality and dignity. It concluded that gay and straight people are equally entitled to freely make intimate and personal decisions central to dignity and autonomy without government compulsion and criminal regulation. The Texas statute was struck down, and *Bowers v. Hardwick* was overruled. The standard the Court applied in *Lawrence* and the conclusion it ultimately reached had significant implications for substantive due process jurisprudence. It suggested what the proper focus of judicial inquiry in due process cases could be: not stagnation, but liberation.

The Supreme Court reaffirmed the logic of *Lawrence* in 2015 when it held that marriage is a fundamental right and liberty that may not be denied to same-sex couples. In *Obergefell v. Hodges,* the Court once again received and refused an invitation to let a narrow version of history determine the case's outcome. Justice Kennedy expressed the Court's reasoning and echoed his analysis in *Law-*

rence: "The nature of injustice is that we may not always see it in our own times." The Court determined that constitutional interpretation can accommodate that reality because the founding charter was "entrusted to future generations" to protect "the right of all persons to enjoy liberty as we learn its meaning."[87] The Court laid out the material and dignitary harms inflicted on same-sex couples by restrictive marriage laws and reviewed precedents like *Loving* and *Griswold* showing that marriage is a fundamental right. Opponents leaned on *Glucksberg* and urged the Court to seek (and not find) a history of a right to same-sex marriage specifically, but the Court declined; *Loving,* after all, did not ask about a historic right to interracial marriage specifically. The majority observed that same-sex couples were "ask[ing] for equal dignity in the eyes of the law." And, it concluded, "the Constitution grants them that right."[88]

For a brief, shining moment, *Obergefell* appeared to be a game changer—for theories of constitutional interpretation, at least, if not for LGBTQ people.[89] (Marriage equality and its attendant benefits are important, but obstacles remain for queer people's full and equal membership in democracy. For instance, in the post-*Obergefell* world, same-sex couples could legally marry but could also still legally be fired from their workplaces because of their sexuality.[90]) Justice Harlan's seminal outline of substantive due process in *Poe v. Ullman* was revived. The history-and-tradition demand of *Glucksberg* had the door slammed in its face. A new door was opened for the public to advance arguments about the constitutional requirements of dignity, equality, and liberty under the Fourteenth Amendment, giving hope to progressive attorneys that Due Process could even go beyond what the government may not deny you and reach what the government must afford to you, like education and housing.[91] Importantly, these interpretive possibilities didn't emerge from the policy preferences and power of the justices alone, as suggested by Chief Justice Roberts in his dissenting opinion in *Oberge-*

fell.[92] They came from decades of dialogue between advocates and the people they represent, the judiciary, and other actors engaged in explicating interconnected constitutional principles.[93] The rights and freedoms the due process cases upheld—including same-sex and interracial marriage, decriminalized same-sex intimacy, contraception, abortion, privacy and autonomy, and equal dignity—built on each other like blocks in human rights Jenga. But then, originalists pulled the *Roe v. Wade* block out. Their legitimation of the dissenting arguments in prior abortion and gay rights cases has destabilized the whole human rights tower, and the country is left wondering which block will be next to fall.

DISMANTLING THE DOCTRINE

The Supreme Court's 2022 decision in *Dobbs v. Jackson Women's Health Organization* did not only decimate abortion access—which, to be clear, would have been a tragedy in and of itself.[94] The opinion was also an originalist Trojan horse, complete with soldiers waiting inside to launch an attack on an array of substantive due process rights. The majority opinion in *Dobbs* is explicitly suspicious of substantive due process's liberty protections; Justice Alito notes that the theory "has long been controversial" and even "at times . . . treacherous."[95] Justice Thomas's concurrence goes further, arguing that the Due Process Clause does not secure *any* substantive rights and should be purged from the Court's jurisprudence expeditiously.[96] Understanding the reasoning supposedly justifying the Supreme Court's rescission of abortion rights in *Dobbs* is critical to understanding the risks originalism poses to other individual rights—like contraception and the right to marry someone of a different race or the same sex—and the pursuit of a just society.

The *Dobbs* opinion states early and often that the word "abor-

tion" is not mentioned in the Constitution. This is unsurprising.*
The word "woman" doesn't appear in the Constitution either.† But
the absence of the word itself is not the end of the conversation. The
Ninth Amendment of the Constitution states directly that "the enumeration in the Constitution, of certain rights, shall not be construed to deny or disparage others retained by the people."[97] This
literally means that just because a right is not specifically spelled out
does not mean it does not exist. The text of the Constitution gives
precious little in terms of guidance, though, about "how to identify
retained rights, how to think about them, or how to enforce them."[98]
The task of constitutional interpretation is, it would seem, up to us.
Courts generally have not interpreted the Ninth Amendment to be
an independent source of substantive rights, perhaps because the
text doesn't readily provide hints as to what that substance would
be.[99] Rather, the main vehicle for defining and protecting unenu-

---

*"The painfully obvious point to make," Professor Khiara Bridges has ob-
served, "is that people with the capacity for pregnancy were not part of the
body politic during the period of the nation's history that the majority believes is decisive of the constitutional inquiry. . . . Because women could not
participate in the democratic process, one could reasonably assume that their
interests were not reflected in *any* of the nation's laws, including the criminal
laws that the *Dobbs* majority read as foreclosing a constitutional right to terminate a pregnancy." Khiara M. Bridges, "Race in the Roberts Court," *Harvard Law Review* 136, no. 1 (November 2022): 35–36.

† Abigail Adams instructed her husband, the future president John Adams, to
"remember the ladies" when crafting the laws that govern the country in 1776,
to no avail. This demand is sometimes characterized as a polite plea from a
wife to her husband, but it was more like a threat: "If particular care and attention is not paid to the Ladies we are determined to foment a Rebellion, and
will not hold ourselves bound by any Laws in which we have no voice, or Representation." National Archives, "Abigail Adams to John Adams, 31 March
1776," Founders Online, founders.archives.gov/documents/Adams/04-01
-02-0241. Original source: L. H. Butterfield, ed., *The Adams Papers: Adams
Family Correspondence, vol. 1, December 1761–May 1776* (Cambridge,
Mass.: Belknap, 1963), 369–71.

merated rights has been the Fourteenth Amendment and its explicit protection of liberty.

Dobbs confronted two arguments for abortion rights grounded in the Fourteenth Amendment. First was an amicus brief submitted by scholars to explain how the prohibition of abortion arguably constitutes sex-based discrimination in violation of the Fourteenth Amendment's Equal Protection Clause.[100] Alito quickly disregarded this argument. Pointing to a 1993 Scalia opinion holding that "the goal of preventing abortion" does not qualify as "invidiously discriminatory animus" against women, Alito concluded that the Equal Protection argument is "squarely foreclosed by our precedents."[101] This is ironic because he said it while he overturned a precedent that had protected bodily autonomy for nearly fifty years.[102] Second was the substantive due process argument that undergirded previous landmark reproductive rights decisions.[103] Rather than follow *these* precedents, the Court held a jurisprudential seance.

The Supreme Court decided that "historical inquiries" were "essential" because of the breadth of the term "liberty" and the need to limit judges from imposing their own policy preferences in lieu of the Constitution.[104] As we've discussed, originalism doesn't actually supply meaningful or valuable constraints on the judiciary. It's a rigged game of hide-and-seek that entrenches the power dynamics and preferences of the eighteenth century. The originalist ideology nevertheless sees itself as Batman: the only thing preventing chaos from reigning in Gotham is the principles provided by the past, quality of the past notwithstanding.

The primary factors in the *Dobbs* majority's analysis were whether the right at issue is "deeply rooted in the nation's history and traditions" and whether it is an essential component of ordered liberty—reviving the test you saw used in the cases saying no to assisted suicide and yes to throwing The Gays ™ in jail.[105] Courts have found these standards satisfied when there's evidence of the right's existence in the country's legal traditions and when they determine that the right is basic to a free society. If you let Justice Alito tell it, the right to an abortion came out of nowhere.[106] He repeats four times that abortion is not grounded in constitutional text, history, or precedent.[107] As for essential liberties, Alito alternately talks around the subject and collapses the inquiry into a historical one, making mushy statements about abortion being "different" because it "destroys" "potential life" and the "historical understanding of ordered liberty" permitting legislatures to regulate abortion.[108]

Even if we accepted Alito's purported standard, *Dobbs* was still wrongly decided on its own terms. The majority's underdeveloped analysis neglects how people capable of pregnancy have always sought to control their reproduction in the United States. Similarly, at no point in its slapdash assessment of what constitutes an essential component of ordered liberty does the opinion fully consider the question, "Essential to whom?"

Black women in America provide stark examples of how the right to an abortion is both grounded in history and essential to a free and fair modern society. The United States was built on a form of racial capitalism where Black women's pregnancy meant profit for white slaveowners. Enslaved Black women were routinely sexually assaulted to produce more slaves—children who would also be owned and from whom they could be separated by sale.[109] Black women resisted and tried to retain ownership of themselves to the extent they could, including by interrupting their menstruation and inducing abortions. Women on cotton plantations, for instance, learned that they could end their pregnancies by chewing the cotton plant's roots.[110] Some enslaved women functioned as midwives of a sort, providing other slaves with herbal remedies and counsel on early abortifacient techniques.[111] We know for a fact that the exploitation of Black women's reproduction was fundamental to the

American system of human bondage, and that abortion, in turn, was a critical form of reproductive resistance to the horrors of slavery.

Congress knew this, too, when it formally outlawed slavery. Importantly, the curtailment of Black people's reproductive freedom and ability to define their own families was indispensable to the oppressive system Congress sought to abolish with the Reconstruction Amendments.[112] And abolitionists both in and outside of the legislature specifically called out the sexual abuse, forced pregnancy, and family separation endured by enslaved people as wrongs that the amendments must address.[113] Senator Charles Sumner, for instance, condemned slavery for violating "the chastity of a whole race . . . while the result is recorded in the tell-tale faces of children, glowing with a master's blood, but doomed for the mother's skin to Slavery through descending generations."[114] Representative John Creswell remarked, "The slave could sustain none of those relations which give life all its charms. He could not say my wife, my child, my body . . . The law pronounced him a chattel and these are not the rights or attributes of chattel."[115] Representative John Farnsworth, too, responded to slaveholders' claims about their so-called vested rights in human property by asking, "What vested rights so high or so sacred as a man's right to himself, to his wife and children, to his liberty, and to the fruits of his own industry? Did not our fathers declare that those rights were inalienable?"[116]

The rich historical record shows that the denial of reproductive control must be counted among the badges or incidents of slavery that Congress is empowered to stamp out under the Thirteenth Amendment, and bodily autonomy must be recognized as a form of liberty protected by the Fourteenth.[117] The Supreme Court's declaration in *Dobbs v. Jackson Women's Health* that there is no constitutional issue with the government conscripting your body into reproductive servitude stands in defiant opposition to the history and liberty on which it claims to rely and exposes cracks in originalism's veneer of credibility.[118] Alito did not mention the Reconstruction even once in his whole tedious opinion. (He did repeatedly make space, however, to discuss famed misogynist Sir Matthew Hale.)

Originalism's seemingly sacrosanct usage of history to determine whether a right exists is a sleight of hand from the start. First, it rests on the assumption that if you didn't have rights in the past, you can't have rights in the present or future. This rips a page straight out of the *Dred Scott* playbook. In *Dred Scott v. Sandford* (1857), the notorious Supreme Court decision that upheld slavery and ruled that Black people could not constitutionally become citizens, the Court explained that its duty was to interpret the Constitution "according to its true intent and meaning when adopted," without regard for any intervening "change in public opinion and feeling" (the feeling in this case being: "Maybe a few Black folks can have a few rights after all").[119] The inescapable consequence of this proto-originalist approach was that the bigotry of the Framers locked Black people into perpetual subjugation. America's racial caste system was always facially irreconcilable with the Founders' soaring demands for a government dependent on the consent of the governed. Yet when the Court observed the blatant hypocrisy between the country's founding documents and the oppression of Black people, this early originalist ruling refused to recognize Black people as part of the human family. The Court instead did as originalism dictates and focused on the dominant original understanding:

> But it is too clear for dispute, that the enslaved African race were not intended to be included, and formed no part of the people who framed and adopted this declaration; for if the language, as understood in that day, would embrace them, the conduct of the distinguished men who framed the Declaration

of Independence would have been utterly and flagrantly inconsistent with the principles they asserted; and instead of the
sympathy of mankind, to which they so confidently appealed,
they would have deserved and received universal rebuke and
reprobation.[120]

Basically, the Court reasoned that it had to pick between protecting the historical choices and reputations of the Framers and
protecting the human dignity of Black people. They decided that
the reputational injury inflicted by acknowledging and repairing the
tears in our national fabric outweighed the degradation of Black
lives. *Dobbs* engages in the same behavior by requiring that we analyze pregnant people's legal rights through the blatantly bigoted lens
of the late-eighteenth and early-nineteenth centuries—a time when,
historians tell us, abortion restrictions accelerated in large part due
to a campaign based on fear and resentment that immigrant populations were growing and white Anglo-Saxon Protestant women were
improperly shirking their so-called maternal duties, as well as efforts
by white male doctors to increase their own professional and financial status by supporting laws limiting access to reproductive healthcare services commonly provided by women.[121] (Alito didn't think
that mattered.) Notably, it is also a time when white women did not
legally exist. The doctrine of coverture proscribed that women had
no legal identity of their own and were instead subsumed under their
husbands, who had exclusive authority to enter contracts and own
property, as well as the prerogative to issue corporal "corrections"—
a euphemism for beatings.[122] (Alito didn't mention that.) Meanwhile,
Black women continued to live under a regime of racialized terror
that constrained their abilities to decide whether to have a child and
to parent that child with dignity—alternatively having motherhood
forced on them or forcibly taken away, among other forms of reproductive cruelty.[123] (Alito didn't touch that with a ten-foot pole.)

It's utterly unsurprising that originalists would consider it constitutional to enact discriminatory laws that curtail women's bodily integrity and reproductive autonomy when their standard for assessing constitutionality comes from an era teeming with discriminatory laws that curtail women's bodily integrity and reproductive autonomy. This is by design. Originalism uses racist, sexist standards in order to achieve racist, sexist results. A major problem present in both the *Dred Scott* Court's rationale and the current Court's focus on the historical depth of a right's roots is that it pays no attention to whether the soil it's rooted in is rotten.

A second problem with this mode of reasoning is that if you break down any right into sufficiently small and specific terms, looking for proof of its historical existence can be like looking for a needle in a haystack. Remember, originalists unsuccessfully tried this trick in *Lawrence v. Texas:* while the majority opinion discussed a right to liberty and to engage in private conduct without government interference, the dissent sneered about a so-called "fundamental right to engage in homosexual sodomy."[124] Instead of attempting to identify a narrow right to terminate a pregnancy, the Court could have sought historical evidence for broader principles like a right to decide if and when to have a family, or a right to bodily autonomy, or a right to self-determination. This is a key advantage of inclusive constitutionalism: starting from the point of principle allows you to adapt fundamental precepts to different circumstances and an evolving world so that we don't leave people out of the democratic project simply because they were not allowed in ages ago.

This isn't a difficult request. The same people who confidently assert that the word "abortion" does not appear in the Constitution have no quibbles about the document's silence on AK-47s or concealed carry. They infer it (quite boldly, I might add) from the sparse text of the Second Amendment:

A well regulated Militia, being necessary to the security of a free State, the right of the people to keep and bear Arms, shall not be infringed.

The Second Amendment historically protected the ability of states to form militias and of white men to own firearms so they could serve in said militias—and so they could terrorize the Black population . . . but I digress.[125] The fact that modern Second Amendment jurisprudence permits almost every Tom, Dick, and Harry to stockpile and brandish weapons of war willy-nilly is a particularly glaring example of how the Court is perfectly capable of extrapolating or reading concepts into laws when it wants to—or even *out* of laws when it wants to, having abandoned the inconvenient language about "militias" that are "well regulated."[126] While I do anticipate some opposition to inclusive constitutionalism as a departure from the methodological status quo, I'm not advocating for something wholly new and unfamiliar so much as recognizing the transformative impact it would have on our democracy if the Court treated women with even half as much care as it does weapons. Instead of asking, "What do we think this meant to rich white men hundreds of years ago?" we can ask, "What do we think this means to an inclusive democratic society today?" Although I find much of the Court's behavior reprehensible, I don't think so little of it to believe this beyond its intellectual capacity.

Inclusive constitutionalism demands an end to the courts' sacrifice of marginalized communities on the altar of originalism. To say we have been sacrificed is not hyperbole. A woman in America has fewer rights over her body than a corpse. Even if someone requires the use of another person's body so they can live, the dead or their surrogate must first authorize whether their organs and tissue can be donated.[127] If you have a uterus, you don't have this luxury. Whether to continue with a pregnancy and childbirth is not your decision to make. Like the Supreme Court's universally denounced majority opinion in *Dred Scott*, *Dobbs* treats millions of people's human rights with contempt and justifies their subordination with poorly substantiated claims about past generations. The dissent in *Dobbs* is clear-eyed about where the majority's position necessarily leads: insisting that the Constitution must be read as it was understood at the time of ratification "consigns women to second-class citizenship."[128] "All men are created equal"—terms and conditions apply to women.

There was a time, not too long ago, when the Supreme Court recognized that people's ability "to participate equally in the economic and social life of the Nation has been facilitated by their ability to control their reproductive lives."[129] But today's Court has abandoned that in favor of singling out a group of people for different legal treatment because of their biological functions. The consequence of this mistreatment is government-facilitated social, legal, and economic inferiority. This should be recognized as an affront to the Constitution's equal protection and due process provisions.

On a more fundamental level, making some people's rights conditional on their reproductive status is plainly incompatible with a functioning free society. Americans who can get pregnant are like Schrödinger's citizens, with legal rights and liberties that may or may not be observable at any time depending on their menstrual cycle.[130] Abortion restrictions introduce a profound tenuousness to people's ability to freely participate in the country's political, social, and economic life, and put their actual lives at risk. *Dobbs* gave no consideration to pregnant people's lived realities and how their very health and safety can depend on access to abortion. Maternal mortality rates in the United States are three times as high as the rates in most other wealthy nations.[131] And for each woman who dies, one hundred more women "suffer a severe obstetric morbidity, a life threatening diagnosis or undergo a lifesaving procedure during their delivery hospitalization."[132] The premier long-term study examining the effects of abortion, unwanted pregnancy, and childbirth found that women denied abortions experience significantly worse physical and mental health and financial and family outcomes.[133] It is unsurprising, then, that the most common feeling expressed by people who get abortions is relief.[134]

It's especially troubling that Black women were left out of the *Dobbs* majority's analysis and had no say in the decision-making process because we will disproportionately suffer the consequences of the ruling. Black women are five times as likely to get an abortion as white women, and we have the unfortunate distinction of having the highest maternal morbidity and mortality rates in the country.[135] Attacks on abortion are direct attacks on Black women's health. Conversely, social science data shows that the Black maternal mortality rate fell at least 28 percent *because* of abortion access.[136] The dual recognition that abortion saves Black women's lives and that abortion did not reach the *Dobbs* Court's standard for an essential and constitutionally protected right has led me to the unavoidable and disturbing conclusion that the originalist justices of the Supreme Court believe Black women's lives are not essential. I can't claim to know whether the Court's conservatives actively want me to die or are merely indifferent to whether I live. But I do know this: there's no legitimate reason to deny Black women and other marginalized populations an equal claim to this country's protections. Abortion plainly could and should have cleared the originalist hurdle for a right deeply rooted in history and essential to ordered liberty. But it didn't, because the touchstone of originalism is delivering victories in the conservative legal movement's war on civil rights. Equality and dignity—not the selective use of history and tradition—should be the core of substantive due process.

SAY IT WITH YOUR CHEST

Dobbs was the first time the Supreme Court formally rescinded a constitutional right.[137] Despite the majority's assurances, we have reason to think it won't be the last. Alito tried to temper public fears about the implications of overturning *Roe* beyond forced pregnancy by saying abortion is different because it presents a "profound moral question" and "destroy[s] a potential life."[138] Setting aside that Americans overwhelmingly support legal abortion and one in four American women get an abortion before the age of forty-five—suggesting it may not be such a profound moral question after all—the traits that make abortion different according to Alito are the same traits that conservatives ascribe to other unenumerated rights.

His proffered carve-out conveniently ignores the fact that birth control, same-sex marriage, and interracial marriage have all historically been framed as profound moral questions, and antiabortion advocates similarly characterize (well, *mis*characterize) birth control as destructive of potential life.[139] Precedents including *Griswold, Loving,* and *Obergefell* would likely fare poorly under the history-and-tradition standard the Court demands in *Dobbs*. And, we shouldn't forget, Justice Thomas's concurrence straight-up says, "Let's get rid of all substantive due process next."[140] The intended casualties of the originalist attack on substantive due process are clear: Jonathan Mitchell—the former solicitor general of Texas, legal architect of the state's abortion bounty hunter law, and conservative culture war consigliere—has explicitly argued that the rights to birth control, same-sex intimacy, interracial and same-sex marriage, and abortion all have no basis in the Constitution's text or history.[141] The conservative legal movement's agenda is not especially subtle.

Dobbs invites the rollback of recognized rights and creates hurdles that prevent the recognition of other rights people are fighting for. Notably, reproductive healthcare and gender-affirming healthcare are two sides of the same bodily-autonomy coin. Both abortion bans and laws that discriminate against trans people use the legal system to enforce stereotypes of how people of a given sex ought to be. Attacks on one are attacks on all.[142] It would be a grave mistake to think that any group's substantive due process rights are safe while originalism rules. Those who claim otherwise are trying to sell us fool's gold, and my mother didn't raise a fool.

Because originalism is stealing our liberties by curtailing substantive due process, some legal scholars propose that we start relying on other parts of the Constitution instead. And Justice Thomas's concurrence in *Dobbs* does suggest that other constitutional avenues may exist that could potentially protect some of the unenumerated rights currently recognized under law. He specifically notes that a long-dormant clause of the Fourteenth Amendment does protect the "privileges or immunities of citizens of the United States."[143]

We should take no comfort in this.

There are a couple of major causes for suspicion, even setting aside the fact that his recommended hook for our rights has been a dead letter since a Supreme Court case took the wind out of its sails in 1873.[144] First, while the Due Process Clause states that no *person* shall be deprived of life, liberty, or property without due process of law, the Privileges and Immunities Clause is explicitly limited to the rights of *citizens*.[145] Tens of millions of green card holders, undocumented persons, and other noncitizen residents of the United States would therefore be shut out of the Constitution's protections and more vulnerable to harmful state actions like prosecution, incarceration, and deportation for behavior that's lawful for citizens. Second, as Thomas says, the Court would still need to decide preliminary questions like "whether the Privileges or Immunities Clause protects *any* rights that are not enumerated in the Constitution and, if so, how to identify those rights."[146] His refusal to commit to the existence of substantive rights under the Clause is a huge red flag.

There's no reason to believe that all or any substantive due process rulings will be neatly transposed into privileges and immunities.

Importantly, conservatives do not oppose the Supreme Court's past rulings on issues like birth control and gay marriage simply because they think the decisions were based on the wrong part of the Fourteenth Amendment. They oppose them because they don't think women should be able to avoid pregnancy and they don't think gay people should be able to get married. And the Court's originalists have already confirmed that they are not going to say, "Ah darn, you got me there," if presented with an argument for abortion under the Privileges and Immunities Clause. The *Dobbs* majority slipped in a footnote concluding that any rights under that clause would still need to be rooted in the nation's history and tradition, citing a two-hundred-year-old case describing unenumerated privileges and immunities as fundamental rights "which have, *at all times,* been enjoyed by the citizens of the several states" (emphasis my own).[147] Thomas concurred that "even if the Clause does protect unenumerated rights, the Court conclusively demonstrates that abortion is not one of them under any plausible interpretive approach."[148]

It's time to change what's plausible.

People committed to the rights of marginalized communities should not allow the Privileges and Immunities Clause to be treated as an acceptable alternative to due process. Originalists would happily yank privileges and immunities away if we were to run toward it, and liberals can't afford to be duped like Charlie Brown with Lucy's football. We have to recognize that originalism remains a problem no matter where we look in the Constitution, and it must be delegitimized as a credible interpretive method. Furthermore, we shouldn't be bullied into backing away from substantive due process—a doctrine already in use to defend our rights. So, instead of distancing ourselves from it, let's double down. Originalists tell us to accept less? We demand more.

Inclusive constitutionalism argues that we should be strengthening rather than shrinking our substantive due process analyses in order to make the Constitution's principles real for all of us. The Due Process Clause should be broadly understood to protect the ability of the country's residents to freely and fully participate in society as equals. Reconceptualizing equality rights under the Due Process Clause should be seen as not just legitimate but welcome and encouraged. Expanding our understanding of due process could help reopen interpretive doors once thought closed and shift our understanding of the government's constitutional obligations to the people. Constitutional interpretation has tended to focus on negative rights, meaning what we may not be subjected to and must be free from, as opposed to what we are due and must be free to do or have. Many scholars have long argued that this negative understanding is woefully insufficient.[149] As Professor Robin West straightforwardly explained decades ago, ensuring that all persons are afforded dignity, concern, and respect "sometimes requires the state to refrain from acting, and sometimes requires it to act."[150] A revitalized Due Process Clause could include, for example, an affirmative right to education, a right to a minimum standard of living, a right to healthcare, a right to counsel in immigration proceedings (ending the cruel farce of literal toddlers "representing" themselves alone in court), and more.

Positive rights such as these have been disfavored by the Supreme Court, to be sure. But the Supreme Court is disfavored by the public, and neither the Founders nor the Supreme Court have the final word in the nation's ongoing dialogue about constitutional interpretation.[151] People interested in harnessing the power of the law for inclusive democracy rather than injustice should not lose sight of the fact that the scope and force of law depends on public assent. It is this fact that underlies scholar and activist Professor Mari Matsuda's decisive statement that "substantive due process can hold multitudes, and someday it will." She explains that the doctrine's detractors "who note the shifting and slippery interpretation of substantive due process miss the point that the entire Constitution [. . .] is a humanmade document subject to epic battles of interpretation."[152] This is a battle we can win if we collectively agree to fight for a just future.

CHAPTER 3

STEALING OUR ELECTIONS

There's a bridge in Selma, Alabama, bearing the name of Edmund Pettus. Pettus was a United States senator, a Confederate general, and a Grand Dragon in the Ku Klux Klan. The bridge was dedicated to Pettus in 1940, thirty-odd years after his death, to celebrate his maintenance of white supremacy and the terror he inflicted on Black Americans even after the Civil War.[1] In 1965, hundreds of activists would be brutalized by police and other armed citizens on that very bridge as they marched in protest of Black people's political and socioeconomic inequality, even after the Civil Rights Act of 1964.[2] The fight for American democracy has been long and bloody. But the late congressman John Lewis—who was nearly killed that day on the Edmund Pettus Bridge as a young man—was known to say that voting is the most powerful nonviolent tool in a democratic society.[3] Importantly, the civil rights heroes of the 1960s did not see the right to vote as an end in and of itself but as a step on the path to freedom. They sought meaningful ballot access in order to produce an actual representative government that would be responsive to their needs and engage in democracy rather than domination. Honest elections should provide a peaceful avenue to express the people's will, allow them to engage in collective decision-making as equals, and hold politicians accountable. People denied a real political voice by means of the vote are forced to speak the language of the unheard; as every Caribbean child has been told at some point as a precursor to consequences, those who can't hear would feel.

Seemingly without consideration for what tools remain when people are deprived of the powerful nonviolent ones, lawmakers across the country have introduced hundreds of pieces of legislation this decade that would change the laws in their states to curtail our ability to participate in free and fair elections. These proposals include limiting access to voting by mail, requiring voters to present official citizenship documents or photo identification at the polls, and allowing partisan actors to conduct fake audits of election results (fraudits, if you will).[4] Dozens of these bills have been enacted into law. The stated purpose of these laws is to combat widespread voter fraud. Because widespread voter fraud does not exist, the laws fail in this regard. But they have proven successful at depressing election turnout, disenfranchising voters, and decreasing confidence in democracy.[5] The present wide-ranging attack on voting rights has frequently been described as Jim Crow 2.0—suggesting that there may be some truth to the adage that the past does not repeat itself, but it often rhymes.[6] Not since the Jim Crow era has there been such a sustained nationwide legislative push making it harder for Americans to vote.[7]

Political figures across the spectrum have contested the Jim Crow analogy—for different reasons. Some on the left eschew the term because of its indelible link to the specific experience of Black Americans post-Reconstruction, while today's voter suppression more transparently affects non-Black people of color and low-income white people, too.[8] On the right, Jim Crow 2.0 is lambasted as dramatic and an exaggeration.[9] For these groups, voter suppression needs to employ the same methods and achieve the same effects with the same level of explicitness and brutality to warrant the title. (Indeed, a supervisor once cautioned me not to use the term so as to not prompt conservative critics to ask where the dogs and hoses were. Apparently, it's only Jim Crow if it comes from the Bull Connor region of France; otherwise it's just sparkling election integrity.) So, fine, the comparison isn't exact. But there are clearly reasonable comparisons to be made, and it is helpful to do so here as echoes of past fights for civil rights reverberate through modern law and politics. Today, the judiciary is embracing legal theories that threaten to turn back time and reverse any progress the country has made toward fuller political representation.[10]

WHY WE CAN'T HAVE NICE THINGS

Let's consider, once again, *Brown v. Board*. In chapter 1, we talked about the formal declaration made by dozens of congressmembers who opposed the integration of public schools. The Southern Manifesto gave rise to originalism and issued a call to use "all lawful means" to resist the implementation of the Court's ruling. The ensuing massive resistance campaign provides a useful frame of reference to better understand the severity of present threats to representative democracy.

When the Supreme Court ruled in *Brown* that the Constitution would not tolerate laws requiring racial segregation in public schools, parts of the country decided we simply shouldn't have public schools anymore. Millions of white Americans resisted the Court's ruling by using a variety of tactics ranging from the ballot box—voting to defund and close schools—to bombs.[11] (Can't integrate a school if there's no school.) Private schools were founded for white children with means. Some Black children had to travel to attend schools in other districts. And some children were forced to go without any formal schooling at all.[12] Education wasn't worth it, in some communities and corners of government, if it had to be shared.

Opponents of an integrated electorate today strum a consonant chord. When people of color and young people used the democratic process in record numbers, helping to usher a Black man into the White House, parts of the country decided we simply shouldn't have a democracy anymore. The first modern wave of restrictive voter legislation came after Barack Obama won the presidency, twice—including laws that federal courts concluded had both the intent and the effect of discriminating against Black voters.[13] Waves swelled into a tsunami of antidemocratic legislation after voters of color overwhelmingly rejected the reelection campaign of a white demagogue: in both 2021 and 2022, lawmakers in dozens of states introduced more than four hundred bills with provisions that would restrict voting access and thwart the electoral process, including some that would allow partisan state officials to interfere in how votes are counted and even directly overturn election results.[14] One bill—which was ultimately defeated, but is the stuff of nightmares nonetheless—would have required Arizona's legislature to convene after an election and vote on whether to accept or reject the election results. Representative John Fillmore, who introduced the bill, further stated, "We should have voting, in my opinion, in person: one day, on paper, with no electronic means and hand counting that day. We need to get back to 1958-style voting."[15]

Election saboteurs in both federal and state legislatures recognize the burgeoning political power of communities of color and have seemingly turned to Joseph Stalin's apocryphal authoritarian advice: who votes, and how, is less important than who *counts* the votes and how they are recorded.[16] One hundred and forty-seven Republican U.S. Congress members baselessly objected to the certification of the 2020 election results, and a deadly mob descended on the Capitol on January 6, 2021.[17] Insurrectionists both in and outside of Congress were unified in their mission of overturning the will of the people and justified their subversion with lies about voter fraud.[18] These claims necessarily privileged the slim majority of white voters who voted for Trump as valid and denigrated the huge majority of voters of color who did not as fraudulent. For adherents of the Big Lie, only the right votes—white votes—should count. Democracy wasn't worth it, in some communities and corners of government, if it had to be shared.

The United States is sometimes described as one of the world's oldest democracies.[19] But political power was not shared in a way that you could describe with a straight face as "rule by the people" until 1965 at the earliest, when Congress passed the Voting Rights Act.[20] The act sought to enforce the Fifteenth Amendment's prohibition on the denial or abridgment of the right to vote based on race, color, or previous condition of servitude, and created a pathway to real political participation for Americans whose votes had been blocked by law and physical violence.[21] Congress reauthorized the act several times, in recognition of its utility and the continuing need for federal enforcement of the Constitution's provisions—first in 1970 for five years, again in 1975 for seven more years, again in 1982 for twenty-five more years, and again in 2006 for another twenty-five more years. There was, for a time, bipartisan consensus: when the act was last reauthorized in 2006, for example, it sailed through the Senate with ninety-eight votes in favor and not a single vote in opposition.[22] The 2006 reauthorization was also the first time a federal voting rights law passed with the participation of Black congressmembers representing each of the former Confederate states.[23] And it was the last reauthorization before the United States had a Black president.

The Supreme Court repeatedly upheld the Voting Rights Act as constitutional throughout its history.[24] But that was before ideologues with other ideas rose to power on the bench. Over the past decade, the Court issued multiple decisions that significantly curtailed the legal protections and structures that once strengthened our fledgling democracy. The Court's weaponization of history and tradition has made it easier for governments to enact and enforce anti-voter laws and harder for the electorate to do anything about it.[25] An antidemocratic movement has been allowed to grow strong. As of 2023, domestic and international experts regard our democracy as "backsliding" and under "significant threat."[26] And over half of respondents to a poll conducted by the Associated Press–NORC Center for Public Affairs Research in October 2022 felt our democracy is working poorly.[27] Our system of governance is the most vulnerable it has been in generations.

Election subversion doesn't always take place in the streets with dogs and hoses, or in dramatic fashion at the Capitol. Sometimes it takes place quietly in the courtroom. Chief Justice Roberts has diligently led the Supreme Court's conservative majority in a years-long effort to steal the crown jewel of the Civil Rights Movement—the Voting Rights Act—and undermine the political power of communities of color. Originalism has sometimes played a supporting role in the Court's construction of an antidemocratic canon; occasionally it's relied upon and at other times it's conspicuously absent. This, too, is an indictment. The selective invocation underscores that originalism is just a tool used when convenient, and that we can choose to decide cases another way.

THE EMPIRE STRIKES BACK

The conservative legal movement struck the first critical blow against the Voting Rights Act when the Supreme Court decided *Shelby County v. Holder*. The local government of Shelby County,

Alabama, filed a complaint in April 2010 suing Eric Holder in his capacity as attorney general of the United States. The county sought to get parts of the act declared unconstitutional and prevent the Justice Department from enforcing them.[28] Sections 4 and 5 of the Voting Rights Act applied specifically to local and state governments, like that of Alabama, that had a track record of discrimination. If a locality was a covered jurisdiction under a standard set out in Section 4(b) called the "coverage formula," Section 5 required it to preclear new laws or changes to existing laws about qualifications or prerequisites to vote with the Department of Justice (DOJ). Covered jurisdictions also had to preclear new laws or changes to standards, practices, or procedures with respect to voting. If the DOJ or a three-judge panel of the D.C. federal district court determined that the voting change did not have a racially discriminatory purpose and would not deny or abridge the right to vote on account of race or color, the locality could go ahead and implement it. The Voting Rights Act also created space for covered jurisdictions to step out from the shadows of their past: a locality could end its preclearance coverage (called "bailing out") if a three-judge panel of the D.C. district court determined no prohibited test or device had been used during the preceding ten years with the purpose or effect of discriminating against voters of color, subject to the condition that an action could be reopened if the attorney general alleged that the locality again used a test or device with the purpose or effect of race-based vote denial or abridgment.[29]

Basically, Sections 4 and 5 were the law's way of saying to a state or local government, You have a history of preventing people of color from voting when left to your own devices, so, until you prove that you can behave yourselves, run voting changes by us so we can make sure everything's kosher; discriminate again, and deal with us again. Section 5 has been described as "the most innovative" provision of the Voting Rights Act but also "the most controversial."[30]

Shelby County alleged in its complaint that it and other covered jurisdictions were, unfairly, being treated worse than other states and political subdivisions based on arbitrary criteria. The formula employed by the Voting Rights Act, Shelby argued, was out of date and did not account for decades of progress and Black Americans' increased political participation. Shelby County contended that Congress exceeded the bounds of its authority to enforce the Fourteenth and Fifteenth Amendments because current needs did not justify the burden created by the Voting Rights Act on the ability of singled-out localities to control their elections. In its view, this mismatch of means and ends amounted to a violation of the purported principle of "equal sovereignty" embodied in the Tenth Amendment and Article IV of the Constitution.[31]

Shelby County's complaint elides the fact that the Voting Rights Act's preclearance provisions treated states differently because those states had actually behaved differently, and those states could end preclearance once they consistently demonstrated that their election laws and policies were not racially discriminatory. Shelby asked the courts to afford greater respect to states as sovereign entities that can run elections as they see fit—at the expense of the people in those states subject to discrimination and disenfranchisement. An inclusive-constitutionalist approach would deny this unseemly request. Instead, it would respect the civil rights activists who, as articulated in an amicus brief invoking the Federalist Papers, "did not spill 'the precious blood' of our people, nor waste 'the hard-earned substance of millions' just so that 'the governments of the individual States might enjoy a certain extent of power, and be arrayed with certain dignities and attributes of sovereignty'" but "did so in the cause of human freedom."[32]

Despite making reference to "equal sovereignty" in its complaint, Shelby County completely misrepresented the source of the concept. Shelby pointed to the Tenth Amendment, which specifies that "the powers not delegated to the United States by the Constitution, nor prohibited by it to the States, are reserved to the States respectively, or to the people."[33] Fun fact, though: the Constitution expressly delegates to Congress the power to regulate federal elections as well as the power to make sure states don't violate citizens' voting rights on account of their race.[34] Shelby also pointed to Article IV, which provides the framework for states' relationships with one another and with the United States. Today this includes things like honoring other states' court judgments, so a couple married in Connecticut is still married in California; and in the pre–Civil War era, it included things like requiring free states to deliver fugitive slaves back to their enslavers.[35] Neither the Tenth Amendment nor Article IV makes explicit or implicit reference to the equal sovereignty idea invoked by Shelby County, so I'd like to take a moment to cut through the obfuscation.

Civil rights legal scholars have traced the origins of this alleged principle in American jurisprudence to *Dred Scott v. Sandford* (1857), a case commonly and without exaggeration reviled as the worst Supreme Court decision of all time. The Court ruled in *Dred Scott* that Black people were not and could not become citizens of the United States under the Constitution, and rationalized this decision in part by claiming that it would infringe on states' equal sovereignty to hold otherwise.[36] The Court reasoned that permitting free states to make Black people citizens would override other states' sovereign right to enslave them.[37] The Court further considered itself "bound, out of respect to the State sovereignties, to assume they had deemed it just and necessary thus to stigmatize" Black people and brand them with "such deep and enduring marks of inferiority and degradation."[38] The Supreme Court concluded that the federal government must sanction Black inequality in order for states to be equal under law.* The *Dred Scott* decision was effectively overturned by the Civil War and formally abrogated by constitutional amendment, but the equal sovereignty idea shuffled onward in a zombie state.

Chief Justice Roberts revived the long-dormant "equal sovereignty" notion in a 2009 Supreme Court decision called *Northwest Austin Municipal Utility District Number One v. Holder,* or just *NAMUDNO* for short. The phrase appears only twice in *NAMUDNO,* with Roberts stating in the first instance that the Voting Rights Act "differentiates between the States, despite our historic tradition that all the States enjoy 'equal sovereignty.'"[39] Traditionalism, as this kind of history-focused approach to constitutional interpretation is sometimes called, is like originalism's fraternal twin—closely related, but not identical. Traditionalism looks to the past and long-standing practices, which can be but aren't necessarily linked to the moment of ratification and the Constitution's original public meaning.[40]

Roberts neglected to mention the role of *Dred Scott* in developing the equal sovereignty concept. He instead supported the proposition by pointing to an antebellum case also cited in *Dred Scott* about new states having the same rights over the navigable waters within their borders and the soil underneath said waters as existing states did when they entered the Union (known as the "equal footing" doctrine), and a case heard soon after the Civil War about Texas's statehood and its contractual obligations in light of its secession and readmission.[41] Neither case was related to voting rights, or even

---

* You may be thinking, "Well, wait a second, set aside other individual states— surely the *United States* can make people citizens." And I like where your head's at. But, while the Court recognized that the federal government does have the power to confer citizenship, it concluded that its naturalization power is only available to foreign-born immigrants as opposed to people imported as property and their domestically born descendants. *Dred Scott v. Sandford,* 60 U.S. 393, 417 (1857).

to federal statutes with different impacts on different states. Both dealt with the status of states trying to enter the Union. And even the equal footing doctrine was somewhat illusory in practice: states *were* often admitted to the Union with different conditions imposed on them—including declaration upon entry as a "free state" or a "slave state" before the Civil War, and several conditions applicable to the former Confederacy after the Civil War.[42] Still, Justice Roberts forged ahead and turned two very old cases about becoming one of these united states into a much grander federalist principle about states' rights. Relying on these cases allowed Roberts to sneak *Dred Scott*-style reasoning into modern civil rights jurisprudence without many people catching a whiff of the *Dred Scott* stench. Roberts further stated in *NAMUDNO* that "a departure from the fundamental principle of equal sovereignty" in the voting rights context "requires a showing that a statute's disparate geographic coverage is sufficiently related to the problem that it targets."[43] This means that if Congress is going to have a voting rights law that treats some places differently than others, it better have an exceedingly good justification for that different treatment. He provided no authority to support this proposition, presumably because none exists.

Roberts claimed in *NAMUDNO* that the preclearance provisions in Section 5 of the Voting Rights Act raised "serious constitutional questions," but that it wasn't the right time to answer them. Thomas alone dissented in part to make Roberts's abstract attacks more concrete, and argued outright that he would find Section 5 unconstitutional because current conditions no longer justified "such an extraordinary remedy."[44] (Racism is over—who knew?) But Roberts's opinion required Thomas to wait just a few more years: the moment to take down Section 5 would come with *Shelby*.

The district court in *Shelby* examined the federalism concerns raised in *NAMUDNO* and observed that the county still had very little to hang its legal hat on. Shelby County argued that the preclearance coverage formula was outdated, and there was insufficient evidence of pervasive current voting discrimination to justify prophylactic federal involvement in some states' regulation of their elections. But Congress had compiled a staggering fifteen thousand pages of evidence of modern, intentional racial discrimination in voting in support of the 2006 reauthorization of the Voting Rights Act, including court decisions, Justice Department findings, reports by civil rights organizations and voting scholars, statistical analyses, firsthand accounts, and more—a feat the court described as "virtually unprecedented."[45] The court reviewed the sizable record and was convinced that Section 5 was still justified by current needs.[46] The court also determined that Sections 4 and 5 were sufficiently narrow—time-limited with a bailout provision and low administrative costs, and connected to jurisdictions with histories of discrimination, for instance—that they plainly remained proportional and congruent responses to the problem of unconstitutional voting discrimination.[47] Shelby County itself was ineligible for bailout because of its own recent history of discrimination against Black voters: a city within the county had created a redistricting plan in 2008 that eliminated the city's only majority-Black district—a district which was created pursuant to a consent decree in a Voting Rights Act lawsuit in 1990—by reducing its Black voter population from 70.9 percent to 29.5 percent.[48] The Department of Justice objected, but the city conducted an election under the unapproved maps anyway. This resulted in the defeat of a Black incumbent, and subsequent legal action by the Justice Department to block the certification of the election results.[49]

Shelby's argument about equal sovereignty was also entirely unconvincing to the district court because the Supreme Court had said it was unconvincing decades ago in a case called *South Carolina v. Katzenbach*. In 1966, South Carolina argued that the Voting Rights Act preclearance provisions violated the fundamental principle of

STEALING OUR ELECTIONS 113

"equality of statehood," which required that federal legislation affecting "political rights and sovereignty" apply "equally, on a nationwide basis, to all sovereign members of the Union."[50] The Supreme Court politely informed South Carolina that it didn't know what it was talking about: "That doctrine applies only to the terms upon which States are admitted to the Union, and not to the remedies for local evils which have subsequently appeared."[51] As I mentioned earlier, nothing in the Constitution says federal voting statutes must apply to all states equally.[52] Ultimately, the *Shelby* district court did not find a valid reason to second-guess Congress's conclusion, made "after many months of deliberation and compilation of a massive record," that Sections 4 and 5 were necessary to fight back against continued state-sponsored discrimination against people of color in the electoral process.[53] The court granted summary-judgment motions against Shelby County, meaning a full trial was deemed unnecessary because Shelby was obviously wrong.[54]

Shelby County appealed the district court's ruling to the D.C. Circuit, where it lost again. The circuit court acknowledged *NAMUDNO*'s questions as to whether the disparate geographic coverage of Section 4(b) was sufficiently related to the targeted problem and whether the current burdens of Section 5 were justified by current needs, and answered both in the affirmative. Parts of its rationale focused on the structure of the law itself, finding it particularly important that jurisdictions could bail out of coverage, and that previously uncovered jurisdictions could become subject to a form of preclearance, too, if a federal court found violations of the Fourteenth or Fifteenth Amendments that warranted such legal relief. Preclearance actually applied equally, then, in that all states could be subject to it if they violated the Constitution's voting protections.

More interesting, though, is the part of the circuit court's rationale that focused on the structure of government and the role of the judiciary. In stark contrast to today's maximalist Supreme Court, which almost never misses a chance to consolidate power, the D.C. Circuit essentially said that it knows when to stay in its lane and let Congress do its job to protect the rights of voters.[55] The modern Supreme Court frequently expands its decision-making power while disparaging and diminishing the power of other branches of government, as documented in scholarship by law professors like Josh Chafetz and Mark Lemley.[56] And while the sheer breadth of the Court's power grab is a recent development, the Court has historically been overeager to curb the legislature's power when it invokes its constitutional authority to confront white supremacy. The Reconstruction Amendments grant Congress extensive power to protect and enforce "rights of belonging," defined by Professor Rebecca Zietlow as rights that promote an inclusive vision of the national community and facilitate equal membership in that community.[57] But with the notable exception of the Supreme Court under Chief Justice Earl Warren's leadership in the 1960s, the high court has often refused to defer to congressional power to define and protect those rights.[58] The D.C. Circuit's decision in *Shelby* refrained from such oppressive judicial activism and instead showed judicial humility.

The appellate court recognized that Congress had acted at "the apex of its power," protecting arguably the most important civic virtue—the right to vote—from possibly the gravest societal sin— racial discrimination.[59] It also emphasized the voluminous record produced by Congress and its "quintessentially legislative judgment" that "Section 5's work is not yet done."[60] The Court did not doubt that the covered jurisdictions were making progress, but it concluded that it owed considerable deference to Congress, which "drew reasonable conclusions from the extensive evidence it gathered and acted pursuant to the Fourteenth and Fifteenth Amendments, which entrust Congress with ensuring that the right to vote—surely among the most important guarantees of political liberty in the Constitution—is not abridged on account of race."[61] In other words, if Congress thinks there is still work to be done to heal the wound of racism, the Court has no right to say, "No there isn't." Thus, the D.C. Circuit affirmed the district court's summary judgment decision. (For anyone keeping score, that's Voting Rights Act: 2; Shelby County: 0.) The court's conclusion that the present conditions warranted substantial deference to the legislature is reminiscent of the idea we talked about in chapter 1, put forth by the Supreme Court in *Carolene* Footnote Four and promoted by John Hart Ely in his important book *Democracy and Distrust*. The judiciary's job is to reinforce democracy and ensure that the political process is open and accessible to minority groups. Inclusive constitutionalism provides an additional, related lesson for the courts: if you see Congress trying to end systems of oppression, mind your business.

Shelby County appealed once again after the appellate court's decision, and its luck changed in 2013 when it faced a friendly audience at the Supreme Court. Chief Justice Roberts authored the opinion for a 5–4 conservative majority. Roberts conceded that the Voting Rights Act's "strong medicine" was warranted by the pervasive and ingenious racial discrimination of the 1960s but nevertheless criticized the act for its "drastic" and "dramatic" departure from the principles of federalism and equal sovereignty.[62] To be clear, Congress frequently enacts laws that impact different states differently or even identify individual states for different treatment. Such laws, which regulate everything from Medicaid to radioactive waste disposal, have frequently been upheld in court.[63] What's more, the Supreme Court explicitly had foreclosed the "equal sovereignty" argument against the Voting Rights Act decades earlier in *Katzenbach* when it clarified that the idea only pertained to admitting states to the Union. Yet Roberts relied heavily on his own passing statements in *NAMUDNO* to reframe the act's disparate treatment of states as a near-unforgivable offense to their dignity (never mind those states' disparate treatment of communities of color). The Court admitted that "any racial discrimination in voting is too much" but said congressional legislation must "speak to current conditions."[64] It concluded that today's conditions couldn't justify the insult of the covered states having to ask the federal government for permission to enact a law while its neighbors could use the normal legislative process.

You'd be forgiven for not knowing what the current conditions actually were; the dissent criticized the Court's majority for its failure to make any "genuine attempt to engage with the massive legislative record that Congress assembled."[65] That record showed that the Department of Justice had blocked more than seven hundred changes to voting laws in the covered jurisdictions between the 1982 and 2006 reauthorizations of the Voting Rights Act after having determined that the changes "were calculated decisions to keep minority voters from fully participating in the political process."[66] Further, between 1982 and 2006, upwards of 800 proposed voting changes were withdrawn or amended after the DOJ requested more information from the submitting jurisdiction.[67] But the Chief Justice did not bother to interrogate why specific states were being treated differently, neither asking nor answering the question as to just how much voting discrimination continued to be attempted in those covered jurisdictions. He instead blithely asserted that the country had changed—voter registration and turnout had improved, more people of color had been elected than ever before, and most appallingly unsubtle barriers to voting had been stamped out—but the coverage formula and restrictions in Sections 4 and 5 had remained the same. That those changes were "in large part *because of* the Voting Rights Act," as Roberts acknowledged, was beside the point.[68] You've met the "I have a Black friend" defense; now meet "We have a Black president."

The Court ruled the coverage formula in Section 4(b) unconstitutional. And with no more formula to identify places subject to pre-clearance, there are now no places subject to preclearance. Thus, the Court's decision left Section 5, which required covered localities to preclear new voting laws and policies, intact but rendered it inoperable—like a car with its wheels boosted off, one of the country's greatest legislative achievements was put up on blocks. Justice Thomas wrote a separate concurrence to again explain that, if it were up to him alone, he would find Section 5 unconstitutional as well.[69] Justice Thomas reasoned that the death-by-a-thousand-cuts incrementalism the Chief Justice is known for "needlessly prolong[ed]" the "demise of that provision."[70] The late justice Ruth Bader Ginsburg sharply criticized the "unprecedented extension of the equal sovereignty principle" as "capable of much mischief." Further, she famously observed in dissent that the Voting Rights Act was a victim of its success and the majority's disingenuous illogical-ity: "Throwing out preclearance when it has worked and is continuing to work to stop discriminatory changes is like throwing away your umbrella in a rainstorm because you are not getting wet."[71]

THE SHELBY SHOCKWAVE

I've lingered on *Shelby County v. Holder* for two reasons. First, it was a lawless and racist decision. The *Shelby* Court abandoned precedent, typical legal principles, and even its precious originalism left and right, bending over backward to actively make life worse for people of color. It failed to give proper weight to the Fifteenth Amendment's express grant of power to Congress to ensure that the right to vote is not abridged because of race. It refused to consider how the Reconstruction Amendments deliberately and fundamentally altered the federalist system in order to foster multiracial democracy—which one might hope self-styled originalists would care about—or how the courts have a responsibility to facilitate the functioning of that inclusive democratic system. It never even contemplated the role of the Constitution's Elections Clause, which explicitly empowers Congress to "make or alter such regulations" that govern federal elections.[72] And just like in *Dred Scott,* the Supreme Court in *Shelby* elevated a make-believe principle of state equality over the very real—and historically infringed upon—right of non-white people to participate in a democratic society as political equals. The Supreme Court should be shamed for these travesties at every opportunity. Every American should have the knowledge to express that shame and, in so doing, relinquish the fiction that the Court is strictly composed of apolitical arbiters possessing unparalleled wisdom.[73] Sometimes the Court is just a handful of old guys in robes doing whatever they want to do and counting on nobody calling them on it. For what it's worth, this is me calling them on it. Their intellectually dishonest affront to democracy demands a new Court with a new jurisprudence grounded in an inclusive constitutionalist vision for the future.

Second, *Shelby County* swung open a door that the supporters of the Voting Rights Act fought for decades to close and keep closed. Once again, there was a clear path for discriminatory laws and judicial opinions chipping away at voting protections. The subsequent legislative assault on our democracy has been comprehensive. Uninhibited state and local governments are now experimenting with new methods of disenfranchisement, like empowering state officials to interfere in the administration of elections and exposing actual election workers to criminal liability for ordinary conduct. Legislatures are also bringing back some old classics, like closing polling places and cutting the hours of those that remain. People of color are uniquely vulnerable to such attacks. Scholarly research shows that restrictive voter legislation in the United States is inextricable from racial resentment. Not only do these laws disproportionately impact people of color, the prevalence of their introduction in the first place depends on the intersection of two factors: Republican control of government and significant nonwhite populations.[74] Scholars and journalists grimly concluded in *Shelby County*'s aftermath that the era of civil rights was over and a new era of reinvigorated white racial hegemony had begun.[75] The Supreme Court's bad decision-making in that case is a major contributing factor to our current loathsome state of affairs.

Voters felt the loss of Section 5 immediately. With Roberts having lit the Disenfranchisement Olympics torch, states raced off to determine who could discriminate the most and the fastest. Texas took an early lead: mere hours after the Supreme Court announced its opinion in *Shelby,* the state announced that it would be reimplementing a burdensome voter identification law that a federal court had previously struck down under Section 5 of the Voting Rights Act.[76] Not to be outdone, North Carolina made an announcement the very next day that it would be moving forward with an omnibus elections bill including strict photo ID provisions, cutting early voting, eliminating same-day registration during early voting, and other restrictions.[77] Section 5 had previously blocked changes like these, but now it was a free-for-all. State and local governments across the country started establishing more and more obstacles to voting. The racial-turnout gap, which had narrowed briefly when Barack Obama was on the ballot, began to grow rapidly in formerly covered jurisdictions.[78] And so the evidence, such as it existed, that Chief Justice Roberts relied on to show Section 5's obsolescence began to disappear altogether in Section 5's absence.[79]

The Justice Department and legal advocates turned to their remaining tools for protecting the franchise. Chief among them is Section 2 of the Voting Rights Act. Section 2 prohibits voting practices or procedures that result in the denial or abridgment of the right to vote on account of race, color, or membership in certain language minority groups. That "result in" language is important; Congress specifically added it when amending the act in 1982 in order to repudiate a bad decision the Supreme Court had made two years earlier. Voters in Mobile, Alabama, had sued the city, alleging that its electoral system discriminated against Black voters in violation of the Constitution and the Voting Rights Act. The Supreme Court disagreed, ruling in *Mobile v. Bolden* that the Fifteenth Amendment doesn't prohibit laws that are racially neutral on their face (meaning laws that aren't explicitly racially discriminatory) unless they're motivated by a discriminatory purpose, and Section 2's protections fully overlapped with those of the Fifteenth Amendment. This meant that a law's discriminatory impact wasn't enough to trigger the protection of either the Constitution or the Voting Rights Act, even if the law demonstrably deprived people of color of equal access to the political process. Justice Marshall made the consequences clear in dissent: "In the absence of proof of intentional discrimination by the State, the right to vote provides the politically powerless with nothing more than the right to cast meaningless ballots."[80]

The Supreme Court had missed the point, so Congress added the new "result in" language to Section 2 to clarify that impact matters even without hard evidence of intent. The Court interpreted the amended act for the first time in *Thornburg v. Gingles* (1986) and acknowledged that Congress had "substantially revised" Section 2 "to make clear that a violation could be proved by showing discriminatory effect alone."[81] More specifically, Section 2 instructed the judiciary to determine whether the "totality of the circumstances" showed that the political process was "not equally open to participation" by members of a protected class, in that those persons had "less opportunity than other members of the electorate to participate in the political process and to elect representatives of their choice."[82]

These amendments met fierce resistance from none other than

John Roberts. Young Roberts worked in the Justice Department and wrote dozens of memoranda urging the Reagan Administration and the Senate to keep Section 2 unchanged, warning that violations of Section 2 "should not be made too easy to prove, since they provide a basis for the most intrusive interference imaginable by federal courts into state and local processes."[83] Roberts also took issue with the national scope of Section 2, arguing that there was "no evidence of voting abuses nationwide supporting the need for such a change."[84]

The amendment prevailed and Section 2 does in fact apply nationwide. So, unlike the coverage formula and preclearance requirement of Sections 4 and 5, it wasn't susceptible to the Court's "equal sovereignty" brouhaha in *Shelby County*. But Section 2 was meant to work in conjunction with Section 5—not in place of it. Section 5 blocked bad laws from going into effect, while Section 2 stops bad laws that are already in effect. And an ounce of prevention is worth a pound of cure. Section 2 litigation is resource intensive. It takes time and money, and puts the burden on plaintiffs to prove discrimination rather than the jurisdictions to prove they're not discriminating. Civil rights organizations and the Justice Department brought Section 2 lawsuits against Texas and North Carolina for their post-*Shelby* suppression spree, for example, which eventually proved that the states intentionally discriminated against people of color. Proof of intent isn't even required under Section 2, to be clear—the laws were just that egregious; a federal court found that the North Carolina law targeted Black voters with "almost surgical precision."[85] But people were disenfranchised for years as the cases were pending, and the lawsuits cost communities millions of dollars. The head of the Department of Justice's Civil Rights Division testified before Congress that "the elimination of Section 5 has increased the cost of protecting voting rights on an order of magnitude similar to the cost of a Ford Fiesta compared to a Boeing 737."[86] Simply put, Section 2 is necessary but not sufficient.

The inadequacy of Section 2 as a replacement for Section 5 has not spared it from the Supreme Court's campaign of democracy destruction. In the summer of 2021, the Supreme Court decided *Brnovich v. Democratic National Committee* (DNC). The DNC and other party affiliates alleged that two Arizona laws violated the Voting Rights Act and the Constitution, and took legal action against Mark Brnovich in his capacity as attorney general of Arizona. One law proscribes that Arizonans who vote in person on Election Day must do so in the precinct to which they were assigned. Across the country, if a voter arrives at a polling place and there are questions about their eligibility to vote, they may cast a provisional ballot. And in many places, if it is confirmed that the voter is eligible, then their provisional ballot is counted like any other—even if they showed up at the wrong precinct. But in Arizona, if a voter mistakenly casts a provisional ballot on Election Day at a precinct other than the one to which they were assigned, even if they are registered to vote in a different place, their ballot will be discarded and not counted.[87] The other law at issue makes it a crime for any person other than a postal worker, an elections official, or a voter's caregiver, family member, or household member to collect a voter's early ballot; a person who picks up their neighbor's ballot and drops it off at the post office has committed a felony in Arizona.[88] Arizona used to be covered by Section 5 of the Voting Rights Act because of its history of discriminating against Native American and Hispanic residents' voting rights.[89] (Despite what you may have been told, the VRA is about protecting voters throughout the United States, not punishing the Deep South.) And plaintiffs believed that the challenged laws in Arizona reflected the state returning to its old ways.

The majority of Arizona's electorate does not vote in person. Still, Arizona consistently leads the country in rejecting in-person voters' provisional ballots.[90] One of the most frequent reasons for provisional ballot rejection in Arizona is that they were cast in the wrong precinct.[91] Precinct mix-ups are the result of a variety of factors including Arizona's high rates of residential mobility and unusually frequent changes to polling locations, especially in areas where people of color live.[92] Indeed, one judge quipped that "the paths to polling places in the Phoenix area [are] much like the changing stairways at Hogwarts, constantly moving and sending everyone to the wrong place."[93] Native American voters also face uniquely high hurdles, as many lack verifiable physical addresses. Voters without street addresses are instructed on Arizona's official voter registration form to "draw a map and/or provide the latitude/longitude or geocode here" in a small box roughly two-by-two inches.[94] The Navajo Nation asserted in an amicus brief that county officials use the tiny maps Navajos draw to estimate the location of their residence, assigning them a precinct that may or may not be correct based on this cartoonish guesswork.[95] The geocode option introduced in 2020 is more precise but less available to many Navajos, who tend to lack computer or internet access.[96] Unsurprisingly, Native, Hispanic, and Black voters cast out-of-precinct ballots at statistically higher rates than their white counterparts. The district court suspected that the out-of-precinct policy might not be a big deal in practice, though, since an overwhelming majority of Arizonans vote by mail and therefore wouldn't be affected by it. (The court did not specify how many voters must be disenfranchised on account of their race before the judiciary would care.)

The second challenged law, however, did affect mail voting. Voting by mail has been a mainstay of Arizona elections since 1991, when the state enacted a law allowing all voters to mail in their ballots without an excuse. Mail-in voting enjoyed bipartisan support for decades because it spared elders from treks to their polling places in the Arizona heat, kept rural voters from having to travel vast distances to vote in person, accommodated residents who live elsewhere for part of the year, and provided flexibility and convenience to voters in need.[97] But in recent years, Arizona Republicans began pushing to restrict people's ability to receive, collect, and return mail ballots. They explained the change of heart by claiming that mail-in voting is a threat to election integrity. There's no proof of that, and evidence suggests the real threat was racism: in 2014, the Republican chair of Arizona's most populous county created a viral video advocating for the outlaw of ballot collection, which featured surveillance footage of a Hispanic volunteer delivering ballots to a polling place. The chair accused the volunteer of ballot stuffing and said he "did not know if the person was an illegal alien, a dreamer, or citizen, but knew that he was a thug."[98] This video was shown at Republican meetings in the lead-up to debate on the ballot collection law.[99]

Some legislators justified the law with other uncorroborated claims about voter fraud; in one story fit for a chain email, a lawmaker said he heard people were collecting ballots and putting them in the microwave with a bowl of water to steam them open and discard the ballots if the vote didn't reflect their preference. Other lawmakers skipped the tall tales and argued that, even though voter fraud doesn't exist, people believe it does, so legal measures are justified to restore their trust in the system. The governor echoed this idea of improving public faith in elections when he claimed that the law preventing friends, community members, and civic organizations from picking up and dropping off ballots ensured "a secure chain of custody between the voter and the ballot box."[100] While difficult to enforce, laws like these inevitably have a chilling effect on would-be voters and those who might otherwise assist them. They also empower vigilantes.[101]

With respect to those Arizonans who voted by mail, the plaintiffs lacked direct data or records indicating the number and demographics of voters who returned their ballots with the help of third parties. Quantitative data is admired but not required by law to prove that a policy disparately impacts racial minorities. Plaintiffs instead provided qualitative evidence in the form of testimony from dozens of witnesses, including political scientists, voters, advocates who collect ballots as part of get-out-the-vote efforts, and advocates who focus on issues affecting the Native American community. The obstacles faced by Indigenous people stand out here, too. Because of both historic and ongoing discrimination, Native peoples frequently live on reservations that are in impoverished and isolated rural areas. There's often no access to transportation or mail delivery. With more than one in four Native people living in poverty and with many miles to drive between them and a post office, they sometimes must choose between buying gas and buying food. These kinds of extreme socioeconomic hurdles lead to Native Americans pooling resources to pick up or drop off mail for one another.[102] The ballot collection ban also defines "household" in a way that excludes traditional Native familial relationships.[103]

The court found that people of color are generally more likely to give their ballots to third parties, but whether they were so much more likely that it created a legally cognizable disparity the court couldn't say. The district court credited testimony that there are significant socioeconomic disparities between Arizona's white and nonwhite populations and that those burdens correspond to reliance on third-party ballot collection. For instance, Hispanic, Black, and Native Arizonans are all much less likely than white Arizonans to have access to secure mail service and to own vehicles, and much more likely to use unreliable public transportation and have inflexible work schedules at hourly-wage jobs. All these factors make nonwhite people more likely to require a third party's help returning their ballot. But the district court concluded that those disparities were imprecise proxies for disparities in ballot collection use. Ultimately, the court was unconvinced by what it described as "circumstantial and anecdotal evidence."[104]

The district court upheld the laws' legality, finding in relevant part that plaintiffs did not meet their burden of showing that the laws disparately impacted minority voters so that they had less opportunity than white voters to meaningfully participate in the political process.[105] The district court's ruling was later reversed by the Ninth Circuit, which held, 7–4, that the challenged practices violated Section 2 of the Voting Rights Act.* The Arizona government and the state's Republican Party then appealed to the Supreme Court.

Although the Supreme Court had heard plenty of Section 2 cases before—cases where, you'll remember, discriminatory results are what counts—this was the first time the highest court was called upon to apply Section 2 to a state's facially neutral and generally applicable rules specifying the time, place, or manner of voting (meaning: regulations that don't expressly single out protected classes and seem to apply equally to everyone, like "The polls are open from nine A.M. to five P.M.").[106] Some experts theorize that the Supreme Court never had an occasion to consider this kind of claim under Section 2 because, prior to *Shelby County,* Section 5 successfully prevented discriminatory laws of this type from being enacted in the first place.[107] Whatever the reason, there wasn't a precisely on-point Supreme Court decision governing this kind of case.

Conclusive guidance from the Supreme Court can be helpful because it mitigates the risk of potential unfairness and unpredictability. Without a uniform understanding, laws that are supposed to apply to the whole country may apply differently depending on where in the country you live. Still, lower courts were gradually developing a consensus on how to analyze Section 2 claims. Before *Brnovich,* most circuit courts would first ask whether the challenged

---

* Attentive readers may have noticed that a seven-judge majority and four dissenting judges means the appeal was heard by eleven judges. That's right: some federal appellate courts have more judges than the Supreme Court, which has no need to be capped at nine justices. *Democratic National Committee v. Hobbs,* 948 F.3d 989 (9th Cir. 2020).

standard, practice, or procedure resulted in a disparate burden on members of a protected class; if so, courts would then ask whether that burden was caused by or linked to social or historical conditions that currently produce discrimination against members of that protected class.[108] This fact-intensive inquiry helped lower courts assess the on-the-ground reality for voters of color in order to determine if a policy caused unequal opportunity for minorities to participate in the political process. These courts arguably did helpful legwork for the Supreme Court. Some theorists argue that our legal interpretative system is stronger when multiple circuit courts can deliberate on a question and craft possible solutions for the Court to choose among.[109] But in *Brnovich,* the Supreme Court did not adopt the test that had been established and accepted by lower courts, nor did it take up any of the other standards proposed in amicus briefs submitted by advocates and academics. Justice Alito instead wrote for the conservative supermajority that it was reasonable for the Court to take "a fresh look at the statutory text" since the Court hadn't applied Section 2 to the type of law at issue before.[110] This is judgespeak for "Forget about the stuff courts have been doing—I'm just going to do my own thing." The new Supreme Court was stacked with arch-conservatives, and they saw an opportunity to debut a brand-new originalist standard. Well, original*ish,* as you'll see.

Congress was explicit when it revised Section 2 that courts should broadly consider the "totality of the circumstances" when interpreting the statute, literally meaning that courts should look at any relevant factor to determine if a law results in discrimination. The Supreme Court acknowledged as much in *Thornburg v. Gingles* (1986), and lower courts shaped this principle into a workable test. But Alito took it upon himself to narrow Congress's focus by highlighting five "guideposts" worthy of special attention, as well as other factors that he thought should not be given much weight. His priorities are alarming. For instance, Alito asserted without any supporting authority that courts should consider the degree to which a voting rule departs from what was standard practice in 1982, when Section 2 was amended. The Court did not claim or imply that election laws in 1982 were paragons of fairness and equal opportunity. Neither did Congress, which presumably amended the Voting Rights Act in order to *change* voting practices—not to lock them into place. Yet the Court suggested that the kinds of regulations that were in place forty years ago are presumptively lawful. This creates obvious and ample opportunities for mischief-making. Many Black churches have organized Souls to the Polls movements since the 1990s, for example, transporting Black parishioners to participate in early voting after Sunday services.[111] But in 1982, many states required nearly all voters to cast their ballots in person on Election Day. Suddenly, that would be relevant in determining whether eliminating early Sunday voting results in racial discrimination in violation of Section 2—despite research suggesting that cutting early Sunday voting decreases minority participation rates.[112] Originalism, evidently, doesn't just constrain constitutional interpretation to the Founding but freezes the world when any law is written and limits its application to make the least change possible.

By way of attempted explanation, Alito said the Court "doubt[s] that Congress intended to uproot facially neutral time, place, and manner regulations that have a long pedigree or are in widespread use."[113] This shielding of time, place, and manner regulations is an astonishing carve-out—exempting countless regulations from judicial scrutiny under Section 2 of the Voting Rights Act—with an equally bewildering rationale. No such exception is contained anywhere in the statutory language. And Congress published a report in 1982 that literally said the purpose of the amendment was "to prohibit *any voting practice, or procedure*" that "results in discrimination" (italics my own). Furthermore, the text the Court was called on to apply wasn't composed of ancient hieroglyphics or written by unknown authors whose thoughts have been lost to history. It was written in the eighties. If you actually wanted to know what the drafters intended, they're still alive and would be happy to tell you. And in fact, that's exactly what they did. A group of former staffers to both Democratic and Republican senators, along with other leaders who worked on the 1982 amendments, submitted an amicus brief to the Supreme Court with the goal of providing "an accurate account . . . of Congress' understanding of the amendments at the time of enactment." In it, the amici emphasized Congress's consistent understanding that Section 2 applies "broadly and pragmatically to root out a wide range of procedures that perpetuate discrimination."[114] The amici elaborated that they always understood and intended Section 2 to reach all facially neutral regulations—including time, place, and manner restrictions—"without a shadow of a doubt."[115] Your guess as to where the Court's conclusion that a whole category of law was exempt came from is as good as mine; I can only assume Justice Alito pulled it out of someplace unmentionable. The Supreme Court's conservatives present themselves as originalists to masquerade as faithful executors of the law, but are quick to discard originalism if it would yield results contrary to their regressive policy goals.

The *Brnovich* Court further prescribed that judges must consider how many opportunities a state provides to vote overall when determining whether any single provision is unlawful. Much like the Court's choice to channel the VH1 series *I Love the '80s* in its first guidepost, this directive makes little sense. The dissent astutely observed that this factor and the terms of Section 2 are inherently contradictory: "Making one method of voting less available to minority citizens than to whites necessarily means giving the former less opportunity than other members of the electorate to participate in the political process."[116] But this guidepost's focus on total opportunities suggests that the state may close any number of doors to the franchise in people of color's faces so long as other doors are ostensibly open.

The difference just a few additional conservative justices can make in the Court's jurisprudence is striking: in *Shelby,* the Supreme Court at least paid lip service to the idea that "any racial discrimination in voting is too much."[117] But in *Brnovich,* the Court essentially decided states can have a little racial discrimination, sometimes, as a treat.

In another guidepost, the Court identified the strength of the state interests served by the challenged voting rule as "an important factor" that courts must take into account. It went on to declare that preventing fraud is a "strong and entirely legitimate state interest."[118] This factor might seem reasonable on the surface, but let's dig a little deeper. Alito is announcing unequivocally that fraud is a valid reason to restrict voter access, right on the heels of insurrectionists lying about fraud to block the ballots of people of color and lay siege to the Capitol. The Donald Trump campaign and its supporters filed dozens of lawsuits in the wake of the 2020 presidential election that questioned the legitimacy of the outcome by falsely alleging fraud and other election irregularities. The claims were debunked and the lawsuits failed. The "widespread voter fraud" Republicans fearmonger about simply does not exist. This resounding rejection notwithstanding, state legislators across the country then validated those same false claims by using them to justify the implementation of laws and policies that make it harder to vote. The Supreme Court now seems to be doing the same thing.

Experts have repeatedly searched for evidence of voter fraud determining the outcome of an American presidential election and found none.[119] (I would accept a counterargument that all elections conducted before the Voting Rights Act enfranchised people of color were inherently fraudulent, but that's not what people typically mean when they talk about voter fraud. Go figure.) Yet the ugly myth of massive voter fraud has been invoked throughout American history to justify the disenfranchisement of disfavored classes of citizens such as Black people, white women, and the poor.[120] For instance, the

New Jersey legislature amended its constitution in 1807 to restrict voter eligibility by changing the voter base from property owners—which occasionally included white women and free Black people—to white male taxpayers. The state claimed that the earlier provision encouraged illegal voting by enslaved people and unpropertied women, and that men were disguising themselves as women in order to vote multiple times.[121] Surely, the real reason was white men's insecurity about their position in the social hierarchy as more groups rose up for democratic rights, but voter fraud was a convenient excuse to tighten their grip on power. Alito's blanket approval of fraud prevention as a reason to uphold laws against Voting Rights Act challenges suggests that even if the plaintiffs had shown a disparate burden caused by the regulation, lawmakers may only have to say the magic incantation "voter fraud" to make their Section 2 liability disappear.

The Court recognized two remaining guideposts as useful in determining whether Section 2 had been violated: the size of the burden a challenged voting rule imposed on members of a protected group, and the size of any disparities in a rule's impact on different racial or ethnic groups. These factors seem mercifully unproblematic, for the most part. It makes sense that an arbiter would have to consider how racial groups are impacted by a law in order to determine if that law has a racially discriminatory impact. Like the district court, though, the Supreme Court's test was more concerned with the *size* of a burden than the *existence* of a burden. The implication that there may be some permissible amount of race-based vote denial remains concerning. To make matters worse, the Court's application of those already subpar guideposts was marred by its apparent bad faith and utter disinterest in honestly assessing the size of the burdens that the law created for people of color.

The *Brnovich* opinion unceremoniously dismissed identifying and traveling to one's designated polling place or dropping off an early ballot oneself as "unremarkable burdens" of voting without taking into consideration the reality of what doing so requires for Arizonan voters of color. In the abstract, that may well be true. But in Arizona, Native communities submitted evidence of how they must rely on election officials' interpretation of small hand-drawn maps to determine their polling place, and how the nearest post office might be located up to two hours away by car—and up to half their households don't have cars to begin with. Those are not the ordinary costs associated with voting, and it is unreasonable to regard them as unremarkable. Still, the Court trivialized the challenged regulations and repeatedly declared that Arizona law generally makes it easy to vote. That is the wrong inquiry. The right question is whether Arizona law specifically makes it harder for some racial groups to vote than others, even if it seems "generally" easy. Evaluating whether a law is discriminatory without accounting for specific group differences is like evaluating whether a food is safe to eat without accounting for allergies.

The *Brnovich* majority tried to downplay the impact of its decision by describing these five guideposts as a nonexhaustive list of considerations for judging Section 2 cases. The dissent warned, though, that we should not be comforted by the Court's "delusions of modesty."[122] The list may not be exhaustive, but the factors the Court identified and prioritized put a thumb firmly on the scale in favor of upholding a state's laws—and against protecting minority voting rights. In contrast to the supposedly "important circumstances" specified in the guideposts, Alito explicitly described the relevance of racial discrimination as "much less direct" in cases involving facially neutral time, place, and manner rules. It's perplexing, at best, that past or present discrimination would not be pertinent to determining if a law results in discrimination. Systemic discrimination affects communities in any number of ways that can impact voting access, even if the franchise was not specifically targeted. Racial discrimination in housing, for example, can influence where someone lives, which in turn influences whether a polling place is a short walk away or a long drive away. Nevertheless, the Court decided that it is "less helpful" to assess whether minority group members suffered discrimination in the past and if the effects of that discrimination persist in the present so long as a time, place, or manner regulation is neutral on its face, meaning the lawmaker had the good sense not to say the quiet part out loud.

Alito's analysis bears no resemblance to Section 2's command to determine if, based on the totality of the circumstances, a law denies people of color an equal opportunity to participate in the political process. The dissent once again made plain the real impact of the Court's rationale. "By declaring some racially discriminatory burdens inconsequential, and by refusing to subject asserted state interests to serious means-end scrutiny," Justice Kagan wrote, "the majority enables voting discrimination."[123]

Justice Gorsuch wrote a concurring opinion in *Brnovich,* joined by Justice Thomas, that threatens to compound the harm that the majority created. The concurrence invites a new line of attack on Section 2 based entirely on one sentence in *Mobile v. Bolden*—the ill-considered Supreme Court decision forty-odd years earlier that prompted Congress to amend the Voting Rights Act. Some laws are only enforceable by certain people or agencies, and in *Mobile,* the Court prefaced its congressionally abandoned conclusion about how to prove Section 2 violations by saying it was "assuming, for present purposes" that the law allows people to allege that their Section 2 rights have been violated and bring lawsuits to enforce those rights.[124] In *Brnovich,* Gorsuch held up that one throwaway sentence as evidence that the Court has, for decades, only "assumed—without deciding" that people have a right to sue under Section 2 (and as they say, to assume is to make an ass of *u* and me). No one seriously doubted that individuals can sue under Section 2. That's a good thing, too: if people couldn't sue to enforce their Section 2 rights, it would be entirely up to already overburdened government attorneys to identify potential violations and initiate enforcement actions nationwide. Since the Justice Department once analogized the cost increase for protecting voter rights after the loss of Section 5 to the cost of a Boeing 737 versus a Ford Fiesta, I imagine losing a fully functional Section 2 as well would put us somewhere in the range of a NASA shuttle. Mind you, that's assuming a presidential administration would actually bother to enforce Section 2 and protect voter rights—which is, disturbingly, not a given with the GOP.

But Gorsuch's concurrence pretends that whether people can bring Section 2 lawsuits is an open question. His evidence was a single case—conspicuously decided the year *before* Congress rejected *Mobile*—where a court referenced *Mobile* and said it, too, would assume without deciding that people have the right to sue under Section 2. Gorsuch admits that literally no one in *Brnovich* argued that plaintiffs didn't have the right to bring Section 2 lawsuits, so the Court had no reason to address the so-called issue. This is how judges say "I haven't decided this yet because no one has asked me to, but I'm asking you to ask me to." Gorsuch invented a controversy virtually out of thin air and invited conservatives to pursue an argument to make Section 2 largely unusable—an argument he and Thomas seem prepared to accept. And at least one appellate court has already taken Gorsuch and Thomas up on their invitation. In November 2023, the Eighth Circuit ruled 2–1 that Section 2 of the Voting Rights Act can only be enforced by the U.S. Attorney General, and that private plaintiffs do not have the ability to sue. If allowed to stand, this would upset decades of practice and precedent, and render the Constitution's prohibition on racial discrimination in voting totally meaningless.[125]

The reasoning used throughout *Brnovich*'s majority and concurring opinion is bizarre. It is also revealing. Congress created and amended the Voting Rights Act in efforts to change an undemocratic status quo. The amici who participated in the 1982 amendments' enactment straightforwardly told the Court that Congress intended Section 2 to "apply broadly and pragmatically to root out a wide range of procedures that perpetuate discrimination," and they urged the Court not to depart from that congressional intent. The Supreme Court rejected this request and instead exposed itself as deeply unserious about interpreting laws as they were written and originally understood if those laws aim to protect democracy. The guideposts created in *Brnovich* bear little to no relationship to the text or principles of the Voting Rights Act or the Constitution, further showcasing originalism's lack of integrity and giving rise to Kagan's iconic description of the opinion as "mostly inhabit[ing] a law-free zone."[126] The Court's new Section 2 jurisprudence dismisses a very real threat to democracy—racial discrimination—as barely worth addressing, and endorses a virtually nonexistent threat—voter fraud—as excusing all manner of democratic ills. The Voting Rights Act fundamentally changed American democracy, and the Supreme Court's destruction of that act is doing the same. The *Brnovich* opinion demonstrates just how vital it is for the United States to adopt a democratizing model of constitutional interpretation that does not lend itself to such failures. If this is the way the Court interprets the law, we need a new way to interpret the law.*

DEMOCRACY'S NOT A GAME, BUT THE REFS ARE RIGGING IT ANYWAY

When the Court isn't actively using its power to make things worse, it's pretending it's not capable of making things better. The Court's

---

* New laws and a new Court wouldn't hurt, either, but I'm taking this one step at a time.

recent decisions regarding gerrymandering are particularly illustrative of how it abdicates its responsibility for the democratic process—and bears responsibility for diminishing people of color's political power. State and local governments use decennial census data to divide the country into hundreds of electoral districts. We can expect some population shifts over the course of ten years, so redrawing districts is an important part of securing equal representation for equal numbers of people. Gerrymandering is what happens when those district maps are drawn in a way to structurally disadvantage some people from the get-go. Sometimes, the people responsible for drawing the maps pack certain groups into a handful of districts, dramatically curtailing their capacity for influence everywhere else. At other times, they may crack the groups apart across many districts, ensuring that they are consistently outnumbered. Whether by packing or cracking, the result is essentially the same: politicians get to pick their voters rather than the other way around.[127] Gerrymandering has been a thorn in the side of representative government since the 1800s.[128] And it remains one of the most pernicious problems in our political system today.

Gerrymandering is particularly likely to occur when redistricting is left to legislatures and one political party controls the map-drawing process.[129] Some state governments delegate redistricting authority to independent redistricting commissions which, when properly designed, offer strong protections against gerrymandering.[130] But the opportunity to structurally create better odds of winning elections and maximize party power is often too good for partisans to pass up. Democrats in Maryland controlled the state's general assembly, governor's office, and most congressional seats after the 2010 census, for example. So they intentionally redrew the maps in order to achieve a seven-to-one Democratic majority among the state's members in the House of Representatives.[131] North Carolina Republicans also gained control of both chambers of the state's legislature at that time. So they enacted a redistricting plan with the express goal of electing ten Republicans and three Democrats; the redistricting committee co-chair explained that he stopped at ten because he didn't believe it would be "possible to draw a map with eleven Republicans and two Democrats."[132] Republican voters in Maryland and Democratic voters in North Carolina sued their respective states, alleging that these partisan gerrymanders violated their constitutional right to an undiluted vote and unconstitutionally burdened their rights to political representation and to freely associate with political parties. The district courts agreed with the voters and found the plans unconstitutional. The states then appealed to the Supreme Court, which agreed with the voters that the plans were partisan gerrymanders; but even so, they did not agree that the Constitution had a problem with that.

The Supreme Court ruled in *Rucho v. Common Cause* (2019) that partisan gerrymandering is a political question, and that federal courts are powerless to address it.[133] Courts have determined that a case poses a "political question" if it must be answered by the political branches of government rather than the judicial branch. Political questions typically arise when the text of the Constitution commits the issue to the legislature or the executive branch, when there are no judicially discoverable and manageable standards for courts to apply, or when the issue can't be resolved without first making a policy decision that should be left to the discretion of the political branches. Political questions are nonjusticiable, which means they can't be decided by legal principles or a court.[134] But *Rucho*'s determination that partisan gerrymandering is nonjusticiable was a departure from precedent: the Supreme Court explicitly rejected the idea that partisan gerrymandering is a political question beyond the courts' reach nearly forty years ago in *Davis v. Bandemer* (1986).[135] There can be valid reasons for courts to remove themselves from the decision-making equation, like if an issue is beyond courts' competency or is a foreign affairs matter, but a majority of the Court in *Bandemer* did not think those considerations were present in the case of partisan gerrymandering. *Bandemer* reasoned that the judiciary wasn't overstepping into a subject more properly decided by another branch of government, and there was no risk of it creating a foreign or domestic disturbance. The *Bandemer* Court also did not think judges were incapable of finding a standard to decide partisan gerrymandering cases.[136] The *Rucho* opinion, then, is little more than weaponized incompetence—and originalism was a weapon in that arsenal of asininity. Today's conservatives on the Court leaned on history to avoid the issues of the present and misstated the problem so they wouldn't have to solve it.

The Supreme Court framed the relevant history as follows: the Founders entrusted district-drawing responsibilities to political branches knowing that they would take partisan interests into account, and without giving a significant role to the judiciary. Chief Justice Roberts claimed that the Framers were perfectly aware of the partisan gerrymandering problem, and "at no point was there a suggestion that the federal courts had a role to play. Nor was there any indication that the Framers had ever heard of courts doing such a thing."[137] Instead, Roberts wrote, the Constitution gives state legislatures the power to set the times, places, and manner of federal elections and gives Congress the power to make or alter such regulations (a congressional power he neglected to mention before dismantling the Voting Rights Act). And, he reasoned, banning legislators from prioritizing partisan agendas when drawing districts "would essentially countermand the Framers' decision to entrust districting to political entities."[138] There's some classic originalist cherry-picking happening here: Roberts's version of history does not mention the Framers' well-documented deep suspicion of political parties and elides their explicit consideration of the judiciary's responsibility to protect against legislative abuses of power.* Roberts also downplayed the fact that the Supreme Court *has* intervened in issues related to a state's drawing of congressional districts—specifically by requiring that districts contain roughly equal numbers of people and by prohibiting racial gerrymandering. But according to the Court, those are different—they're straightforward, while partisan gerrymandering is difficult.

Rucho reasoned that population inequality among congressional districts is justiciable while partisan gerrymandering is not because the Court has a workable standard to decide population inequality cases; decades ago, the Court ruled on Equal Protection grounds that one person's vote should be worth the same as another's.[139] And partisan gerrymandering claims differ from racial gerrymandering claims, Roberts argued, because partisan gerrymandering claimants are asking for their political party to receive "a fair share of political power and influence," while racial gerrymandering claimants are only asking for the government to stop impermissibly using their race as a factor in drawing districts. You can prohibit map-drawers from taking race into consideration when redistricting, Roberts tells us. But partisanship is a permissible factor, and the Court has no way to determine how partisan is *so* partisan that permissible partisanship becomes unconstitutional, he says. The Framers did not provide federal courts with a clear, manageable, politically neutral standard to apply and never required that "groups with a certain level of political support should enjoy a commensurate level of political power and influence."[140] In fact, the Court recalled, for decades after the Constitution was ratified, parties could and

---

*With that said, I, like Chief Justice Roberts, am not a historian. But I'm willing to listen to those who are. See, e.g., "Brief of Historians as Amici Curiae in Support of Appellees," at 6–10, 30–33, *Rucho v. Common Cause,* 139 S. Ct. 2484 (2019). See also "Brief of Constitutional Accountability Center as Amicus Curiae in Support of Appellees" at 6–13, 29–31.

sometimes did get nearly half of the vote statewide and not a single seat in Congress. (The implication here is "It could be worse—what are you complaining about?") So the Court's majority threw its hands in the air and denied the existence of constitutional authority and legal standards that would let it do anything else. The result was preserving district plans they recognized as "highly partisan, by any measure"—and a status quo they admitted was "incompatible with democratic principles."[141]

The credibility of Roberts's claim that partisan gerrymandering cases must be distinguished from racial gerrymandering and population inequality cases collapses upon closer inspection, as it rests on multiple faulty premises. First, it distinguishes partisan and racial gerrymandering by falsely equating racism with the simple acknowledgment of race and failing to consider the diminishment of people of color's political power. This is a childlike conception of racism that frees the Court of any responsibility to address all but the most blatant forms of discrimination. Second, it treats racial gerrymandering and partisan gerrymandering as if they're different in meaningful ways. But once you consider how racially polarized voting is in this country, it becomes clear that they're not. In every presidential election in the nearly sixty years since the passage of the Voting Rights Act, Republicans have won at least a plurality of the white vote and Democrats have overwhelmingly won the Black vote.[142] Partisan gerrymandering and racial gerrymandering are the same thing, for all intents and purposes. And slapping a different label on the same harm shouldn't make it any less unlawful and deserving of judicial intervention.

Rebranding racism is a real risk: jurisdictions sometimes try to defend themselves from allegations of racial gerrymandering by claiming that they're engaging in partisan gerrymandering. The Lawyers' Committee for Civil Rights Under Law has warned that holding partisan gerrymandering nonjusticiable would allow states to "diminish the voting strength of racial minorities with impunity merely by couching their gerrymandering in political terms."[143]

Even if a state says it's targeting Black voters because they're Democrats rather than because they're Black, it's still targeting Black voters.

I freely admit that determining appropriate legal standards can be challenging. But courts decide upon and apply standards all the time. *Rucho* distinguished partisan gerrymandering from the functioning standard in population-equality cases as if the one person, one vote principle just emerged from the Constitution fully formed like Athena from the head of Zeus. Not so. It had to be forged and made workable by the Court.[144] The *Rucho* Court, in contrast, equated its unwillingness to adopt a standard with the impossibility of a standard. This false equivalence is underscored by the amicus briefs that submitted possible standards that the Court might adopt, and by Justice Kagan's dissent, which points out that "What [the majority] says can't be done *has* been done . . . courts across the country, including those below, have coalesced around manageable judicial standards to resolve partisan gerrymandering claims."[145] Not only are courts frequently capable of sussing out standards in general, they have specifically done so in the precise type of case where the Court chose to feign helplessness instead. The Court's argument that it has neither the power nor the ability to address partisan gerrymandering is therefore laughably unconvincing.

The dissent generously credits the *Rucho* majority for not actually describing what it did as "originalism."[146] I do not. The influence of the ideology is clear even if it is not explicitly invoked. The opinion emphasized its version of Founding Era history and made the case that the Constitution was not understood to prohibit partisan gerrymandering or empower the court to enforce such a prohibition when it was originally promulgated. Legal scholars have observed that this reliance on originalism—meaning, the Court's half-hearted search for definitive historical proof that the Framers intended courts to resolve gerrymandering issues—created a presumption of nonjusticiability, and thus, an obstacle for those seeking judicial relief.[147] (I can't claim to know if the Court will use "Prove to me George Washington heard of this" as the analytical starting point to confirm the justiciability of issues other than gerrymandering, but there could be wide-ranging consequences if so.) The majority also suspiciously failed to cite *Reynolds v. Sims* (1964), a seminal redistricting case that developed the one person, one vote principle, and which some argue was incompatible with originalism and therefore wrongly decided.[148] Only the dissent references *Reynolds*'s conclusion that the Supreme Court is required to remedy constitutional violations caused by politicians' redistricting decisions.[149] As such, prominent originalist law professor John O. McGinnis praised *Rucho* for refusing to even mention *Reynolds,* much less give effect to its principles, and lifted *Rucho* up as a welcome example of "silent originalism."[150] This isn't a conclusive sign about *Reynolds*'s future, but it is an ominous one. The consequence of originalism, whether silent or loud, is that injustice is not the justices' problem.

WHAT IF WE DID GOOD THINGS INSTEAD OF BAD THINGS?

It didn't have to be like this. The Court's ruling in *Rucho* was not foreordained and does not reflect what the law is or what the judiciary should be. Courts have a responsibility to act as a bulwark against intrusions on our democratic rights rather than simply acquiescing to them. Gerrymandering damages the very foundations on which our government rests by denying voters an equal opportunity to participate in the political process, and it cannot be that the Constitution simply forfeits the democracy it is supposed to facili-

STEALING OUR ELECTIONS 143

tate. These concerns are absent from the *Rucho* opinion, but they are central to an inclusive-constitutionalist analysis. Inclusive constitutionalism requires that when we interpret the Constitution, we honor the transformative mission of the post–Civil War Amendments to establish a functioning, diverse, democratic society in which we can all participate as equal members. This overriding purpose should inform and guide our understanding of what any given constitutional commitment means.

Doing so would demand a different result in cases like *Rucho, Brnovich,* and *Shelby County.* Let's stick with *Rucho* as an example. Imagine the opinion had an alternative rationale that began by recognizing the right to vote as the bedrock of a democratic society. This is not far-fetched—the Supreme Court has long characterized the vote as the fundamental right that preserves all others.[151] And the Fourteenth Amendment protects citizens' right to participate in elections on an equal basis.[152] If we accept that the Constitution demands equality and does not permit a "preferred class of voters," as the Court once said decades ago, we would have to recognize that gerrymandering—including partisan gerrymandering—interferes with that right.[153] Partisan gerrymandering treats voters unequally simply because of their party affiliation and allows one party to win representation with fewer votes than another. State-sponsored discrimination designed to produce "representatives" who do not reflect the country's will is an unreasonable perversion of democracy that cannot be reconciled with the liberatory goals of the Reconstruction Amendments. The Constitution is violated when power is entrenched at the expense of the people.

These principles aren't limited to claims brought under the Thirteenth, Fourteenth, and Fifteenth Amendments; inclusive constitutionalism provides a lens through which the whole Constitution should be viewed. Let's take the First Amendment, which is short enough that I'm going to reproduce it here in its entirety:

Congress shall make no law respecting an establishment of religion, or prohibiting the free exercise thereof; or abridging
the freedom of speech, or of the press; or the right of the people peaceably to assemble, and to petition the Government for
a redress of grievances.

"Hey, wait a second," you may be thinking. "I don't see the word
'gerrymandering' in there." I know you don't, and that's okay. The
Constitution is full of phrases like "freedom of speech" that Supreme Court justices have sometimes described as "majestic generalities."[154] They're important! They're powerful! They're . . . vague.
So we have to construct their meaning—which is to say, determine
what all they cover, both explicitly and implicitly. My theory is that
we can and should use multiracial democracy itself as a source for
identifying that meaning. We can ask ourselves, What would this
provision mean if we took the Reconstruction Amendments' striving for an inclusive democratic society seriously? This framing lets
us look at the Constitution anew, like noticing Rubin's vase between
two faces. Where before we only saw a negative command not to
abridge the freedom of speech, we can instead see an affirmative obligation on the government to make sure all people can exercise their
freedom of political expression on equal terms.

The pro-democracy and antisubordination goals of the Reconstruction Amendments can be read to bolster First Amendment
legal claims against gerrymandering, which are currently underdeveloped in the Supreme Court's jurisprudence. Justice Kennedy authored a concurring opinion twenty years ago in which he recognized
that governments run afoul of the First Amendment when they
enact laws that have the purpose and effect of subjecting voters to
disfavored treatment because of their views. Kennedy suggested
that this applies to how electoral districts are drawn, too, and noted
that democracy depends on citizens' ability to band together in fur-

therance of their political beliefs.[155] Fourteen years later, in a case called *Gill v. Whitford*, Justice Kagan expanded on Kennedy's argument in a concurring opinion joined by Justices Ginsburg, Breyer, and Sotomayor. Kagan highlighted that gerrymandering burdens the ability of like-minded people to "affiliate in a political party and carry out that organization's activities and objects" and, in doing so, burdens the First Amendment.[156]

The Court has repeatedly found that the First Amendment protects the "freedom to associate with others for the common advancement of political beliefs and ideas."[157] Similarly, the Court has "rejected government efforts to increase the speech of some at the expense of others" on multiple occasions.[158] Voting is arguably the pinnacle of political speech, as it is how people express their political preferences and hold elected officials accountable in a democracy. Gerrymandering can then be understood as implicating the First Amendment, because it diminishes the value of some people's political expression and privileges others because of their political associations.[159] Taken together with the egalitarian underpinnings of the Reconstruction Amendments, the Constitution cannot abide state-sponsored discrimination to artificially distort the electoral process and weaken the political power of disfavored groups.

Inclusive constitutionalism may consider the past in its analysis, but it gives more weight to the democratic principle at issue. It doesn't allow a judge to wriggle away from remedying a harm simply because the government has been harming people in that way for a long time. The Constitution does not bind us to repeat mistakes in perpetuity. Inclusive constitutionalism also considers the present realities that determine whether it's possible for people to access their constitutional rights. For example, even if we were to concede that the Founders were not overly concerned with gerrymandering in the past, their analysis would not have factored in today's access to sophisticated technological tools and precise, detailed data about populations and their voting behavior. "With such tools," Justice Kagan observed in her concurrence in *Gill v. Whitford* (2018), "mapmakers can capture every last bit of partisan advantage."[160] Partisans today can and routinely do win over a minority of voters but a majority of political representation. These unearned advantages are durable. Under a gerrymander in Pennsylvania that lasted from 2011 until 2018, for instance, Democrats received between 45 percent and 51 percent of the statewide vote in three congressional elections but consistently won only 28 percent of House seats. As Justice Kagan put it in her dissent in *Rucho,* "These are not your grandfather's—let alone the Framers'—gerrymanders."[161] It's election rigging. And it isn't fanciful to believe in a Constitution that has something to say about that.

I'll be honest: I get worked up about this sort of thing. But this isn't just based on my personal feelings about what's right and what's wrong. It's based on law—with the added bonus of common sense.

To illustrate: zoom out a bit and think about what's so bad about racial gerrymandering. The real offense isn't the formal racial classification in and of itself; it's the enforcement of a racial hierarchy. It's that some people are made to be less-than and robbed of a say over the direction of their communities because the right to self-governance is subordinated to a desire for power. The Declaration of Independence is also instructive here, albeit not legally binding. It tells us that government legitimacy requires consent of the governed.[162] Gerrymandering is antithetical to that consent. And that means the judiciary has an obligation to act.

The only recourse recommended by the Court in *Rucho* is Congress. The majority tells voters, "Partisan gerrymandering is *a* problem but not *our* problem, and state and federal legislatures can do something about it." Mind you, the thing many legislatures are doing about gerrymandering *is* gerrymandering. It's become more common over time for legislatures and partisans to take charge of line drawing for legislative and congressional districts—an exercise conducive to shenanigans.[163] Requiring us to rely on legislatures to fix the problem ignores the fact that some politicians aren't eager to end a practice that helps them get in office and stay there.

Our democracy train is getting robbed, and the Court is telling us the only thing we can do is call up Butch Cassidy and the Sundance Kid. I'm telling us we can have better. Courts have a job to do. The Supreme Court recognized decades prior to *Rucho* that nothing in the Constitution "gives support to a construction that would immunize state congressional apportionment laws which debase a citizen's right to vote from the power of courts to protect the constitutional rights of individuals from legislative destruction."[164] The Constitution must be read to facilitate rather than thwart democracy. Courts have the power to do this, and we have the power to accept nothing less.

The *Rucho* Court's denial of a constitutional remedy for partisan gerrymandering theoretically leaves the Voting Rights Act's protections against racial gerrymanders in place. But "in place" is not the same as "invulnerable." Conservatives are actively working to neutralize Section 2 of the Voting Rights Act, either by explicitly ruling it unconstitutional or just rendering it useless (à la *Shelby County*'s impact on Section 5). The right wing came dangerously close to succeeding in *Allen v. Milligan* (2023).[165] In that case, Black Alabamian voters challenged their state's electoral map as an illegal racial gerrymander under the VRA. The case was heard by a three-judge district court, including two Trump-appointed judges, who agreed that the map unlawfully diluted Black residents' voting power. The court issued an order blocking Alabama from using the map in the 2022 midterm elections and directing the state to draw a new map.[166] Alabama then appealed to the Supreme Court with an audacious argument, claiming: first, the map was drawn race-neutrally and did not violate Section 2; and second, even if Section 2 did prohibit the map and require a new one that re-empowered Black voters, Section 2 was unconstitutional because it put racial considerations before race-neutral redistricting criteria. According to the state, fixing a racial gerrymander would also be a racial gerrymander because it would be taking race into account. Equating the remedy of harm with the imposition of harm is transparently dangerous and disingenuous. Nevertheless, the Supreme Court lifted the order that blocked Alabama from using the map, inexplicably forcing Black voters to participate in an election under conditions that were *too racist for Trump judges in Alabama* while the case proceeded.[167] People feared that this signaled an imminent and terrible shift in the legal landscape, like when the ocean recedes before a tsunami, and were relieved months later when the Supreme Court ruled 5–4 that the lower court got it right after all: Section 2 was legal, Alabama's map wasn't.[168] Still, those four dissenting justices—Thomas, Gorsuch, Barrett, and Alito—made clear that they're itching to strike down Section 2, describing the provision as "on a collision course with the Constitution."[169] Justice Kavanaugh suggested in his concurring opinion that he would entertain a "temporal argument" that Section 2 was constitutional when it was enacted but it has since outlived its legality (again, à la *Shelby County*). As for Alabama, the state continued to play in people's faces, drawing a new map that was just as discriminatory as the old map, and was slapped with more lawsuits.[170]

The cases discussed in this chapter amount to nothing less than a full-fledged judicial assault on the foundation of democratic governance: the ability of the people to pick who represents them. And the consequences of simultaneously facing more threats to democracy and having fewer tools to defend against them are as grim as they are predictable. The Supreme Court's current approach to elections jurisprudence starkly contrasts with its 1991 determination that the judiciary should interpret the Voting Rights Act "in a manner that provides the broadest possible scope in combating racial discrimination."[171] The intended and achieved result of the ongoing antidemocratic movement is the reduced political power of people of color. Rejecting originalism and adopting inclusive constitutionalism is a critical step toward taking our power back.

I recognize that this proposal may upset the sensitive stomachs of legal formalists who believe that judges should apply the law without regard to public policy or social interests, so allow me to offer some constitutional Imodium: democracy contains legal principles that have been insufficiently applied during originalism's reign of terror. Inclusive constitutionalism is not the same as following your own prerogatives at the expense of the law; rather, it's embracing a fuller and richer understanding of the law so that it serves all of us. I concede that this is not value-neutral. But that's sort of the point. Originalism is also not value-neutral. It values preserving a system with few protections for individuals other than wealthy white men, who it assumes should be free to legally impose their will on everyone else. Inclusive constitutionalism values protecting and promoting a modern, multiracial, democratic society in which we can all freely participate. Laws and legal interpretation are tools, and it's okay to think about how to use those tools to bring about a better, more just world.

CHAPTER 4

STEALING THE CENSUS

E ver since the words "We the People" were written in those big calligraphic letters on a sheet of parchment in 1787, Americans have debated what they mean. Who are "we," exactly? Who are people, and who among them should have any say over their own lives or the lives of others? These aren't abstract questions. In tangible ways, people's ability to participate in society depends on who is seen as a legitimate member of that society in the first place. One of the most direct ways the Constitution helps define who counts as a member of the American community is the census: the Constitution requires an "actual enumeration" of the country's population every ten years, and "the census" is what we call that once-a-decade count.[1] And the importance of the census has turned the decennial count into a decennial target.

The census is commonly described as the largest peacetime mobilization in the world.[2] With support from state and local governments as well as innumerable community-based organizations and advocacy groups, the federal government marshals a massive quantity of resources and mobilizes hundreds of thousands of workers each decade in an effort to count every person who resides in the country. In conducting the 2020 census, for instance, the Census Bureau hired a workforce of over three hundred thousand people to help identify all addresses where people could live, and personally visit tens of millions of households to follow up if they didn't respond to earlier enumeration attempts.[3] Residents are included in the census whether they're adults or children; citizens, green card holders, or undocumented; homeowners or homeless; and so on, making the census the most inclusive thing the United States does together as a country.

This decennial ritual is more important than people tend to realize. For people to count in our democracy, you have to count the people. The census is established in Article I of the Constitution—which details the structure and responsibilities of Congress—as the direct link between the country's population and representation in the House. This was an American innovation: no other nation in the history of the world had ever before taken a census of its population and used it to allocate seats in government accordingly.[4] The population count is also constitutionally linked to states' tax obligations. As James Madison summarized in the Federalist Papers, "Numbers are the best scale of wealth and taxation, as they are the only proper scale of representation."[5] In addition to its constitutionally defined purpose of obtaining an accurate portrait of the country so federal representation and taxation can be divvied up along those lines, the census is used today for redrawing the boundaries of legislative districts, allocating trillions of dollars to local, state, and tribal governments, and more.[6] It allows the government to distribute funds for critical resources like hospitals and food assistance all across the country in proportion to population.[7] Counting everyone is a necessary first step to making sure everyone gets their fair share.

When it's done right, the census allows communities to quantify inequities they face, advocate for better allocation of resources, and engage in evidence-based policymaking. A new experiment from the Census Bureau, for example, uses census data to identify specific areas in the country that are most vulnerable to disasters including Covid-19 and extreme heat exposure.[8] The census can literally show Americans who we are and what we need. The laws governing the census, and the values and principles we decide are worth considering when interpreting those laws, set the floor on which we can build an inclusive, equitable democracy—or an exclusionary imitation of one.

Despite the census's noble goal, the Census Clause of the Constitution was initially written in an ignoble way. It read, in relevant part:

> Representatives and direct Taxes shall be apportioned among the several States which may be included within this Union, according to their respective Numbers, which shall be determined by adding to the whole Number of free Persons, including those bound to Service for a Term of Years, and excluding Indians not taxed, three fifths of all other Persons.[9]

"Indians not taxed" referred to Indians who lived within their tribes' sovereign territories.[10] Native populations were excluded from the census until 1860, when the census first counted Indigenous populations who lived outside tribal land.[11] A more accurate enumeration is something to be celebrated today, but this was not a positive change at the time; in the 1870s, census data was used to help forcibly relocate Native people from their land.[12] The "other persons" alluded to in the original Constitution—not free persons, not untaxed Indians, but a secret third thing—were slaves. The odious "Three-Fifths Clause" regarded enslaved Black people as existing in a liminal space, simultaneously a little more than property and a little less than human. The partial count was a "compromise" made between white politicians in the North and South that artificially inflated the political power of the communities that held Black people in bondage. The enslaved-population boost gave slave states extra seats in the House of Representatives and more Electoral College votes without allowing for Black political participation or conferring any actual representation. Simultaneously, slave states' tax liability was reduced because it was based on the number of residents, and they did not count Black people as full persons.[13] From its inception, the government compromised its stated principles by using democratic instruments like the census to racist and undemocratic ends. (For an interesting alternative view, though, consider that Frederick Douglass buttressed his argument for abolition by claiming that the Constitution encouraged freedom—not slavery— and observing that even the Three-Fifths Clause was "holding out to every slaveholding State the inducement of an increase of two-fifths of political power by becoming a free State."[14])

One of Congress's legislative objectives after the Civil War was to rid the Census Clause of its accommodation to slavery. The Fourteenth Amendment issued a firm command to count the "whole numbers of persons in each state," not just fractions thereof.[15] And, aiming to deter former slave states from disenfranchising freedmen, it mandated that states that deny or abridge eligible residents' right to vote—for reasons apart from rebellion or other crime—shall be penalized with a proportional reduction in their representation.[16] Here's Section 2 of the Fourteenth Amendment in full:

> Representatives shall be apportioned among the several States according to their respective numbers, counting the whole number of persons in each State, excluding Indians not taxed. But when the right to vote at any election for the choice of electors for President and Vice-President of the United States, Representatives in Congress, the Executive and Judicial officers of a State, or the members of the Legislature thereof, is denied to any of the male inhabitants of such State, being

twenty-one years of age, and citizens of the United States, or in any way abridged, except for participation in rebellion, or other crime, the basis of representation therein shall be reduced in the proportion which the number of such male citizens shall bear to the whole number of male citizens twenty-one years of age in such State.[17]

Importantly, the Penalty Clause says a state that disenfranchises eligible voters should get fewer congressional representatives overall, but that representation would still be equally allocated to residents within the state. Think about it this way: a penalized state may get four seats in Congress instead of five, but each of those four elected would represent a quarter of the state's population. No one in the state is suddenly without a legislator, nor is any one of the state's legislators representing way more people than another. The whole population of the state remains entitled to equal representation. Both the Penalty Clause and the Census Clause further the principle that enumeration, representation, and the Constitution itself are for all residents as opposed to just voters or a subset thereof.[18]

One might hope that, because the Fourteenth Amendment cleared things up, federal benefits and burdens would be allocated along total population lines without a hitch from then onward. But America had no such luck. The census has remained a site of government contestation over who makes up the people and who can be excluded.

KOREMATSU AND ITS KINDRED SPIRITS

At times, the exclusion has been quite literal. On February 19, 1942, President Franklin Delano Roosevelt signed Executive Order 9066, authorizing the secretary of war and his designees to "prescribe military areas" from which people could be forcibly relocated, in or out. Under that authority, U.S. Army lieutenant general John DeWitt issued proclamations making military areas out of the whole West Coast, and giving Japanese Americans an immediate eviction notice.[19] DeWitt justified this course of action when recommending it to Henry Stimson, the secretary of war, by arguing that Japanese Americans didn't really count as American: "The Japanese race is an enemy race and while many second and third generation Japanese born on United States soil, possessed of United States citizenship, have become 'Americanized,' the racial strains are undiluted."[20] Between 1942 and 1945, over one hundred thousand people of Japanese ancestry were detained in American concentration camps. Nearly seventy thousand of these internees were American citizens.[21] And, according to DeWitt in a 1943 report, the "most important single source of information prior to the evacuation was the 1940 Census of Population." The Census Bureau prepared "several special tabulations," including the numbers of residents with Japanese ancestry and their locations, which "became the basis for the general evacuation and relocation plan."[22]

The Supreme Court then approved this revocation of membership in "we the people" in its 1944 decision for *Korematsu v. United States*. Fred Korematsu was a native-born American citizen of Japanese descent who was convicted for his failure to report for imprisonment. He challenged his conviction and the military's proclamations as unconstitutional on many grounds, including Due Process (both procedural and substantive) and Equal Protection. The Court affirmed his conviction—and tacitly upheld the internment of over one hundred thousand Japanese Americans during World War II as legal. Supreme Court justice and former Ku Klux Klan member Hugo Black wrote for a 6–3 majority that the case was not about imprisoning citizens in concentration camps simply because of racial prejudice, which would clearly be wrong, but about appropriate wartime security measures.[23] Dissenters observed the obvious: tens of thousands of people were being deprived of equal protection of the laws and subjected to indefinite detention without due process, for no reason other than their ancestry. One dissenter, Justice Frank Murphy, outright said that the Court legalized racism—a word that had never before appeared in a Supreme Court opinion.[24] While the other dissenters emphasized the mistreatment of American citizens, Murphy's concern extended to *all* individuals of Japanese descent who lived in the United States and were subjected to unconstitutional "blanket condemnation." Murphy's righteous dissent in particular points us toward an inclusive constitutionalist road not taken, as he concludes that "all residents of this nation" must "be treated at all times as the heirs of the American experiment and as entitled to all the rights and freedoms guaranteed by the Constitution."[25]

The ghosts of these betrayals by the Census Bureau and the Court continue to haunt both institutions.[26] Following the September 11 attacks, for instance, the Census Bureau alarmed many by sharing datasets about Arab American populations with the Department of Homeland Security. A spokeswoman for Customs and Border Protection (an agency within the department) claimed that the information was not being used for law enforcement in any way, and that the requests were only made to help the agency identify which airports needed signs and pamphlets in Arabic. Many were skeptical and likened it to the compilation and sharing of information on Japanese Americans during World War II.[27] *Korematsu* accusations also resurfaced in 2018 when the Supreme Court decided *Trump v. Hawaii,* a case about the legality of an immigration policy designed to effectuate Donald Trump's proposed "total and complete shutdown of Muslims entering the United States until our country's representatives can figure out what is going on."[28] Like the order in *Korematsu,* the Muslim ban was an exclusionary directive issued by the executive branch targeting people based on a core personal characteristic. Fred Korematsu's daughter, Karen, and other children of Japanese Americans who famously (and unsuccessfully) challenged their mass incarceration and removal before the Supreme Court, highlighted these similarities.[29] But Chief Justice Roberts wrote for a 5–4 Republican majority that *Korematsu* was neither analogous nor relevant to the case at hand, reasoning (if you can call it reason) that the "forcible relocation of U.S. citizens to concentration camps, solely and explicitly on the basis of race" had nothing in common with a "facially neutral policy denying certain foreign nationals the privilege of admission."[30] The Court upheld the legality of the order and, as with *Korematsu,* invoked the talisman of unsubstantiated national security concerns to spirit away explicit evidence of bigotry.

These Supreme Court decisions weren't grounded in originalism—or any other discernible school of thought, for that matter, beyond "prejudice is good sometimes." Yet they offer a revealing history that should inform our thinking about the census and inclusive constitutionalism. The shortcomings of the Census Bureau and the Court in relation to Japanese Americans in the 1940s and Muslim Americans today are a canary in a coal mine that should alert us to broader democratic shortcomings. The fact that threats aimed at one group injure people of another underscores that our liberation is bound together.[31] The echoes of *Korematsu* in *Trump v. Hawaii* make clear how legal weapons forged against one group will later be repurposed against another if we do not unequivocally reject their use. We cannot afford to leave one another behind. As famed writer and activist James Baldwin once wrote in a letter to then-jailed activist and scholar Angela Davis, "If they take you in the morning, they will be coming for us that night."[32] Our collective future depends on our active construction of an inclusive alternative to originalism, and any other half-baked legal theory trotted out to justify marginalization.

WAITING TO EXCLUDE

The Census Bureau has worked diligently to repair its reputation and focus on its mission to serve as the nation's leading provider of quality data about the country. Laws and policies have also been revised in order to strengthen the census's confidentiality protections and prevent the sharing and misuse of sensitive information.[33] But it hasn't always been easy. Most recently, rampant political interference from the Trump White House—including meddling in the bureau's collection, processing, and publication of census data—intersected with a global pandemic and numerous chronic issues to endanger the ability of the 2020 census to accomplish its constitutional purposes. Protecting the census in future decades will require comprehensive structural reform. While the primary responsibility for such legal change lies with Congress, each branch of government has a role to play in keeping the census aligned with law and democratic objectives. And the Supreme Court is not doing its part. Several legal threats to the 2020 count exposed the hollowness of the Supreme Court's current legal interpretative methods, the necessity of a new practice of inclusive constitutionalism, and the capacity of legal interpretation to shape who we as a nation choose to be.

The Trump Administration waged a multifront campaign to manipulate the census to bolster the political power of white Republican communities at the expense of people of color. This isn't hyperbole. They wrote a surprising amount of this down! In 2018, Stephanie Hofeller discovered the files of her late father—a Republican strategist named Dr. Thomas Hofeller, who was described in *The New York Times* as "the Michelangelo of gerrymandering."[34] Hofeller advised Republican lawmakers and party operatives to be discreet as they planned how to cartographically capture outsized political influence and warned that "emails are the tools of the devil." But after his death, his estranged daughter found several years' worth of inculpatory emails and at least seventy thousand files.[35] Among the treasure trove was evidence that likely altered the course of litigation about the Trump Administration's effort to add a question to the 2020 census asking every person residing in the United States whether they're a citizen.

Dr. Hofeller conducted a study in 2015 about shrinking the population base used for redistricting from all residents to only citizens of voting age. The Fourteenth Amendment, you'll remember, explicitly says to count all residents for the apportionment of congressional representation among the states. Technically, it doesn't literally specify that total population is also the correct basis for drawing districts within the state; but courts and legislatures have long understood the Constitution to require equal representation for equal numbers of people, and total population redistricting to satisfy that requirement. Using the citizens-of-voting-age population (also known as CVAP data) instead of the total population essentially aims to work around the Constitution's requirement that people receive equal representation by, once again, redefining who counts as people. Hofeller recognized that the shift would be a "radical departure" from constitutional principles and concluded that it would provoke significant resistance from "Democrats and the major minority groups in the nation," but it would be "advantageous to Republicans and Non-Hispanic Whites."[36]

Adult citizens are presently more white and more Republican than the American population as a whole, while noncitizens and youths are more likely to be (and to live near) people of color and Democrats. To wit, an analysis of 2020 census data showed that one in four children in the United States are Latino.[37] CVAP-based redistricting would treat millions of young people, lawful permanent residents, and other noncitizens as if they do not exist, thereby diminishing political power in places where more people of color and children reside and privileging aging white people who live in more sparsely populated areas.[38] In order to obtain data allowing map drawers to most precisely redistrict based on citizens of voting age—by which I mean: data allowing map drawers to produce electoral maps structurally designed to benefit conservative white people—Hofeller reasoned that a citizenship question would need to be added to the 2020 census.[39]

In December 2017, the Department of Justice (DOJ) sent a letter to the Commerce Department—the executive agency that currently houses the Census Bureau—in which the DOJ formally requested the addition of a citizenship question to the 2020 census. The DOJ claimed that the data would be "critical to the Department's enforcement of Section 2 of the Voting Rights Act and its important protections against racial discrimination in voting."[40] (Voting rights! Remember those?) This was a puzzling explanation, considering that the Trump Administration had shown literally no prior interest in enforcing the Voting Rights Act, as evidenced by its failure to file any new Voting Rights Act cases until May 2020.[41] The justification also contradicted the wishes and vast experiences of organizations that actually engaged in voting rights litigation and advocacy, nearly two hundred of which would go on to say that gathering citizenship data from the decennial census not only was unnecessary but would actually undermine their ability to enforce the act by worsening the quality of the data they rely on.[42] Experts within the Census Bureau additionally expressed concern that the citizenship question did not undergo the bureau's usual rigorous vetting process, and cautioned that imposing the question would likely prompt lower response rates in already undercounted communities and necessitate more extensive nonresponse follow-up operations, thus causing the census to be both less accurate and more expensive.[43] Nevertheless, the Commerce Department announced in March 2018 that it would be moving forward with the citizenship question in response to the DOJ's request so that it could more effectively protect minority voting rights.[44]

You might be thinking, "Why would an Administration with a demonstrated commitment to racism suddenly claim to be interested in protecting people of color's voting rights?" The answer was simple: the Administration was lying. And in *Department of Commerce v. New York,* the Supreme Court actually recognized as much.[45]

Department of Commerce v. New York reached the Supreme Court after immigrants' rights organizations, state and local governments, and other parties challenged the legality of the citizenship question on both statutory and constitutional grounds. Courts usually review the actions of executive agencies like the Commerce Department with a pretty deferential standard, but those agencies *are* required by a statute called the Administrative Procedure Act (APA) to be reasonable when exercising their authority and explaining their decisions. The APA empowers courts to block agency actions that are "arbitrary, capricious, an abuse of discretion, or otherwise not in accordance with law."[46]

The Trump Administration steadfastly maintained that the sole reason for the citizenship question was a request initiated by the Justice Department in order to enforce the Voting Rights Act. Yet the Administration's own records showed otherwise. Documents revealed over the course of the lawsuit showed that the Commerce Department had badgered other agencies and asked them to make a request for citizenship data. Eventually, Attorney General Jeff Sessions agreed that the Justice Department would make the phony request. The Voting Rights Act rationale was manufactured after the fact and handed off to the DOJ. Actual statisticians within the bureau continued to recommend against the citizenship question and tried to discuss alternative options with the DOJ but were iced out— Sessions personally directed Justice Department officials not to meet with them.[47] A federal district court ruled that there was "a veritable smorgasbord of classic, clear-cut APA violations" and blocked the addition of the citizenship question to the 2020 census questionnaire.[48] The Trump Administration then appealed to the Supreme Court.

After the Court heard oral arguments but before it announced its decision, the Hofeller files were released. The files showed that Dr. Hofeller, not the Department of Justice, was the origin of both the citizenship question and the fake Voting Rights Act justification for its inclusion. Hofeller had also ghostwritten sections of a draft letter theoretically from DOJ to the Commerce Department, requesting the citizenship question and putting forth the explanation about protection for minority voters. That draft was incorporated into the final letter sent from the Justice Department to the Commerce Department. Attorneys and legal commentators observed that the revelations put pressure on the Supreme Court and would make it much more challenging for the Court to produce a coherent opinion permitting the citizenship question to appear on the decennial census form.[49]

The Supreme Court issued its opinion in *Department of Commerce v. New York* a few weeks later and affirmed the lower court's decision blocking the citizenship question, on the grounds that the Commerce Department's explanation was pretextual. The decision was written by Chief Justice Roberts, and his desperation bubbles just below the opinion's surface. The chief justice was on the Administration's side. Much of the decision actually reads like it is going to uphold the agency's action. (Indeed, Professor Robert Tsai suggested that the chief justice may have drafted an opinion that was favorable to the Commerce Department and hastily revised it after he was shaken by news of the Hofeller files.)[50] The opinion announces that there's no constitutional issue with the citizenship question, emphasizes the breadth of the Commerce Department's discretion over the census, and reminds the reader that the Court's review is deferential. But the Court then asserts that it is "not required to exhibit a naiveté from which ordinary citizens are free."[51] This is judge-speak for "I was born at night, but not *last* night." And the record before the Court contained extensive evidence of a "significant mismatch between the decision the Secretary made and the rationale he provided."[52] You can almost hear the chief justice telling the Trump Administration, "Please, all I need is a reason. Just give me a single reason to uphold the citizenship question that I can say with a straight face." He received none. The Court found that "here the VRA enforcement rationale—the sole stated reason—seems to have been contrived."[53] Despite bluster from Trump, who asked lawyers if they could delay the census until they dug up a reason the Supreme Court would accept, the citizenship question was kept off the 2020 census—a big win for accuracy and inclusivity, as experts predicted the inclusion of the question would have caused nearly nine million people to not complete the census.[54]

In important part, I agree with the Court's ruling. I was relieved, in fact, with its conclusion that "reasoned decisionmaking under the Administrative Procedure Act calls for an explanation for agency action" and "what was provided here was more of a distraction."[55] But this determination always struck me as incomplete. Although the Court recognized the Trump Administration's stated reason as pretext, it never said pretext *for what*. Minority voting rights was obviously not a truthful explanation, but the Court suggested it didn't have the foggiest idea of what the real reason could be, earlier disclamation of naïveté aside. The Trump Administration had told a darkly ironic lie—the Voting Rights Act is supposed to protect people of color's political power, but the federal government was deliberately setting out to weaken that power. This is a direct threat to the constitutional purposes of the Census Clause as revised by the Fourteenth Amendment, which is clear about who should be counted, as well as the amendment's command that all people are entitled to equal protection under the laws. Neither of these concepts was present in the opinion. Instead, the Court implied that it would have allowed the citizenship question to undermine the census, if only the Trump Administration's sabotage weren't so sloppy.

It is a mistake, from an inclusive constitutionalist perspective, that the antisubordination goals of the Reconstruction Amendments were not even part of the Court's discussion. Without that foundation in the citizenship question case, all Chief Justice Roberts is saying is, effectively, "I can excuse racism, but I draw the line at Administrative Procedure Act violations." The Court missed the opportunity to say something much more meaningful by invoking democratic values and openly opposing thinly veiled white supremacy. Instead, the case's lesson for future bad actors is to have a more competent cover-up.[56]

IF AT FIRST YOU DON'T SUCCEED

The Trump Administration's loss in the citizenship-question case did not deter it from its mission of transforming the census, and the Constitution, into tools to reward friends (conservative white people) and punish enemies (everyone else). In July 2019, just a couple of weeks after the Court's decision in *Department of Commerce v. New York,* Trump published an executive order directing executive agencies and departments to share as much information as legally possible with the Commerce Department to help the Census Bureau "establish citizenship status for 100 percent of the population." No longer hiding the Administration's motives, the order said outright that "a more accurate and complete count of the citizen population" would enable states to more effectively "design State and local legislative districts based on the population of voter-eligible citizens."[57] A year later, in July 2020, the Administration issued a memorandum announcing that—for the first time ever—it was the policy of the United States to categorically exclude undocumented residents from the count used to apportion seats in the U.S. House of Representatives.[58] Trump claimed an unheard-of authority to cast aside the work of the Census Bureau and essentially craft his own DIY census, taking out a marker and unilaterally scratching out swaths of the population as if they weren't really people who lived here, or as if they weren't really people, period: an impractical means to illegal ends.

Inexplicably, some originalists argued that this unprecedented far-right policy was actually what the Framers wanted all along. The Trump Administration itself knew that such an argument was dubious. Back in 2017, at the direction of Commerce Secretary Wilbur Ross, senior political appointee and lawyer James Uthmeier drafted a legal memorandum analyzing how the Commerce Department might add a citizenship question to the census and use the data for apportionment. At first, Uthmeier warned that citizens-only apportionment likely violated federal statutes and the Constitution. The Fourteenth Amendment, as we've discussed, says apportionment must be based on the "whole number of persons." Noncitizen residents are obviously persons. And on top of that, apportionment has literally never been conditioned on citizenship, a fact that undercuts the idea that the original understanding was to do otherwise. "Over two hundred years of precedent, along with substantially convincing historical and textual arguments, suggest that citizenship data likely cannot be used for purposes of apportioning representatives," Uthmeier determined in his draft.[59] He then seemingly got with the program and dramatically revised his draft to reach the opposite conclusion: the final memo stated that "there is nothing illegal or unconstitutional about adding a citizenship question" for apportionment purposes and "there are bases for legal arguments that the

Founding Fathers intended for the apportionment count to be based on legal inhabitants." He provided no examples or citations to support this claim, probably because the claim is insupportable.[60] Apparently, the Trump Administration reasoned that an appeal to the Founding Fathers' purported intent was a Get Out of Constitution Free Card. Uthmeier seemed aware that his memo was an exercise of advocacy, not objectivity: he emailed his revised draft to another political appointee and wrote, "Feel free to let me know if this is sugar coating the analysis too much."[61]

The week after Trump issued the Exclusion Memorandum, the House Oversight Committee held a hearing about safeguarding the 2020 census and counting every person.[62] The committee, which was led by a Democratic majority at that time, invited testimony from four previous directors of the Census Bureau, who had served under Democratic and Republican presidents alike; collectively, they'd served under Richard Nixon, Gerald Ford, Jimmy Carter, Bill Clinton, George W. Bush, Barack Obama, and Donald Trump. Each director was asked if they believed, based on their knowledge and experience, that the Constitution requires the census to count all United States residents, including those who are undocumented. All directors said yes. Each was asked if total population is the apportionment base required by law, if all previous censuses and apportionment counts in history have included both citizens and noncitizens including undocumented residents, and if Trump's memorandum appeared to violate both statutory and constitutional law.[63] Again, all directors said yes. Yet John Eastman, the once-esteemed originalist scholar turned would-be election overthrower, disagreed with their assessments and testified before Congress in defense of the former president's scheme, even going so far as to claim that the exclusion memorandum should go bigger and encompass "non-citizens more broadly, not just non-citizens who are unlawfully present in the United States."[64] (Yes, months before co-conspirator number two wrote his now-famous legal memos in an effort to help Trump steal the 2020 presidential election, he wrote congressional testimony in an effort to help Trump steal the 2020 census.[65])

It seems simple on its face that the Constitution's instruction to count "the whole number of persons in each state" would mean all the people residing in all the states. Undeterred by this plain meaning, Eastman testified before Congress that the Constitution's use of the word "persons" was only a stylistic change from the word choice "inhabitants" in an earlier draft, and "inhabitants" was understood at the time to mean "domiciled," and "domiciled" meant "legally and permanently present, part of the body politic." And *that* meant, he said, that noncitizen residents were not part of "we the people" and should be excluded from the census count used to apportion congressional representation. In short, Eastman made an originalist argument that people in the seventeenth century thought apportionment was just for citizens entitled to participate in the electoral process, and so we should, too.[66]

There are many things that make this facially absurd. First of all—and for the umpteenth time, I know—"this is how things worked hundreds of years ago" is not in and of itself a good enough reason to do the same things today. And second, his characterization of how things worked hundreds of years ago is unambiguously incorrect. Most obviously, enslaved people—oppressed noncitizens vulnerable to the possibility of sale and forced relocation domestically or overseas in the trans-Atlantic slave trade—were specifically enumerated and included in antebellum apportionment bases, each as three-fifths of a person. And fugitive slaves who escaped and illegally resided in the North were then counted in those northern states.[67] Enslaved people's inclusion in the apportionment base from the time of the drafting, despite lacking all the traits Eastman claimed were necessary, is proof of the claim's silliness.

In reality, neither the legislative nor the judicial nor the executive branches before Trump have ever bought what Eastman was selling—with good reason. The Constitution's drafters knew how to say citizens when they meant citizens. Indeed, the document says "citizens" in plenty of other places. But here, it said "persons" instead, and Congress expressly rejected amendments to make apportionment conditional on citizenship. Representative James Blaine of Maine explained in 1866: "As an abstract proposition no one will deny that population is the true basis of representation; for women, children, and other non-voting classes may have as vital an interest in the legislation of the country as those who actually deposit the ballot."[68] Furthermore, Representative Roscoe Conkling of New York, who was instrumental in drafting the Fourteenth Amendment, literally stated on the House floor that the drafters considered and decided against a suggestion to rely on citizenship status and concluded that "persons, and not citizens" have always been the appropriate constitutional basis for representation and apportionment.[69]

Congress also knows how to make exceptions when it wants to do so. Crucially, untaxed Indians are the only group explicitly excluded from the apportionment count in the text of the Constitution, and undocumented residents are not "Indians not taxed." Eastman likened the two groups and claimed undocumented residents are in the same position as "Indians not taxed" with respect to representation without acknowledging the fact that there's a major difference between tax-paying noncitizens residing in the United States and tribal members residing in their tribes' sovereign territories. The National Congress of American Indians strongly opposed the invocation and mischaracterization of tribes' political and legal status to once again denigrate a whole class of people as not "persons" under law—a harm with which Indigenous people are all too familiar.[70]

That undocumented persons are in fact persons should not be

open to dispute. The Supreme Court has even recognized as much repeatedly throughout history. For instance, in *Yick Wo v. Hopkins* (1886), a case about discrimination against noncitizen Chinese residents, the Court stated:

> The Fourteenth Amendment to the Constitution is not confined to the protection of citizens. It says: "Nor shall any State deprive any person of life, liberty, or property without due process of law; nor deny to any person within its jurisdiction the equal protection of the laws." These provisions are universal in their application, to all persons within the territorial jurisdiction, without regard to any differences of race, of color, or of nationality; and the equal protection of the laws is a pledge of the protection of equal laws.[71]

The Supreme Court referenced *Yick Wo* a century later in *Plyler v. Doe* (1982) when it struck down a Texas law that authorized local school districts to keep undocumented children out of schools and denied those children school funding—funding that just so happens to be allocated based on the census count, which includes those same children. While the Court declined to outright recognize a right to education, it said that such a deprivation would take an "inestimable toll" on "the social, economic, intellectual, and psychological wellbeing of the individual," and held that the "denial of education to some isolated group of children poses an affront" to the Equal Protection Clause of the Fourteenth Amendment.[72] The Court continued to describe the inclusiveness of the Constitution: "Whatever his status under the immigration laws, an alien is surely a 'person' in any ordinary sense of that term. Aliens, even aliens whose presence in this country is unlawful, have long been recognized as 'persons' guaranteed due process of law by the Fifth and Fourteenth Amendments."[73]

In addition to recognizing undocumented people as people, the Supreme Court has also repeatedly recognized that total population is a reasonable apportionment basis. Similarly, presidential administrations on either side of the aisle have long counted—and understood that they are constitutionally required to count—all persons who reside in the United States.[74] Not persons with papers. Persons. As Depeche Mode confirmed in their 1984 hit song, "People Are People."

Many state and local governments, immigrants' rights groups, democracy organizations, and others challenged the legality of the Exclusion Memorandum in court. A three-judge federal district court in New York unanimously found the memorandum unlawful and described the merits of the parties' dispute as "not particularly close or complicated."[75] The federal government appealed that decision and asked the Supreme Court to decide whether the Exclusion Memorandum was illegal in *Trump v. New York*. The Court dodged the question. Erasing undocumented people from the apportionment count was statistically unsound in addition to legally questionable: the bureau did not actually have a reliable, scientific methodology to identify and exclude people from apportionment based on their immigration status, and the Trump Administration expressed some uncertainty during the litigation as to whether and how well it would be able to pull its plan off in practice. For the Court's conservative majority, that meant the groups who sued to challenge the memo did not suffer any real legal injury yet and an attempt to resolve the dispute judicially would be premature. Essentially, the Court decided that it could decide later, once it was clearer how many people Trump would be able to exclude and in which states.

Another way to phrase the Court's conclusion is "Come back when more damage is done." This was a cop-out. It wasn't the worst-case scenario, to be clear—worse would have been the Court fully abandoning the pretense of law and upholding the policy as constitutional—but it wasn't particularly good, either. It created further uncertainty where there should have been none and left Trump free to give breaking the law his best shot. The liberal justices made the absurdity plain in their dissent: "Where, as here, the Government is acknowledging it is working to achieve an allegedly illegal goal, this Court should not decline to resolve the case simply because the Government speculates that it might not fully succeed."[76] Mercifully, the clock on Trump's presidential term was ticking, and the Administration eventually ran out of time to effectuate its scheme. President Joe Biden rescinded Trump's census directives on his first day in office.[77]

To avoid painting with too broad a brush, I should note that a couple of originalists have acknowledged that the Constitution's text and original public meaning clearly command the inclusion of undocumented persons within the category of "persons."[78] But Eastman and other professional lackeys in Trump's employ aren't the only ones making lawless originalist claims to the contrary. For example, the state of Alabama and Congressman Mo Brooks of Alabama's Fifth District filed a lawsuit in 2018 challenging the legality of counting all United States residents in the population base used for apportionment.[79] Alabama argued both that it would be unconstitutionally harmed by the inclusion of noncitizen residents (claiming that they would have received another congressional seat if not for the Californias and Texases of the world, with their larger noncitizen populations) and that noncitizens were never meant to be included. Alabama alleged in their complaint that "the phrase 'persons in each state' was understood at both the Founding and in the Reconstruction era to be restricted to aliens who have been lawfully admitted to the body politic constituted by the Constitution."[80] In other words, "when they said people, they didn't mean *those* people." Alabama eventually voluntarily dismissed their action, so a court didn't have the opportunity to assess and decide Alabama's claim on the merits, but its stark conflict with standard legal interpretive principles suggests that any judge worth their robes should recognize it as bogus.

THE INCLUSIVE REBUTTAL TO THE EXCLUSION MEMO

The notion that the Constitution permits or even requires the exclusion of some people who reside in the United States from the apportionment count is based in bigotry, not law. But even if the memorandum's illegality weren't so clear-cut—if there were ambiguities such that a person interpreting the law had to make a choice—inclusive constitutionalism would consciously consider which choice supports robust representative government and is conducive to an equitable democracy. Hint: it's not the choice that returns to America's dark and dehumanizing history of literally counting some people as *fractional* people. The Reconstruction Amendments rejected this sort of degradation when they repealed the Three-Fifths Clause and nullified the Slave Trade and Fugitive Slave Clauses—constitutional provisions highlighted by Chief Justice Roger B. Taney in *Dred Scott v. Sandford* to justify law's treatment of "the negro race as a separate class of persons" who were "not regarded as a portion of the people or citizens of the Government then formed."[81] (And even so, those enslaved "noncitizens" were still counted for apportionment!) At home and abroad, history has repeatedly shown us the atrocities that are possible when people are legally cast out of the human family. The Constitution cannot be taken seriously as the touchstone of American democracy if it does not recognize real, living, breathing humans as persons.

Conservatives' push to exclude people who live here from the census solely on the basis of citizenship would also undermine our democratic society because noncitizen residents are still residents with a right to representation. The whole "idea of the Constitution," Senator William Fessenden of Maine said in 1866, is "that the whole population is represented; that although all do not vote, yet all are heard."[82] A lack of citizenship doesn't make a person any less of a member of the community. Noncitizen residents live in our neighborhoods, pay into our government coffers, learn and teach at our schools, receive and provide treatment at our hospitals, observe faiths in our houses of worship, work at our businesses, and more. They are us. They have a real stake in public life and, for that matter, how their tax dollars are spent. It would be obscene for the government to count noncitizens as residents when it comes to taking their money and when they risk their lives in the U.S. military but not when apportioning representation.

Excluding noncitizens from apportionment would not make their community ties any less enduring or change the reality that they are constituents. But it would spread their elected representatives much more thinly, as states with larger noncitizen populations would have a larger population per congressional district than districts in other states, and make their communities' concerns much more likely to go unaddressed. When analyzing the census citizenship question case as well as the Muslim ban case, Stanford Law professor Jennifer Chacón drew attention to the Trump Administration's effort "to take advantage of the legal vulnerabilities of the classic legal outsiders—noncitizens, and particularly those lacking formal legal immigration status—to limit the political power and official protection of legal insiders."[83] Erasing noncitizens from the apportionment count would inflict harm to the dignity and material interests of noncitizens and other residents they live among by diminishing their access to democratic institutions and public services—access the Reconstruction Amendments set out to expand.[84]

Again, this isn't some wacky idea I've pulled out of nowhere.

Rather, this sort of inclusive understanding is entirely consonant with the Supreme Court's unanimous 2016 decision in *Evenwel v. Abbott*. In that case, a truly absurd cast of characters sought a court order that would block Texas from holding elections using its district map and require the legislature to draw a new one. One plaintiff was a local Republican Party chairperson who once authored an op-ed warning about the Constitution becoming usurped by Islamic law, and who has amplified the conspiracy theory that former president Barack Obama is a secret communist who wasn't born in this country. The other plaintiff was an openly antisemitic and homophobic YouTube personality who, separately, believes that unicorns are real.[85] But the most important player to know is the man who recruited the plaintiffs: Edward Blum. Blum is a notoriously litigious conservative activist whose name you might recognize from his ongoing, very well-funded, and often successful legal crusade to disempower communities of color. Blum's credits include wrecking the Voting Rights Act in *Shelby County v. Holder* and wrecking affirmative action in *Students for Fair Admissions v. Harvard College* and *Students for Fair Admissions v. University of North Carolina,* like some kind of horseman of a white-supremacist apocalypse.[86] In *Evenwel v. Abbott,* Blum spearheaded a challenge to Texas's use of the total population measured by the decennial census as the basis for drawing legislative districts rather than the voter-eligible population. Texas produced maps after the 2010 census with districts that were substantially equal in size if you compared total populations, but not if you compared citizens aged 18 and up. The plaintiffs argued that the Equal Protection Clause required equalizing the districts' voter-eligible populations so that their votes would have equal value.

Remember, Republicans have repeatedly explicitly tried to obtain and use CVAP data in order to make democracy less representative and better serve the interests of a shrinking white conservative minority. Invoking the Equal Protection Clause here was an attempt to transform an amendment designed for confronting white supremacy into a tool for entrenching it. And the entire Court shut it down, holding that history, precedent, and practice all demonstrated that it was "plainly permissible" under the Constitution to base redistricting on total population.[87] Even Justices Thomas and Alito agreed with this! With that said, they just concurred in the judgment, so their agreement was limited to the conclusion and not the reasoning. At the heart of the Court's reasoning was, importantly, the principle of representational equality. The *Evenwel* majority emphasized that the census enumerates, and elected representatives serve, all residents—not just those who are eligible or registered to vote.[88] This reasoning provides another source of support to the argument that a proper interpretation of the Census Clause requires the inclusion of all residents in the apportionment base, including noncitizens. It's a simple, democracy-enhancing principle: everyone counts, so count everyone.

Yes, it's true that noncitizen residents can't vote in federal elections. But that's hardly a convincing reason to exclude them from apportionment when you consider how many citizen residents can't or don't vote. There are millions of people who have been disenfranchised because of certain criminal convictions. There are people who have the legal right to vote but not the ability because they face significant obstacles to the ballot; people who are too young to vote; people who just aren't interested in voting.[89] The list goes on. And despite these varying circumstances, they are all still constituents entitled to political representation because of their residency. Elected officials aren't supposed to represent solely the people who voted for them, or solely people eligible to vote. They are supposed to represent we the people. That means all of us. When asked if the Constitution's command to count "the whole number of persons in each state" includes noncitizen persons, a democratizing interpretive model says yes, because they are literally persons residing in the states, and democratic principles would be undermined if we declared otherwise and decided not to enumerate noncitizen residents like we do any other resident.

Back during that congressional hearing on Trump's exclusion memorandum, Representative Gerry Connolly of Virginia pointed out how absurd it was "for a crowd that talks about originalism" to latch onto such an obviously ahistorical, atextual, unconstitutional argument.[90] The whole charade underscores that originalism's primary objective is to launder right-wing reactionary politics. If and when originalists, anti-immigrant advocacy groups, and other bad actors try this dehumanizing stunt again in the lead-up to the 2030 census and beyond, we can and should shut it down by giving inclusive constitutionalism the force of law.

COUNT ME IN

Originalist (or, perhaps, *faux*riginalist) arguments about the census are not limited to questions regarding which people get counted. Conservatives have invoked originalism to question how people are counted as well. The Constitution specifically requires an "actual enumeration" of the population, but it is silent on what it means to actually enumerate. Enumeration methods have been a matter of some legal debate over the last few decades. And courts have occasionally been called to resolve the question: How do we count who counts?

The precise way the census count is conducted has varied throughout its multicentury history. The aim remains the same—to count every person once, only once, and in the right place—but the best available tools with which to do so change. The bureau continually researches and updates its methods to collect and protect data as technological and statistical fields evolve. We've come a long way from the 1790 census conducted by U.S. Marshals traversing the Eastern Seaboard by horse or on foot.[91] In 1960, for example, the census was delivered by mail to all occupied housing units and then tabulated almost completely by computer for the first time.[92] And the 2020 census was the first for which respondents had the option to complete the census online rather than on paper.[93]

With each census comes lessons learned. One thing census takers have learned over a couple of centuries is that they're better at counting some people than others. The Census Bureau describes "hard-to-count" communities as "population groups for whom a real or perceived barrier exists to full and representative inclusion in the data collection process."[94] Groups may be hard to count because they're hard to locate, like households that don't appear in the bureau's master address file; hard to contact, like people who move a lot or are experiencing homelessness; hard to interview, if there are impediments to communication like language barriers, limited internet access, or low literacy; or hard to persuade, like people who are suspicious of the government or just plain apathetic.[95] Many communities of color, children (especially those under the age of five), and low-income people, among others, have persistently been disproportionately undercounted.[96]

This reality can be obscured by the census's excellent national coverage results. The 2020 census, for instance, got the national population total almost exactly right. After each census, the Bureau performs various quality checks to determine how close it got. And its post-enumeration survey showed that the 2020 census did not have a statistical undercount *or* an overcount at the national level—a particularly remarkable feat in light of the unique challenges posed by a global pandemic and extreme political interference, on top of chronic threats like underfunding.[97] But, even though the bureau got the overall count precisely right, it overcounted some groups and undercounted others. Black people were undercounted by 3.3 percent in 2020. Latino people were undercounted by 4.99 percent—a huge jump from their 1.54 percent undercount in the 2010 census. And Native people living on reservations were undercounted by a whopping 5.64 percent.[98] People who rent their homes were also undercounted, by 1.48 percent.[99] And children under the age of five had the worst undercount in decades.[100] All told, the 2020 census omitted 18.8 million people.[101] It would be one thing if these undercounts were distributed evenly across groups, but they're not. The 2020 census overcounted white people by 1.64 percent, up from 0.83 percent in 2010. Asian people were neither overcounted nor undercounted in 2010, but in the 2020 census they were overcounted by 2.62 percent.[102] The last census ultimately produced statistically significant undercounts in six states—Arkansas, Florida, Illinois, Mississippi, Tennessee, and Texas—and overcounts in Delaware, Hawai'i, Massachusetts, Minnesota, New York, Rhode Island, Utah, and Puerto Rico.[103] Overcounting some communities and undercounting others means resources get sent to the wrong places. This differential undercount has historically meant wealthier and whiter areas get more than their fair share of money and power, and poorer and browner areas get less. Even a perfect national count, then, can conceal inaccuracies, which translate into inequities across the country.

The Census Bureau has long pursued a variety of strategies in order to reduce or eliminate differential undercounts. Of these, originalists have been particularly concerned with the bureau's use of a statistical technique called sampling. Sampling is a data-collection method that examines a representative sample of a population in order to gain information about the characteristics of the broader population.[104] Think of it sort of like an advanced version of sticking a fork into food that you're cooking to check if it's ready yet: looking at pieces can help you learn more about the whole. Statistical experts within the Census Bureau advocated for the use of sampling in conjunction with traditional census-taking for the 2000 census, noting that samples provide "richer, more complex, accurate, inexpensive, and timely information."[105] Similarly, in the lead-up to the 2000 census, the National Academy of Sciences concluded that "any coverage measurement program designed to reduce the differential undercount would require sampling."[106] But the conservative legal movement had other ideas. Various elected officials and voters brought a lawsuit challenging the legality of sampling for calculating the apportionment population under both the Census Act and the Constitution.

The relevant part of the Census Act, added in 1957, reads: "Except for the determination of population for purposes of apportionment of Representatives in Congress among the several States, the Secretary shall, if he considers it feasible, authorize the use of the statistical method known as 'sampling.'"[107] Challengers argued that the statute amounted to a ban on sampling for apportionment but permitted sampling for other purposes, like generating datasets about household demographics or other characteristics. Proponents contended that the law meant the secretary must use sampling when feasible for purposes other than apportionment and had discretion to use or not use sampling when it came to apportionment. Basically the disagreement is over whether the "except for" language should be interpreted as "This is not *allowed*" versus "This is not *required*." The Supreme Court sided with the challengers and ruled in *Department of Commerce v. House of Representatives* (1999) that the Census Act disallowed sampling for apportionment purposes.[108] Because the Court decided the case based on an interpretation of the Census Act, the Court's majority did not evaluate whether the Constitution permitted sampling.[109] Justice Scalia wrote a concurring opinion volunteering his thoughts on the matter anyway, joined in full by Justice Thomas and in part by Chief Justice Rehnquist and Justice Kennedy.[110] Scalia found it "unquestionably doubtful" whether statistical sampling satisfies the constitutional requirement of an actual enu-meration.[111] Relying on three dictionaries published in 1773, 1796, and 1828, he concluded that enumeration means counting individu-als one by one and forbids statistical estimation.[112] Scalia recognized that the professional field of statistics did not yet exist, but said the Framers did know about the advantages of estimation, generally. So, he reasoned, if previous congresses didn't avail themselves of esti-mation's benefits, it was probably because they thought they couldn't constitutionally do so.[113] There are (at least) two grievous flaws with this reasoning. It treats the Framers' rudimentary knowledge of esti-mation and reliance on one-by-one counting as equivalent to an awareness and rejection of modern statistics. And by creating a pre-sumption against legality if a known beneficial policy hadn't been implemented before, Scalia and the originalist company he kept ef-fectively said that we can't do smart things now if we didn't do them sooner, turning "You snooze, you lose" into a constitutional rule. The dissenting justices criticized the constitutional argument as "without merit" and "absurd."[114]

Another case about statistical adjustment of the census reached the Supreme Court a couple of years later in *Utah v. Evans* (2002). Utah sued the Census Bureau over its use of a statistical method in the 2000 census called "hot-deck imputation." Hot-deck imputa-tion was a process used in the 2000 census to fill in gaps and resolve conflicts in the data by using information from the current census, as opposed to cold-deck imputation, which uses information from prior censuses. If someone filled out the census but didn't include their age, for example, the bureau might use hot-deck imputation to infer what their age is based on the response of a nearby household with other similar characteristics.[115] There are important method-ological differences between hot-deck imputation and sampling, but both use information about part of a population to infer information about the population as a whole, so Utah argued that it, too, violated the Census Act and, separately, ran afoul of the Constitution.[116]

The Court disagreed on both counts. Regarding the Census Act, the Court found that the statute banned sampling but that sampling and imputation are two different processes, with different technical meanings and objectives.[117] With respect to the Constitution, the Court rejected the idea that the Census Clause prescribes a precise method for determining the population—especially not one known to be much less accurate.[118] The Court reasoned that the point of the clause was to tie representation to population, not to establish exactly how the population will be counted forevermore.[119]

Justice Thomas authored a dissent joined by Justice Kennedy, arguing that statistical estimation techniques are at odds with the original and unchanging meaning of the Constitution. (Justice Scalia dissented separately, focusing on procedural issues.) Again consulting a few dictionaries published between 1773 and 1828, Thomas and Kennedy determined that "an actual enumeration" was understood at the Founding to mean really counting people one by one.* "From the first census," they wrote, "Congress directed that the census be taken by actually counting the people. . . . Congress enacted a series of requirements for how to accomplish the counting; none mention the use of sampling or any other statistical technique or method of estimation."[120] For Thomas and Kennedy, accuracy didn't matter much (or, more specifically, it was "not the dispositive factor in the constitutional consideration").[121] The more important concern for them and the Framers, they claimed, was avoiding political manipulation. They contended the phrase "actual enumeration"

---

*I think of this as the Little Bunny Foo Foo method, since it basically says enumeration should be conducted by scooping up all the residents and bopping them on the head. *Utah v. Evans,* 536 U.S. at 492–93 (Justice Thomas dissenting in part).

served to preclude the potential for abuse accompanying any use of estimation such as imputation or sampling.[122] Apparently, fixing the census's inaccuracies is manipulation, but deliberately making the census inaccurate is not. Funny how that works out.

Let's be clear. Sampling, imputation, and the like are extremely sophisticated estimates performed by statistical experts—not politically motivated guesswork. And one could reasonably understand the "actual" part of "actual enumeration" to mean you can and should use the enumeration method that produces an actual, accurate population count rather than one we know misses *millions* of people who actually reside in the country. Originalists argue that we must instead commit ourselves to ignorance, purposefully undercounting and underserving marginalized people, because a colonizer's neural pathways might short-circuit if you handed him a graphing calculator.

Imputation survived the legal challenge in *Utah v. Evans,* but the prohibition on sampling recognized in *Department of Commerce v. House of Representatives* is still in place today. Advocates have called for Congress to get rid of the statutory ban. (Full disclosure: "advocates" includes yours truly in the course of my work as a professional democracy nerd.)[123] In the absence of a statute, the only remaining legal question would be whether sampling is constitutional. Inclusive constitutionalism contends that the Constitution clearly permits sampling for apportionment purposes. Two reasons in particular stand out—one more practical, and one more philosophical. First, our constitutional system of governance requires equal representation for equal numbers of people, which cannot be fulfilled if we don't actually know how many people there are. It would be nonsensical for the Constitution to require an actual enumeration of residents but require us to not use tools that produce the actual number of residents. It's similarly unreasonable to read the Constitution as foreclosing innovation that could improve census response rates. Second, if your chosen method of constitutional interpretation requires you to intentionally underserve communities of color, then your method is illegitimate. We know that the current enumeration method harms historically marginalized groups, and it is perverse to interpret the Constitution as compelling such harm or preventing us from remedying it.

Let's review: the far right regularly invokes originalism, which says, "We must go where history leads." I suggest we start responding with inclusive constitutionalism, which says, "Whose history—and where, pray tell, are you leading us? Because we might need to reset the GPS." The legal debates surrounding the census make strikingly clear that the way we choose to interpret law has direct and lasting impacts on the way we constitute the people of the United States. "Sometimes," Professor Reva Siegel writes, "judges decide cases recognizing us as the kind of people we are; and sometimes judges decide cases recognizing us as the kind of people we aspire to be. Both forms of interpretation, backward- and forward-looking, can express the identity of the American people."[124] Especially in an era of resurgent ethnonationalism, we must resist those who would use the law to shrink we the people and steal away people's equal claim to the American community. We shouldn't allow bad actors to use originalism and other legal niceties to explain away antidemocratic policies. Justifying the deliberate undercounting of communities of color, children, and the poor by maintaining that the Constitution actually requires you to do so when more accurate and equitable methods exist is bewildering and unacceptable. Inclusive constitutionalism demands that we read laws to embrace our diverse total population rather than privilege the few over the many.

CHAPTER 5

TAKING IT ALL BACK

Originalism is a trap used by the conservative legal movement to steal the Constitution. This heist has, in turn, enabled the right wing to steal much that Americans hold dear, including the ability to live freely as equal members of our communities and the agency to make decisions about the future of those communities. Originalism has curtailed bodily autonomy, hollowed out the meaning of liberty and equality, and acted as an obstacle to evolving understandings of justice, as we discussed in chapter 2. It has directly undermined our ability to participate in elections and made it harder for Congress to confront voter discrimination, as we saw in chapter 3. And it has contested people's status as a real part of our society—as real people, even—threatening the human dignity of whole communities and their ability to receive the political representation and basic services that they are due, as we just talked about in chapter 4. This is, clearly, the bad news. But the good news is: we don't have to live like this. We *weren't* living like this as recently as the 1980s. Federalist Society co-chair Professor Steven Calabresi once recalled of that decade, "You could have gathered all of the originalists in the country around a kitchen table quite comfortably. It was a small group of people."[1] Originalist legal scholarship was practically nonexistent before the concerted efforts of Ronald Reagan's Justice Department. The rapid rise of the ideology is itself proof that we can decide for ourselves what constitutes legitimate legal thought.

As I wrote at the beginning of this book, there is no one objectively correct way to interpret the Constitution. Some of its directives are explicit, but others are generalities about which people are free to argue; the arguments that win over time are what we understand as constitutional law. A given interpretation essentially becomes "correct" when enough people are convinced to accept it as such. Again, take originalism: the conservative legal movement wanted people to think about the law in a different way and found that they could make that happen with sufficient numbers of sufficiently organized people. (And money. Money doesn't hurt.) They turned the Department of Justice into an originalist think tank and public-relations firm and made a coordinated effort to identify and groom conservative law students and young lawyers for judgeships and higher office. With people in the right places, they created infrastructure that led the legal community and the general population to accept originalism as valid. By activating academics and social movements, making the ideology politically salient, developing a pipeline of originalists to be elevated to positions of power, and constantly publicly discussing originalism in the media as if it weren't unadulterated foolishness, the conservative legal movement successfully reset the range of publicly acceptable policies and moved their ideas "from laughable to legitimate."[2]

The conservative legal movement would like you to think that originalism has existed forever, on a higher plane outside of politics and collective action. Presenting originalism as something that just *is* rather than something that was created by political actors helps disguise the resulting injustice as the natural output of a legitimate system. Such a belief can be demotivating: the public may think that something natural can't be beaten, or even if it could, that it shouldn't be. But the present legal hellscape isn't some naturally occurring phenomenon. Newton's laws I respect. Alito's laws? Not so much. The harmful legal system that exists today was made by people, and people can unmake it.

I know it's frustrating to think that the country's current mess was, in nontrivial part, spoken into existence by conservatives—that it didn't have to be this way, but a small minority wanted it to be. On the other hand, there's something freeing in the knowledge that law is a construct that is subject to change. We can find strength in our capacity to be the agents of that change. Laws mean things if we make them mean things. And the courts have power to the extent that we give them power. Before you fix your fingers to write an op-ed accusing me of threatening the rule of law, please know this isn't an extreme or radical idea. It's an empirical reality, wholly consistent with democracy. Legal and political elites have recognized as much for ages. President Abraham Lincoln demolished the case for judicial supremacy over 165 years ago when he gave a speech methodically explaining why he believed the country did not need to follow the Supreme Court's decision in *Dred Scott:*

> If this important decision had been made by the unanimous concurrence of the judges, and without any apparent partisan bias, and in accordance with legal public expectation, and with the steady practice of the departments, throughout our history, and had been in no part based on assumed historical facts which are not really true; or, if wanting in some of these, it had been before the Court more than once, and had there been affirmed and reaffirmed through a course of years, it then might be, perhaps would be, factious, nay, even revolutionary, to not

acquiesce in it as a precedent. But when, as it is true, we find it wanting in all these claims to the public confidence, it is not resistance, it is not factious, it is not even disrespectful to treat it as not having yet quite established a settled doctrine for the country.[3]

Lincoln recognized that Supreme Court opinions do not possess any intrinsic correctness or finality. They have to earn it, and contested partisan decisions that rely on false retellings of history and diverge from public expectations and institutional consensus—decisions like, say, *Dobbs* and *Shelby*—are particularly unworthy of deference. The skeptical reader may think here, "Well, Lincoln was president, so this may just reflect nonjudicial branches of government jockeying for power," but even a member of the Supreme Court has recently espoused this court-critical view. Justice Sotomayor dissented from the Court's decision striking down affirmative action and wrote that "the Court's unjustified exercise of power . . . will serve only to highlight the Court's own impotence in the face of an America whose cries for equality resound."[4] Here, too, we see a member of the elite acknowledging that the Court is not the ultimate legal arbiter, especially when it acts in a way that inhibits people's movements for a just and egalitarian democratic society. Disabuse yourself of the notion that the law is only what the Supreme Court says it is. The people—the *demos* in democracy—will always have the final word.

As I've shown throughout this book, there are many instances of the Court interpreting the Constitution in ways we now recognize are clearly wrong. And as I'll show in this chapter, there are also instances of ordinary, organized people forcing the Court to get it right. There's nothing stopping us from doing the same. Inclusive constitutionalism calls on lawyers and laypeople alike to collectively think about and interpret the law so we fulfill the Constitution's democratic ideals in such a way that we may all be free. The theory encourages us to define legitimate legal interpretation as that which takes the liberatory mission of the Reconstruction Amendments seriously—and to apply those equitable principles in the real world. Together we can create the inclusive constitutionalist future we want to live in. Reclaiming the Constitution starts with us.

MAKING CONSTITUTIONAL MEANING

American legal education typically treats Supreme Court justices as the only actors whose thinking warrants consideration in determining what the Constitution means. The Court's opinions are pored over as definitive statements of the law, and the undercurrents of political contestation and agitation by social movements locally and nationwide remain largely out of view. Basically, law schools serve students hot dogs but don't show how the sausage was made. These shortcomings notwithstanding, there's a growing body of legal scholarship that analyzes how constitutional meaning is constructed and considers it a collaborative process between actors both inside and outside the court system.[5] Yale Law professor Douglas NeJaime, for example, writes succinctly that "constitutional meaning becomes authoritative not because a court decided so independently, but because social movements have persuaded political forces, opinion leaders, the public, and judges that a new position is reasonable and, in fact, correct."[6]

This theory of change is borne out by American history. The Supreme Court did not simply wake up one day and realize segregation was a mistake, for instance. The relevant text of the Constitution didn't change, either, in between the Court saying it was A-OK for a state to make sitting in a train car while Black a crime and the Court recognizing that segregation is unconstitutional. But the way people interpreted that same text and insisted it be understood did change. It would be impossible to fully explain the Supreme Court ruling in November 1956 that the racially segregated bus system in Montgomery, Alabama, was unconstitutional without accounting for the nearly fifty thousand Black city residents who had been refusing to ride the bus since December 1955.[7] The Montgomery Bus Boycott was a community expression of principle backed by power: regular people collectively declared that segregated buses were unacceptable, and put severe economic pressure on the government by boycotting those buses and depriving the city of fares. By the time the Supreme Court formally changed the law, a mass movement had already transformed the legal terrain by putting its constitutional vision into practice.

Changing hearts and minds is useful for changing the meaning of the Constitution, even when the words within the four corners of its pages remain the same. There were no pertinent amendments in between 1986, when the Court said there was no constitutional issue with criminalizing private, consensual gay intimacy; 2003, when the Court said that, actually, the Constitution prohibits the criminalization of private consensual gay intimacy; and 2015, when the Court recognized that the Constitution protects same-sex couples' fundamental right to marry. What changed over those twenty-nine years was the way that the people demanded the Constitution be read.

The campaign to legalize same-sex marriage nationwide was open and direct about its strategy: win the freedom to marry in more states, thereby increasing the campaign's momentum and proving that the earth does in fact keep spinning when same-sex couples are afforded the same rights as different-sex couples; build and grow majority support for marriage equality, creating conditions that encourage policymakers and other people in power to do right by same-sex couples; and repeal federal marriage discrimination laws, again paving the way for outright recognition of the freedom to marry.[8] The

LGBTQ movement's work directly influenced the attitudes and behavior of the general public, lawmakers, and judges. When the Supreme Court struck down a Texas law that made gay intimacy a crime in 2003, as we discussed in chapter 2, it specifically acknowledged that its decision-making was influenced by the evolution of laws over time and new thinking about the expansiveness of liberty.[9] "We think that our laws and traditions in the past half century are of most relevance here," Justice Kennedy wrote. "These references show an emerging awareness that liberty gives substantial protection to adult persons in deciding how to conduct their private lives in matters pertaining to sex."[10] Utah's federal district court similarly went on to explain when it struck down the state's prohibition on same-sex marriage in 2013, "Here, it is not the Constitution that has changed, but the knowledge of what it means to be gay or lesbian. The court cannot ignore the fact that the Plaintiffs are able to develop a committed, intimate relationship with a person of the same sex but not with a person of the opposite sex. The court, and the State, must adapt to this changed understanding."[11] Remember, just a few decades before, the Supreme Court was asserting with complete confidence that there was "no connection" between "homosexual activity" and marriage, and claiming that criminalization was justified because the majority of the electorate thought it was immoral to be gay.[12] Social movements can shape what constitutes common knowledge—and when you know better, you do better.

Sometimes, justices learn quickly and are forced to immediately course correct. A Supreme Court ruling on flag salute mandates and the scope of the First Amendment once generated so much outrage that the Court reversed itself only three years later. In *Minersville School District v. Gobitis* (1940), the Supreme Court heard a case about children who were expelled from public school because they refused to salute the American flag and recite the pledge of allegiance. The local school board required that students and teachers salute the flag every day, but twelve-year-old Lillian Gobitas and her ten-year-old brother Billy were practicing Jehovah's Witnesses who believed doing so would violate biblical commands against idolatry.* (Billy wrote a letter to his school directors explaining, "I do not salute the flag not because I do not love my country, but I love my country and I love God more and must obey His commandments."[13]) The students were punished for their refusal with expulsion, and their parents had to enroll the children in private school at the family's own expense.[14] The Gobitas family argued that this violated their constitutional rights under the First and Fourteenth Amendments. The Supreme Court ruled 8–1 that it did not. The Court recognized that there were free speech and religious liberty interests at stake but argued that a free society and liberty itself are predicated on national cohesion. Lawmakers' authority to cultivate democratic loyalty and fellowship was particularly important for the Court at that moment because of its unstated but underlying anxiety about the rise of Nazi Germany and World War II.[15] "The flag is the symbol of our national unity," the Court reasoned, and "national unity is the basis of national security."[16]

The sole dissenter expressed serious concern that the young Jehovah's Witnesses were "politically helpless minorities" coerced to "express a sentiment which, as they interpret it, they do not entertain, and which violates their deepest religious convictions."[17] But the eight-justice majority concluded that it should not intrude on a legislature's decision-making authority so long as democratic channels remained open for the public to pursue political change and there was no obvious infringement of constitutional liberty. The

---

*The family's name is Gobitas, but it was misspelled as "Gobitis" in the Court's records.

Court wasn't so much requiring the pledge as determining that legislatures could require the pledge, and free people could "fight out the wise use of legislative authority in the forum of public opinion."[18]

The majority did not predict that people would also fight out in the streets, and with shocking brutality: the Court's ruling precipitated a sharp increase in violence against Jehovah's Witnesses. The ACLU documented attacks against nearly 1,500 adherents to the faith in 355 separate instances across 44 states in 1940. In one such instance, about a month after the *Gobitis* decision, journalist Beulah Amidon observed a group of vigilantes forcibly relocating the town's resident Jehovah's Witnesses while a sheriff looked on with seeming approval. When she asked what was happening and why, the sheriff replied, "Jehovah's Witnesses . . . They're running 'em out of here. They're traitors—the Supreme Court says so. Ain't you heard?"[19] New laws requiring that public school students salute the flag also surged in the wake of *Gobitis,* along with a corresponding dramatic increase in expulsions.[20] In some places, the parents of expelled children no longer attending school were also vulnerable to fines and prosecution for their children's purported delinquency.[21]

Outside of this spate of laws and violence, *Gobitis* found few friends. The decision was criticized by writers at nearly two hundred newspapers. It was roundly condemned by legal scholars in dozens of academic journals.[22] The author of the *Gobitis* opinion, Justice Felix Frankfurter, described in his diary being "literally flooded with letters" from people saying that he in particular as a Jewish person should have understood the need to protect a minority group from the hostilities of the public.[23] Within months of the decision, some justices who were in the majority began to publicly express their misgivings. When one justice told Frankfurter that another member of the eight-justice majority was having second thoughts, Frankfurter asked if the regretful justice had been rereading the Constitution. "No," Frankfurter's colleague replied, "he has been reading the papers."[24] Some lower-court judges used the Supreme Court's apparent conflictedness as an opportunity to openly reject *Gobitis* as precedent, saying that they didn't have to accept the Court's ruling as binding authority under the existing circumstances.[25] Like Lincoln after *Dred Scott,* official actors publicly announced that a Supreme Court decision was illegitimate and refused to give it precedential effect.

The Roosevelt Administration also quickly distanced itself from the Court's ruling. Days after *Gobitis,* Solicitor General Francis Biddle gave a radio address condemning violence against Jehovah's Witnesses and announcing that the attorney general had ordered an investigation into the attacks. "We shall not defeat the Nazi evil by emulating its methods," he admonished listeners.[26] (A little rich coming from the administration that also put thousands of Japanese Americans in internment camps, I know.) A few weeks later, First Lady Eleanor Roosevelt published a column urging national self-reflection to avoid getting "swept away from our traditional attitude toward civil liberties by hysteria." She specifically referenced an incident where six Jehovah's Witnesses were pulled out of their houses and forced to march with and pledge allegiance to the flag, and posed the rhetorical question, "Must we drag people out of their homes to force them to do something which is in opposition to their religion?"[27] Around six months after that, President Roosevelt delivered a State of the Union address now known as the Four Freedoms speech. The speech committed the country to fighting against global authoritarianism and identified four freedoms deemed foundational to free societies. The first two were "freedom of speech and expression" and "freedom of every person to worship God in his own way," which most obviously referred to Nazi Germany and the genocide of Jewish people but had unmistakable domestic implications as well.[28] By 1942, prominent Department of Justice attorneys were publicly stating that *Gobitis* was not "accepted as a firmly rooted precedent" and urging for the case to be reexamined "in the light of the immediate public reactions."[29]

In the public imagination, after these columns and speeches, flag salute mandates rapidly shifted from "something that could beat the Nazis" to "something Nazis would do." They no longer demonstrated a commitment to democratic ideals and national unity, to the extent they ever did, but a troubling totalitarian imposition.[30] The question of the constitutionality of such mandates came before the Supreme Court again in *West Virginia State Board of Education v. Barnette* (1943). This time, the Court considered the issue as being squarely about the government's authority over speech. There was then no need to examine if Jehovah's Witnesses should have a special exception from otherwise mandatory flag salutes if the government doesn't have the power to make the salute a legal duty in the first place.[31] The Court also recognized that it has a responsibility to act when liberty is infringed. *Gobitis* was overruled with a 6–3 vote.

Of the eight justices who previously made up the *Gobitis* majority, two had retired before the Court heard *Barnette,* three changed their minds, and three were left to dissent. The lone dissenter in *Gobitis,* Harlan Stone, had also become chief justice by the time of *Barnette*. The *Barnette* opinion was written by Justice Robert Jackson, but some legal scholars contend that credit for the decision really belongs to "those who refused to accept the Court's 1940 pronouncements on the meaning of the Constitution, minority rights, and religious liberty."[32] There is evidence for this assessment in the opinion itself. The decision cites several law journal articles that were written by people who weren't Jehovah's Witnesses and nonetheless opposed *Gobitis*. "Many citizens who do not share these religious views hold such a compulsory rite to infringe constitutional liberty of the individual," Jackson wrote.[33] Further, contemporary records now reveal that earlier drafts of the decision included references to the violence perpetrated against Witnesses in both Nazi Germany and the United States, as well as the Justice Department's public statements opposing the *Gobitis* ruling. This recognition of outside influence was removed at the explicit urging of Chief Justice Stone to avoid "the impression that our judgment of the legal question was affected by the disorders which had followed the *Gobitis* decision."[34]

A common thread unites these examples of legal change around flag salute mandates, anti-gay discrimination, and segregated buses. They all show that actors outside of the Court and Congress can use nontraditional channels to change what the Constitution means. *Barnette* in particular demonstrates that justices' decisions are informed by more than their own sterile analyses of the law, despite them pretending otherwise. People shape what's possible. *Barnette*'s legacy also serves as a reminder that constitutional change can happen quickly—hastened by social and political conditions—and the public is not just stuck with repugnant precedent. Indeed, four Supreme Court justices invoked this idea when dissenting from the Court's 1986 decision blessing the criminalization of same-sex intimacy: "It took but three years for the Court to see the error in its analysis in *Minersville School District v. Gobitis* . . . I can only hope that here, too, the Court soon will reconsider."[35]

In a technical and legalistic sense, a Supreme Court case becomes precedent the moment it is decided. But in reality, as we've seen, people can reject it. Movements that successfully construct new constitutional meanings treat Supreme Court decisions less like decrees and more like part of an ongoing dialogue. Because they consider a prior decision by the Court unacceptable, they refuse to relinquish the authority to interpret the Constitution to an untrustworthy Supreme Court alone. These movements instead assert in multiple forums that their alternative understanding is correct—and increase pressure on a wide range of actors to validate their interpretation and restructure society accordingly.

Building and mobilizing a constituency to put an inclusive constitutionalist vision into practice is critical because constitutional rights don't just vindicate themselves. Legend has it that when the Supreme Court ruled roughly two hundred years ago in *Worcester v. Georgia* that the state did not have the right to regulate Cherokee land, President Andrew Jackson quipped, "John Marshall has made his decision, now let him enforce it." More recently, even before *Dobbs* explicitly overruled *Roe v. Wade,* decades of conservative advocacy had eroded the right and made abortion inaccessible throughout much of the country. The fight doesn't actually stop after we win our rights—we have to fight to protect them. Scholars of law and pro-democracy movements like Professor Lani Guinier and Professor Gerald Torres remind us that "culture shifting, not just rule shifting" is required to bring about lasting social change.[36] There is no one weird trick to achieve this. We will need multiple messengers and persuasive approaches in order to influence and shift power within a culture as diverse as America's, and to create social and political conditions that are conducive to new constitutional meanings.

A FEW TACTICS FOR LAYPEOPLE

You're probably already familiar with at least one of the tools out there for shaping constitutional meaning: national elections. Federal judges are nominated by the president and confirmed by the Senate. Judges appointed by Biden and Obama tend to interpret the Constitution very differently than judges appointed by Trump and Bush (pick a Bush, any Bush). It matters who is in the White House and in Congress, and voting is an important way for eligible members of the population to engage in harm reduction.* Still, national elections aren't the only way you can influence the Constitution; they're not even the only elections! And there are plenty of opportunities for you to affect constitutional interpretation beyond one day at the ballot box.

The overwhelming majority of all cases in this country (95 percent!) are filed in state courts. Therefore, judges in state courts play a significant albeit underappreciated role in interpreting and applying Supreme Court precedents, the U.S. Constitution, and the state's constitution. And in most states, judges are subject to elections. These elections work a bit differently from state to state. Some states have partisan elections where judicial candidates openly run as Democrats or Republicans, other states have nonpartisan elections where candidates' political affiliations are not disclosed, still others have judges who are initially appointed by their state's governor and must then sit for retention elections once their term is up, and so on.[37] Each of these elections presents possibilities. Organized members of the public can work together to make the Constitution a campaign issue and withhold votes from originalist candidates. This matters. If elected, judges who are aligned with inclusive constitutionalist social movements can push activists' ideas into the legal and political mainstream and develop jurisprudence that strengthens democracy.[38] Judicial elections, then, provide a direct avenue for reshaping constitutional values close to home.[39]

Significantly, ideas know no borders. Opening up new interpretive possibilities locally can help us think more broadly about our national constitutional commitments. The state constitution of Hawai'i, for example, includes an express and enforceable "right to a

---

* "Eligible members" is currently limited to citizens aged eighteen and up without certain criminal convictions, but there are ongoing movements both to lower the voting age and re-enfranchise incarcerated people.

clean and healthful environment," which the state's courts have held encompasses an affirmative right to a life-sustaining climate system. In a concurring opinion in one of those cases, *Matter of Hawai'i Electric Light Company* (2023), a judge went further and emphasized that the substantive due process right to life, liberty, and property also includes the right to a life-sustaining climate because all other constitutional guarantees are meaningless without a habitable planet.[40]

Few federal courts have heard such an argument, and fewer still have been receptive to it—with one notable exception. In 2015, a group of young people ages eight to nineteen sued the heads of several government agencies in a federal district court in Oregon. They alleged that the government violated their due process rights by knowingly imperiling their health and welfare via its fossil fuel policies and impermissibly discriminated against them as youths, most of whom could not vote, and who would disproportionately experience the dangerous consequences of the destabilized climate system. The federal agencies tried to get the young people's lawsuit dismissed and, when that failed, tried to get the court to rule against the young plaintiffs without a full trial. But district courts in Oregon refused, recognizing that a stable climate system capable of sustaining human life is a fundamental right without which civilization would not exist, and that the youths had made viable claims that could be redressed in court.[41] In *Juliana v. United States* (2020), the Ninth Circuit overruled the district court 2–1 and dismissed the case. The majority agreed with the youths that "the problem is approaching the point of no return" and "absent some action, the destabilizing climate will bury cities, spawn life-threatening natural disasters, and jeopardize critical food and water supplies," but pointed out that these injuries couldn't be resolved just by declaring the government's actions unconstitutional: "Any effective plan would necessarily require a host of complex policy decisions entrusted, for better or worse, to the wisdom and discretion of the executive and legislative branches."[42] However, the one dissenter forcefully disagreed and argued that "the mere fact that this suit cannot alone halt climate change" doesn't mean the court can't hear and resolve the case.[43]

Citing the *Juliana* dissent extensively, the concurring opinion in *Matter of Hawai'i Electric Light Company* gave serious consideration to how the constitutional right to be free from catastrophic and irreversible climate change could bump up against the limits of judicial competency. It ultimately concluded that there is a substantive due process right to a stable, life-sustaining climate system, and it was within the court's power to issue an order like "reduce greenhouse gas emissions" that the politically accountable branches would then determine how to implement. The court analogized this to *Brown v. Board* issuing a broad directive to "desegregate schools" and governments then developing specific plans to actually do so. State courts can offer formal recognition of rights and serve as a productive forum to spur government deliberation and dialogue about what is required to vindicate those rights, within and outside the judicial branch.

To be sure, these conversations can't be left to elites alone. A maxim among activists and community organizers is that the people closest to the problem are closest to the solution. And social-movement scholars emphasize that more significant and sustainable change is possible when the people who are most affected by unjust power structures organize themselves to challenge those structures together.[44] Organizers who are interested in fostering lasting and equitable constitutional change should build on the work they're already doing to meet their communities' material needs by linking it to constitutional claims that advance a broader conception of their rights and reject the legal ideologies that justify and perpetuate their oppression. For instance, if you're organizing tenants to fight for repairs in their apartment complex, you can introduce the idea that they have a substantive right to housing itself. Making this connection would make the law real for people who probably wouldn't be invested in constitutional change in the abstract (legal doctrine doesn't get most people out of bed in the morning) but do care about their living conditions. Plus, by contextualizing their demands in terms of the government's foundational obligations to the people, organizers can appeal to broader audiences, open up new avenues for persuasion and mobilization, and bridge the divide between how elites conceptualize the law and how regular people experience the law. The concept of constitutional rights broadly resonates with the American people. Weaving appeals to the Constitution into your advocacy can shift what people think of as constitutionally acceptable—or even constitutionally required.[45]

When workers fight for better wages and employment conditions, for example, they can also claim that they have the right to collectively organize and strike under the Constitution. The Thirteenth Amendment prohibits forced labor, after all, and one can argue that this necessarily implies the freedom to stop working and negotiate your work conditions.[46] Has the federal government recognized that yet? No, not yet. The right of private employees to organize and strike is guaranteed, though limited in many ways, by a statute called the National Labor Relations Act, and courts have not recognized labor-protest rights for private or public employees under the Constitution. But activists could say it anyway, tapping into the reverence with which many Americans regard the Constitution by normalizing an understanding of workers' rights as a constitutional commitment. There is power in putting your constitutional interpretation into practice and acting as if it is already recognized as correct. (Put another way, fake it till you make it. It worked for originalists!)*Just take the West Virginia teachers who went on strike in 2018 *despite* a state law prohibiting public-sector employees from collective bargaining and striking: the teachers won a 5 percent pay increase for state employees. When the president of the West Virginia Education Association was asked if the strike was illegal, he replied, "We have a right to have our voices heard."[47] This principle echoes a union slogan from the 1960s and '70s: there is no such thing as an illegal strike, just an unsuccessful one.[48]

It's important to advocate for laws and policies aligned with inclusive constitutionalism—even if (or perhaps especially if) your proposed policy conflicts with the Supreme Court. The conflict can even be explicit. Long before *Dobbs,* for example, conservative legislatures were passing "trigger laws." These were antiabortion laws that would be triggered when specified conditions were met, like "*Roe v. Wade* is unconstitutional, and this abortion ban will go into effect when the Court strikes it down." Though the laws were unenforceable by their own terms, they had a powerful mobilizing and signaling effect, as if forces were aligning to announce, "*Roe*'s days are numbered." Instead of trigger laws against abortion, proponents of inclusive constitutionalism should consider trigger laws for democracy.

Here's an example. Arizona voters passed a ballot initiative in 1998 in the wake of a public corruption scandal in which 10 percent of Arizona's legislators were exposed as having accepted bribes. In order to reduce corruption, increase electoral competition, and expand political speech, the ballot initiative created a voluntary public

---

*For all my *Doctor Who* fans out there, remember the episode when Amelia Pond has to keep her eyes closed while crossing a forest full of Weeping Angels so the Doctor tells her to "walk like you can see"? That line is, in a way, my touchstone for legal change: it always comes to mind when I think about moving to an inclusive-constitutionalist future by acting out its principles as if we were already there.

financing system for candidates in statewide elections. Candidates who used the program would receive an initial sum of funding, and if a privately financed opponent exceeded the allotted state funding, the state would provide matching funds. Republican candidates and funders sued, arguing that their First Amendment rights were violated because they had to spend less money if they wished to avoid triggering the release of matching funds to their publicly financed opponents. The Republicans on the Supreme Court agreed, ruling 5–4 in *Arizona Free Enterprise Club's Freedom Club PAC v. Bennett* (2011) that matching funds amounted to an unlawful burden on privately financed candidates' free speech, which was paid for fair and square. A sample trigger law in Arizona could read, "The voter-approved and democracy-enhancing program providing matching funds for publicly financed candidates will be reimplemented within thirty days of the Supreme Court overruling *Arizona Free Enterprise Club PAC v. Bennett*."

Building support for democracy-enhancing trigger laws that advance constitutional change would require activists to engage in voter education and outreach work premised on the idea that an equitable policy is within reach and can be implemented once a wrongly decided Supreme Court opinion is overruled. In doing so, advocates would be simultaneously building public support for a particular policy, asserting that the public can legitimately interpret the Constitution in a different way, and resetting what the public expects and is willing to accept from the courts and the legislature. If people were encouraged to imagine how the Constitution should be read and what the government should do, it would bring into focus the ways the existing Constitution and its interpretation are falling short and would benefit from formal amendments and reinterpretation. The advantages of this tactic apply equally to ballot initiatives and referenda, which are unique vehicles for an organized public to express a new constitutional vision. Roughly two dozen states have processes by which citizens can directly enact new laws or constitutional amendments. Some activists have embraced these tools in the new post-*Dobbs* world so the people themselves can protect abortion in the face of recalcitrant politicians. In both Ohio and Michigan, voters passed ballot initiatives amending the constitutions in their states to guarantee a constitutional right to abortion.[49]

On top of the substantive policy goals that can be achieved, community-driven advocacy is inherently valuable because it allows and encourages people to use their own power. People power also meaningfully distinguishes this kind of legal clash—advocating for laws that courts currently think are illegal—from the kind of conservative lawlessness I described in chapter 1. Overriding the will of majorities in pursuit of inequality is different from mobilizing the masses in furtherance of egalitarianism.

Another possible avenue for regular people to act out their constitutional vision is one that a lot of folks try to avoid: jury duty. Jury duty gets a bad rap. This is understandable. It hauls you away from your life for hours or even days at a time; it gives you only a token pittance, if you're lucky enough to be in a state that compensates jurors for their time at all; and, honestly, it can just be dreadfully boring sometimes. But it also can give people a direct opportunity to reject the government's understanding of the Constitution and decline to enforce an unjust law. "Jury nullification" is a term typically used to describe the power of juries to declare someone accused of a crime "not guilty," even if the evidence suggests they broke the law. It has also occasionally been used to describe jurors refusing to impose the death penalty, even if the convicted person met the legal requirements for execution, and choosing the sentence of life imprisonment instead. Jurors might nullify for various reasons, such as a belief that the person's conduct shouldn't be a crime to begin with or that the sentence is otherwise unconscionable—such as the death penalty or excessively long mandatory minimums. Jury nullification expresses a rebuke of state power by effectively refusing to give a law any practical force.[50]

The legal system is generally tight-lipped about the practice—sometimes forbidding defense attorneys from telling jurors they have that option, and even prosecuting advocates who distribute pamphlets about jury nullification to passersby near a courthouse.[51] But none of that erases the fact that jurors can *always* prevent a conviction by choosing to say "not guilty."[52] Juries' power to refuse to convict is especially important in this political moment marked by rampant criminalization and repression of dissent and other freedoms. In September 2023, for example, the attorney general of Georgia announced a sweeping indictment that charged dozens of activists under the state's Racketeer Influenced and Corrupt Organizations (RICO) Act. The indicted people are a diverse assortment of advocates supporting racial justice, environmental defense, Indigenous rights, economic justice, and more, all of whom oppose the government's plan to spend $90 million to destroy hundreds of acres of the Weelaunee Forest and build a sprawling police training complex. The indictment conflates the protesters' shared aim with evidence of a conspiracy and has been described by the Center for Constitutional Rights as a "ludicrous and terrifying" criminalization of speech.[53] The threat of prosecution for exercising your rights has also increased in the aftermath of *Dobbs* as more and more people are subjected to criminal liability for their pregnancy outcomes—including but not limited to abortion—and for assisting people in accessing the reproductive healthcare they need.[54] Recognizing that policing is always a state weapon of choice against social movements and other disfavored groups, nullification provides a tool to dull that blade and keep people out of the clutches of the criminal legal system. Perhaps it could even pressure prosecutors to think more conscientiously about the criminal charges they are willing to file. Law professor and former prosecutor Paul Butler once astutely observed that criminal conduct is extrajudicially excused all the time by cops and prosecutors who exercise their discretion, and "ironically, it is only when 12 jurors do it, as opposed to one police officer or prosecutor, that a hue and cry ensues."[55]

A powerful example of jury nullification occurred at the trial of a group of protesters who the government called the Camden Twenty-eight. In August 1971, a predominantly Catholic group of twenty-eight leftists opposed to the Vietnam War planned and carried out a raid of a draft board office in Camden, New Jersey. The group broke into the building and destroyed Selective Service documents. This tactic supported the antiwar movement both symbolically and substantively by sabotaging the draft process that sustained the war. Unbeknownst to the protesters, there was an informant in their midst: one group member had reservations about the plan and alerted the Federal Bureau of Investigation (FBI) with hopes of minimizing the group's criminal exposure, potentially limiting it to conspiracy charges alone.[56] But that's not what happened: the FBI instead provided the group with much of the funds and tools needed to execute the raid, and waited to arrest the protesters until the break-in occurred. Dozens of agents caught the protesters red-handed. The Camden Twenty-eight were arrested on a litany of charges, and some faced possible sentences up to forty-seven years in prison and $46,000 in fines.[57]

The protesters put out a statement before their trial that didn't contest whether they committed the criminal conduct they were accused of—they proudly claimed responsibility for their actions—but challenged the idea that their conduct was really a crime. "We do not believe that it is criminal," they wrote, "to destroy pieces of paper which are used to bind men to involuntary servitude, which train these men to kill, and which send them to possibly die in an unjust, immoral, and illegal war."[58]

The protesters explicitly treated their trial as a referendum on the Vietnam War, even presenting video of destruction in Vietnam and dilapidation in Camden as evidence of the wrongs they were mobilizing against, including a government that always has money for bombs but not for housing.[59] The mother of one of the protesters testified about her son who was killed in Vietnam; the war's cost in human lives and money that could have been better spent at home; and her belief that, if there were "any criminals in this case, it's the middle-class America who sits by" and sends boys to die "for tin, rubber and oil."[60] Historian and political scientist Howard Zinn testified about civil disobedience as an honorable American tradition that has been essential to building a more just society, as when antebellum Americans refused to cooperate with the Fugitive Slave Act. Zinn also argued that the determination of criminal violations should be weighed against the human consequences, the motive for breaking the law, and the social evils challenged by breaking the law.[61] Repeatedly, the protesters directly asked the jury to nullify the law and acquit them in order to express opposition to the Vietnam War and to the FBI's role in encouraging the raid. The judge cautioned the jurors that "protest is not an acceptable legal defense," and that it would be improper to base their decision on their stance on Vietnam.[62] Nevertheless, the judge took the unusual step of telling the jurors they could acquit if they believed the FBI went to "intolerable" lengths that were "offensive to the basic standards of decency and shocking to the universal sense of justice" in facilitating the crime—even though the protesters began planning the raid before the informant got involved, and though they did the break-in without him.

When the trial concluded, the jury found the defendants not guilty on all counts. According to one of the jurors, the jury both agreed that the government went too far and wanted to join the defendants in opposing the Vietnam War.[63] The protesters convinced the public of the rightness of their cause, and the public had the protesters' backs. One of the Camden Twenty-eight remarked after the verdict that they were now the Camden Forty, counting the jurors among their ranks.[64]

This brings us to what may be the most important point: there is strength in numbers. There is an abundance of tactics that mass movements can and do use to facilitate social and political change that would similarly benefit a movement for inclusive constitutionalism. Professor Robert Tsai has observed that constitutional actors—people who shape the Constitution's meaning, whether in a formal sense, like judges, lawyers, professors, or elected officials, or a more informal sense, like activists and regular motivated people— are "susceptible to prodding, cajoling, praise, and threats," just like anybody else.[65] Civil disobedience (deliberately breaking a law), uncivil obedience (following the letter of the law in a manner that is very inconvenient and unexpected), strikes, marches, sit-ins, sabotage, and other forms of defiance are all tried-and-true tactics in activists' toolboxes. And new tactics will surely be invented to adapt to new circumstances. But you can't have a mass mobilization without a critical mass. Connecting with people and identifying your common goal is a prerequisite for collective action. You can start by building on your existing relationships with people right where you are: your family, friends, neighbors, or classmates; people who share your faith or are in your union or community organization or play on your roller derby team—whatever's your thing. Wherever you are is where your part in creating legal and political change begins.

A FEW TACTICS FOR LAWPEOPLE

My emphasis on the role of the general public is not to suggest that attorneys should just relax while others do all the hard work. Like Liam Neeson in *Taken,* lawyers have a very particular set of skills.

The most obvious tool, one uniquely suited to lawyers, is a lawsuit. Little more needs to be said at this point in the book about the ability of court cases to shape the way the country thinks about the law, and their potential to tangibly impact social, political, and economic life. A word of caution, though: litigation is somewhat analogous to voting, in that American liberals tend to valorize both at the expense of other tactics. They've produced victories before, so now litigating and voting are sometimes treated as the only avenues for lawpeople and laypeople, respectively, to effect change. And while they certainly have value and can advance strategic goals, they can't sustain constitutional change all by themselves. We attorneys can do other things, too!

For starters, we need to collect our people. Attorneys sometimes forget that we are not simply passive participants in a legal system that dangerously underserves the public. We have a say in making it. Attorneys who recognize the currently dominant mode of legal thinking as transparently unreasonable, unworkable, and unsafe need to develop and promote alternative models of constitutional thought. And then we must spread the word, informing and persuading other lawyers. I like to think this book is a solid push in the right direction, but there are several more steps to take. It's my hope that attorneys accept this invitation to broadly explore how inclusive constitutionalism can and should apply to different areas of law. Legal journal articles and conferences are spaces where we can start building up and normalizing these ideas within the legal profession. And amicus briefs, particularly at the state court level (which gets dramatically less attention than federal courts, as discussed), could provide an opportunity to introduce and field test some of these concepts in front of judges and start informing jurisprudence. There are also groups that pull together legal academics, practitioners, students, and non-legal actors to lay this kind of intellectual groundwork, such as the Constitutional Democracy Initiative at Columbia

Law School, the Law and Political Economy Project housed at Yale Law School, the Systemic Justice Project at Harvard Law School, and the People's Parity Project—housed wherever you want it to be! (PPP has chapters across the country.) More lawyers should get involved in efforts like these to reimagine a more equitable legal system and support the work of social movements. Lawmakers must also begin to publicly recognize originalism as an unwelcome intrusion on their ability to do their jobs—preventing them from addressing modern problems or crafting new solutions—and reject originalist judicial nominees.

I know (oh, do I know) that law is inherently a risk-averse profession, so the idea of challenging established norms may induce some mild anxiety, but be brave!* We cannot afford to meekly maintain an intolerable status quo. Now is a time for boldness and creativity. And you can't make a constitutional-interpretation omelet without cracking a few legal-doctrine eggs.

Another major responsibility for lawyers will be to act as translators for the nonlawyer public. Too often, legal writing and commentary treats the law like one big esoteric thought experiment and not something that determines whether real people have a roof over their heads and food on their tables. The judiciary relies on jargon and legalese that can obscure the harm caused by its constitutional interpretation. Mainstream media has been slow to cover the courts critically, and frequently fails to center the people most impacted by laws' inequities. The Supreme Court in particular has long coasted on an unearned reputation of legitimacy—in part because people haven't been adequately informed, in language they understand, about what the Court is doing and why they should care. And even when lawyers recognize injustices caused or enforced by law and

---

* My nephew, who is currently five, often advises, "Don't be scared, be bwave!" and I have taken his erudite guidance to heart.

theorize alternatives, those necessary conversations rarely break out of our small circles—the testing grounds of ideas I mention above—and get through to the public at large. The idea that knowledge is power is cliché but true. We can help build power by sharing our knowledge and making the law accessible and digestible to regular people. Public engagement and media commentary are going to be critical for shaping a new narrative about what's possible, and for building up an informed and activated constituency—one that's empowered to fight for a new constitutional vision that improves their lives. Lawyers have a responsibility to plainly explain to people how they are affected by the Constitution and communicate to the public that constitutional change is possible, desirable, and their right.

In addition to producing scholarship, legal academics have a role to play in their teaching. Law schools inculcate the next generation of attorneys with ideas about right and wrong ways to think about the law. Professors should make clear to students that originalism is one of multiple competing methods of interpretation. Students should be encouraged to identify and evaluate the different values and motives that drive various interpretive approaches, and to think about how the choice of interpretive method can impact the legal conclusion.

Attorneys should also provide social movements with legal support to help ensure that their claims are taken seriously, and that their demands are translated into the law of the land. There are many ways to get involved, including but not limited to litigation. Advocates may be interested in creating model legislation, for example, so they can supply local lawmakers with a bill they would like introduced and enacted. The American Legislative Exchange Council (ALEC) has been doing this for conservatives for years; between 2010 and 2018, members of the U.S. Congress and legislators in all fifty states introduced nearly 2,900 ALEC bills, with more than 600 becoming law.[66] Progressive lawyers with policy experience could similarly assist advocates with legislative drafting. Moreover, if activists want to provide a formal comment on a proposed regulation or submit testimony at a governmental hearing, attorneys could help guide them through that process.

Protesters sometimes face the possibility of arrest and could benefit from education on what their rights are and the potential legal consequences of their actions. Please note that I said education—I did not say persuasion to change their tactics, or preemptive encouragement to comply with state authority. You should certainly provide legal services to keep them out of jail and minimize any collateral consequences if they're arrested. But sometimes protesters are willing or even planning to get arrested (yours truly once got arrested on purpose with a couple dozen others while protesting for the Freedom to Vote Act). Again, be brave! Cowardice is not one of the requirements under your state's rules of professional conduct. By sharing legal information, you're empowering advocates to make informed decisions for themselves. In addition to our technical skill set, lawyers are likely to have capital—political, social, and otherwise—that may be inaccessible to activists. We may be better positioned to identify and navigate institutional hurdles keeping social movements from achieving their goals. Organizations like Law for Black Lives and the Advancement Project are strong examples of how attorneys can be deeply embedded within movement work and a boon to grassroots activists. These groups act as legal infrastructure, providing racial justice advocates on the ground with technical assistance, legal and policy research, and other resources. Go where the work is being done and ask groups what they need; you may be able to give it to them.

Finally, it is critically important for attorneys to develop a demographically and professionally diverse pipeline of future state and federal judges at the trial, intermediate, and appellate levels. The judiciary is a monochromatic maelstrom of corporate and carceral interests. This is unsurprising, because the legal system fast-tracks white guys who worked as prosecutors or represented massive corporations to judges' chambers. Worse yet, the Federalist Society starts training baby conservatives to become judges before they can even spell "Reaganomics." The bench desperately needs new perspectives. Inclusive constitutionalists should be both arguing and deciding cases. Every seat matters, and we need people prepared to fill them.

I'm not so arrogant as to claim that the recommendations I've made here will guarantee victory all by themselves. Martin Luther King, Jr., himself once observed that "there is no tactical theory so neat that a revolutionary struggle for a share of power can be won merely by pressing a row of buttons."[67] But I am confident that there are questions that our tactics must seek to answer if we are to have a successful people's movement; namely: How can currently marginalized people build power, and how can people who currently hold power over us be influenced or confronted? The suggestions for bringing about inclusive constitutionalism that I've put forth here— fighting to change laws and the people who make and execute laws, and reshaping the legal and political battlefield on which we fight— reflect my initial attempts to answer those questions.

YES, IT'S WORTH IT

America's first Reconstruction gave rise to the heart of inclusive constitutionalism: a commitment to wholly reimagining the country's legal foundation so that oppressed people could know freedom, equality, and justice. That commitment tragically faltered while white supremacists remained resolute, and Reconstruction slipped into Redemption (as white southerners called their return to power after the Civil War) and Jim Crow. But the spirit of liberation was not extinguished. The second Reconstruction, by which I mean the Civil Rights Movement, began to follow through on that long-unkept promise as countless persistent Americans mobilized to achieve civil, political, and economic equality. Those great strides were followed by a long backlash, which has worsened in recent years with originalism's takeover of the Supreme Court. But the reason originalists have worked so feverishly is that the country has come closer to achieving a real, inclusive democracy than ever before.

The conservative legal movement is threatened by the successes of people's movements for freedom and the progress those movements have made in discarding undemocratic hierarchies. So originalists dig through the trash bin of history like racist raccoons looking for leftover oppression. Then they try to intellectualize this garbage behavior so they can maintain a veneer of legitimacy. Yet their mask is slipping. Now, as Americans resist the extremists who want to send the nation hurtling backward into a dangerous and cruel time—endangering people of color, women of all races, the queer community, the working class, and people who live at the intersections thereof, in particular—a third Reconstruction must begin. And we are at its cusp.

The precipitous decline in the Supreme Court's approval ratings suggests that the image it fabricated for itself as an impartial and trustworthy legal arbiter is breaking down. Its own bad actions are priming the public for comprehensive reform. At the same time, the police-brutality protests of 2020, the voting rights movement in 2021 and 2022, the worker strikes across multiple industries in 2023, and other challenges to the existing structures of power all provide evidence of a public that hungers for justice and equality. This is the moment to educate, empower, and mobilize the general public and legal practitioners alike around remaking the legal system so that we may build a just democracy that works for all of us.

Inclusive constitutionalism—a framework that interprets the whole Constitution in light of the Reconstruction Amendments' promise to build a functioning multiracial democracy—can help bring about and sustain the transformation that our legal system needs. If we are to have the democracy we deserve, we the people must free ourselves from the originalism trap. All Americans have a stake in our democracy, and in ensuring that we don't set fire to the future because of misstatements about the past. If we develop and promote a positive alternative method of constitutional interpretation free from originalism's artificial constraints, then we can shift what lawyers and the general public come to expect and demand from the law and simultaneously assert that the Supreme Court is not guaranteed the last word on democracy. This in turn would create new and improved tools with which we can build a stronger, more inclusive, and more equitable society.

All of this may sound overly optimistic, and I admit that I am an optimist by definition. If you're trying to make the world a better place, you have to believe the world can indeed get better. I also understand why people may be reluctant to share that belief. A genuinely pluralistic democratic society hasn't existed yet, so you may wonder if it can exist at all. But any doubts I have are diminished by the knowledge that generations of freedom fighters turned impossibilities into realities. After all that oppressed people have dreamt and achieved, under much worse conditions, we would have to be staggeringly unimaginative to think a better world is out of reach. We should not disrespect ourselves or their legacy by resigning ourselves to myopia. We don't have the power yet? Fine, then we make the power. Each of us can contribute to this essential liberatory project, and together we seize our freedom.

I also understand that this journey will not be without obstacles. There are currently only three Democratic appointees on the Supreme Court. And while I hope to have convinced you that reorienting constitutional interpretation around the goals and principles of the Reconstruction Amendments is a smart way to reimagine jurisprudence, I am unconvinced that we can simply outsmart power. The six justices who overturned *Roe v. Wade* would have done so regardless of whether the right to abortion was covered by the penumbra of privacy or grounded in equality. And they would have done so for the simple reason that they *could* have done so; they'd wanted to for years and finally had the numbers to pull it off. Regrettably, there's no sufficiently clever or well-reasoned argument you can make that will convince people who are firmly committed to oppressing you not to do so. However, once you understand the role of the Constitution as facilitating an inclusive democracy, structural reforms targeting the parts of our political system that don't serve the public are revealed as possible, necessary, and constitutional. That includes expanding the Court and ending life tenure.* It is facially absurd for a government that calls itself a democracy to permit a driblet of wealthy, well-connected, mostly white old men to rule over a diverse nation of over 331 million people as wannabe philosopher kings for the rest of their natural lives.[68] We must remember, though, that even if we were to expand the Supreme Court with four more justices tomorrow, those justices would still need a model of what to do beyond "not that." As long as the courts have any power to say what the law means, they need a better way of doing so. Inclusive constitutionalism and other democracy-enhancing priorities work together hand in hand.

Even if the Supreme Court as currently constituted initially confines inclusive constitutionalism to the dissent, it would nonetheless be an improvement over the status quo. The power to merely write

---

* By no means should this be taken as an exhaustive list. The Electoral College, severe Senate malapportionment, and everything else that allows a minority of the country to wield a majority of political power would also be near the front of the line for my personal chopping block.

dissents is obviously not ideal, but it's also not nothing. Dissents can validate and energize opponents of the Court's rulings. They can help persuade lawmakers, other attorneys, the media, and the public that the majority got the issue wrong, and spur political action as a result.[69] They can reframe the issue and provide guidance on how to limit the impact of the majority's decision—a tactic the right wing has sometimes used in dissent with shocking success, as when it turns discrimination cases into "states' rights" cases.[70] They can expose falsehoods in the opinion and set the record straight.* And—this is the big one—they can present entirely different alternatives for the future.[71] Case in point: Clarence Thomas was writing one-man dissents for years that have now been adopted as the Republican party line, as his style of strict originalist analysis has been used to promote expansive gun rights, permit forced birth, and decry race-conscious remedies as "the real racism."[72] Dissents can be roadmaps for future majority opinions. Dissenting liberal justices should use their platform to start doing some progressive cartography that utilizes an inclusive constitutionalist framework rather than countering conservatives' arguments on their own terms alone. The country will outlive this iteration of the Court, and once we are in a position to make better decisions, we will need clear and firm thinking regarding what to do and how to do it. We don't have to limit ourselves to cleaning up Chief Justice John Roberts's mess, nor should we. We can create our own jurisprudence—one that does not

---

Kennedy v. Bremerton School District comes to mind: Justice Gorsuch wrote for the majority that a football coach "lost his job" for "pray[ing] quietly while his students were otherwise occupied." Justice Sotomayor's dissent caught him in 4K. It includes a photograph of the coach delivering a religious speech to dozens of students kneeling in a circle around him, following the coach's solicitation of media coverage. *Kennedy v. Bremerton School District,* 597 U.S. __ (2022).

leave people behind, recognizes that we all have a claim to the Constitution, and maintains that it should work for all of us.

Inclusive constitutionalism can also provide helpful guidance to state courts, and to lower-court judges seeking to narrow the Supreme Court's harmful decisions from below. Lower-court judges should take every opportunity to distinguish the Supreme Court's bad opinions into oblivion. By "distinguish," nonlawyers, I mean the practice whereby attorneys say, "That precedent may seem, at first glance, like it should apply here, but it's actually not quite analogous for assorted reasons and should not govern the outcome of this case." If judges distinguish the Court's opinions by limiting them to their distinct facts, judges can start building up new doctrine. Of course, I expect that many such rulings would be appealed. But the Court may struggle to keep up with its new workload if narrowing precedent becomes sufficiently widespread among lower courts. What I'm getting at is: this isn't Pokémon—the Supreme Court may be unable to catch 'em all—and an onslaught of creatively interpreted opinions could have a valuable signaling and politically mobilizing effect. Besides, federal judges in the lower courts currently have lifetime appointments, too. And with job security that enviable, they could be bolder about putting their positions to use.

Now let's take a step back away from the courtroom. I would be thrilled if inclusive constitutionalism became a core part of judicial decision-making, but the decisions that courts make are less important than what we the people do with them.[73] The judiciary doesn't have the power of the purse or the sword. It has no armies to enforce its decisions. The power of the judiciary—like the meaning of the Constitution—is contingent on public acceptance and conferral of legitimacy.[74] Real power comes from us.

Together, we have the power to say no to a Supreme Court that brazenly works to entrench the political and economic domination of the many by the few and to eliminate subordinated groups from public life. The wealthy elites who push and defend such harmful policies want the rest of us to fight one another rather than fight *for* one another. But a democratic society is not a zero-sum game. The raw material of the Constitution supports an inclusive vision, not an exclusionary one. All of this country's residents are part of the people who the Constitution is supposed to serve. And by harnessing our collective power, we can actually make it do so.

When we foster that solidarity, that strength in numbers and, importantly, that hope, we make a better world possible. I'm not referring to a passive hope of acquiescence, like, "Maybe everything will turn out fine," but an active hope of righteous refusal. This hope is subversive, because it requires us to believe that we can live in a different world than this and inspires us to challenge the status quo. Fatalism is much like originalism: both tell us not to dream bigger and that we can have no better. Both keep us from achieving a functioning democracy. Both lie. The truth is, we can choose to interpret the Constitution so that it serves all of us—guided by the Reconstruction Amendments' revolutionary purpose and their expansive conceptions of liberation and egalitarianism. Rejecting the extremism of originalist ideology is a step toward taking back the Constitution. And taking back the Constitution is a step toward the inclusive and equitable democratic society we deserve.

ACKNOWLEDGMENTS

My goodness, I owe so much to so many.

It seems strange to be able to pinpoint the exact moment when the course of my life changed. On June 24, 2022 (at 3:43 P.M., to be precise), I received an email from Jennifer Reitman introducing me to Kera Bolonik. Kera would go on to introduce me to her agent, Sarah Burnes. Sarah would soon become *my* agent, championing me and my work and helping me navigate the unfamiliar waters of publishing. And she would introduce me to Molly Turpin, my editor. Molly blew me away with her fervor for getting my ideas and my voice out into the world, and for making my book the best version of itself.

This book rests on an intellectual foundation created by generations of thinkers and doers who struggled for liberation. Some are well known, others have surely been lost to history. I'm indebted to them all the same: *The Originalism Trap* would not be possible if not for the people, past and present, fighting for freedom.

My book, like me, would also not exist without my family. I feel very lucky to have had the constant support of my grandparents,

parents, sisters, aunts and uncles, and cousins throughout this process. I also want to acknowledge my precious niece and nephew who, to be honest, were generally unhelpful in allowing me to get work done, but who always helped me know what I was working for and why. And I am incredibly grateful for Nicholas, my love, who has steadfastly been a shoulder to lean on, a brain to bounce ideas off, and so much more.

This book was also shaped by countless conversations with people who helped me think through the substance of what I wanted to say or the process of how to say it, or even just offered a kind word and let me know they were rooting for me. Please forgive me for what I know will be a nonexhaustive list (a good problem resulting from an abundance of support): Nicole, Elizabeth, Sonali, Jackie, Alyssa, Chisun, Dillon and Karenna, Alec and Wendy, Gabe, Bri, Gabi, Turquoise, Stuart, Julia B., Julia K., Mekela, Jasleen, Kelly, Clara, Yurij, Ames, Ruth, Hernandez, Sara, Nuzhat, Ashok, Amy, Kate, Audrey, Bani, the People's Parity Project crew—thank you all.

And finally, I owe a debt of gratitude to Brooklyn Perk, my beloved coffee shop, where much of this book was written. I'll be in for an iced latte and pastry tomorrow.

NOTES

Chapter 1: Heist

1. H.L.A. Hart, "Positivism and the Separation of Law and Morals," *Harvard Law Review* 71, no. 4 (1958): 593, 607.
2. See, e.g., "Intro 8.1 Interpreting the Constitution Generally," *Constitution Annotated,* https://constitution.congress.gov/browse/essay /intro.8-1/ALDE_00001302/#essay-15. See also Philip Bobbitt, *Constitutional Fate: Theory of the Constitution* (New York: Oxford University Press, 1982) (discussing what he terms "modalities" of interpretation—structural, textual, ethical, prudential, historical, and doctrinal).
3. See, e.g., Justice Neil Gorsuch, "Why Originalism Is the Best Approach to the Constitution," *Time,* Sept. 6, 2019, https://time.com/5670400 /justice-neil-gorsuch-why-originalism-is-the-best-approach-to-the -constitution/.
4. See, e.g., Jonathan Easley, "Scalia: Constitution Is 'Dead, Dead, Dead,'" *The Hill,* Jan. 29, 2013, https://thehill.com/blogs/blog-briefing-room /news/140572-scalia-constitution-is-dead-dead-dead/.
5. Randy E. Barnett, "The Misconceived Assumption about Constitutional Assumptions," *Northwestern University Law Review* 103 (2009): 615, 660.
6. Keith E. Whittington, "Originalism: A Critical Introduction," *Fordham Law Review* 82 (2013): 375, 377.
7. Robert H. Bork, *The Tempting of America: The Political Seduction of the Law* (New York: Free Press, 1990), 143.

8. See, e.g., Erwin Chemerinsky, "Even the Founders Didn't Believe in Originalism," *The Atlantic,* Sept. 6, 2022, www.theatlantic.com/ideas /archive/2022/09/supreme-court-originalism-constitution-framers -judicial-review/671334/. See also Wilfred Codrington III, "The Framers Would Have Wanted Us to Change the Constitution," *The Atlantic,* Sept. 30, 2021, www.theatlantic.com/ideas/archive/2021/09/framers -would-have-wanted-us-change-constitution/620249/.

9. U.S. Const. Amend. XIII.

10. U.S. Const. Amend. XIV.

11. U.S. Const. Amend. XV.

12. See, e.g., Amy Dru Stanley, *From Bondage to Contract: Wage Labor, Marriage, and the Market in the Age of Slave Emancipation* (Cambridge: Cambridge University Press, 2010).

13. Eric Foner, "The Strange Career of the Reconstruction Amendments," *Yale Law Journal* 108 (1999): 2003, 2006.

14. For instance, scholars like Professor Dorothy Roberts argue that the Reconstruction Amendments and the historical movement to abolish slavery and its attendant conditions should be relevant to our understanding of the Constitution's utility in abolishing policing and incarceration. See, e.g., Dorothy E. Roberts, "Foreword: Abolition Constitutionalism," *Harvard Law Review* 133, no. 1 (2019). See also Brandon Hasbrouck, "Reclaiming the Abolition Amendments," American Constitution Society, Feb. 6, 2023, www.acslaw.org/expertforum /reclaiming-the-abolition-amendments/.

15. David E. Pozen, Eric L. Talley, and Julian Nyarko, "A Computational Analysis of Constitutional Polarization," *Cornell Law Review* 105 (2019).

16. Saul Cornell, "*Heller,* New Originalism, and Law Office History: 'Meet the New Boss, Same as the Old Boss,'" *UCLA Law Review* 56 (2009): 1095.

17. See, e.g., Jill Elaine Hasday, "On Roe, Alito Cites a Judge who Treated Women as Witches and Property," *Washington Post,* May 9, 2022, www .washingtonpost.com/opinions/2022/05/09/alito-roe-sir-matthew -hale-misogynist/. See also G. Geis, "Lord Hale, Witches, and Rape," *British Journal of Law and Society* 5 (1978): 26, 30–35.

18. *Dobbs v. Jackson Women's Health Organization,* 142 S. Ct. 2228 (2022).

19. Brief of American Historical Association and Organization of American Historians as Amici Curiae in Support of Respondents at 2, 5–10, 30, *Dobbs v. Jackson Women's Health Organization,* 142 S. Ct. 2228 (2022).

20. *Dobbs v. Jackson Women's Health Organization,* 142 S. Ct. 2228, 2253–54 (2022).

21. "History, the Supreme Court, and Dobbs v. Jackson: Joint Statement

from the AHA and the OAH," American Historical Organization, July 2022, www.historians.org/news-and-advocacy/aha-advocacy/history -the-supreme-court-and-dobbs-v-jackson-joint-statement-from-the-aha -and-the-oah-(july-2022).

22. Khiara M. Bridges, "Foreword: Race in the Roberts Court," *Harvard Law Review* 136, no. 1 (2022): 23, 39.

23. *New York State Rifle & Pistol Association, Inc. v. Bruen,* 597 U.S. ___ (2022).

24. *New York State Rifle & Pistol Association, Inc. v. Bruen,* 597 U.S. ___ (2022).

25. Saul Cornell, "Cherry-Picked History and Ideology-Driven Outcomes: Bruen's Originalist Distortions," *SCOTUSblog,* June 27, 2022, www .scotusblog.com/2022/06/cherry-picked-history-and-ideology-driven -outcomes-bruens-originalist-distortions/.

26. See, e.g., Erwin Chemerinsky, *Worse Than Nothing: The Dangerous Fallacy of Originalism* (New Haven: Yale University Press, 2022), 92–105 (explaining originalism's "abhorrence problem").

27. *United States of America v. (1) Litsson Antonio Perez-Gallan,* No. PE:22-CR-00427-DC, 2022 WL 16858516, at 3 (W.D. Tex. Nov. 10, 2022).

28. See, e.g., Emily J. Sack, "Battered Women and the State: The Struggle for the Future of Domestic Violence Policy," *Wisconsin Law Review* (2004): 1657, 1661.

29. See, e.g., Reva B. Siegel, "'The Rule of Love': Wife Beating as Prerogative and Privacy," *Yale Law Journal* 105 (1996): 2117, 2129.

30. See, e.g., Carolyn B. Ramsey, "Firearms in the Family," *Ohio State Law Journal* 78 (2017): 1257. See also "Statement on Gender Violence and the Prison Industrial Complex (2001)," INCITE! Critical Resistance Statement, https://incite-national.org/incite-critical-resistance -statement/; Deborah Epstein, "Effective Intervention in Domestic Violence Cases: Rethinking the Roles of Prosecutors, Judges, and the Court System," *Yale Journal of Law and Feminism* 11 (1999): 3, 10.

31. *United States of America v. (1) Litsson Antonio Perez-Gallan,* No. PE:22-CR-00427-DC, 2022 WL 16858516, at 6 (W.D. Tex. Nov. 10, 2022).

32. Jacquelyn C. Campbell et al., "Risk Factors for Femicide in Abusive Relationships: Results from a Multisite Case Control Study," *American Journal of Public Health* 93, no. 7 (2003): 1089–1097.

33. *United States v. Rahimi,* 59 F.4th 163 (5th Cir. 2023).

34. United States Court of Appeals for the Fifth Circuit, "About the Court—Brief History," www.ca5.uscourts.gov/about-the-court/circuit -history/brief-history.

35. *Id.*

36. *United States v. Rahimi,* 59 F.4th 163 (5th Cir. 2023).

37. See, e.g., *United States v. McGinnis,* 956 F.3d 747 (5th Cir. 2020).

38. *United States v. Rahimi,* 59 F.4th 163, 176 (5th Cir. 2023).

39. Madiba Dennie, "Originalism Is Going to Get Women Killed," *The Atlantic,* Feb. 9, 2023, www.theatlantic.com/ideas/archive/2023/02/originalism-united-states-v-rahimi-women-domestic-abuse/672993/.

40. *New York State Rifle & Pistol Ass'n, Inc. v. Bruen,* 142 S. Ct. 2111, 2181 (2022) (Breyer, J., dissenting).

41. See, e.g., "The Unwritten Rights Issue," *Washington Post,* Nov. 30, 2022, www.washingtonpost.com/magazine/interactive/2022/unwritten-rights-substantive-due-process/.

42. *Dobbs v. Jackson Women's Health Organization,* 142 S. Ct. 2228 (2022).

43. *Dobbs v. Jackson Women's Health Organization,* 142 S. Ct. 2228, 2301 (2022) (Thomas, J., concurring).

44. See, e.g., Devin Dwyer, "What the Respect for Marriage Act Does and Doesn't Do," ABC News, Dec. 13, 2022, https://abcnews.go.com/Politics/respect-marriage-act-same-sex-interracial-couples/story?id=95181737.

45. See, e.g., "Alliance Defending Freedom," Southern Poverty Law Center, www.splcenter.org/fighting-hate/extremist-files/group/alliance-defending-freedom; *303 Creative LLC v. Elenis,* 600 U.S. __ (2023).

46. *Id.*

47. Brief for 236 Members of Congress as Amici Curiae in Support of Respondents at 12, *Dobbs v. Jackson Women's Health Organization,* 142 S. Ct. 2228 (2022).

48. See, e.g., Kenneth Berman, *Stare Decisis and the Supreme Court's Undoing Project, Litigation,* Fall 2022, at 56, 57.

49. Jeremy C. Young and Jonathan Friedman, "America's Censored Classrooms," PEN America, Aug. 17, 2022, https://pen.org/report/americas-censored-classrooms/.

50. See, e.g., Noah Berlatsky, "An Uncomfortable Truth about GOP Anti-Trans Bigotry," *Public Notice,* June 7, 2023, www.publicnotice.co/p/gop-transphobia-eliminationist-rhetoric-genocide; Jeff McMillan, Kavish Harjai, and Kimberlee Kruesi, "Many Transgender Health Bills Came from a Handful of Far-Right Interest Groups, AP Finds," Associated Press, May 20, 2023, https://apnews.com/article/transgender-health-model-legislation-5cc4a7cb4ab69150f670d06fd0f361ab; Kavish Harjai, Jeff McMillan, and Kimberlee Kruesi, "Transgender Health: Comparing Model Bills to Real Proposals," Associated Press, May 23, 2023, https://apnews.com/article/transgender-health-model-legislation-bills-4eb5e34c72f8a0d91d00158586289ba3; "Mapping Attacks on LGBTQ Rights in U.S. State Legislatures," American Civil

Liberties Union, www.aclu.org/legislative-attacks-on-lgbtq-rights, last updated June 2, 2023.

51. See, e.g., "2023 Anti-Trans Bills Tracker," Trans Legislation Tracker, https://translegislation.com/; *Parents Defending Education v. Linn Mar Community School District* 2022 W1 16908242 (C.A.8), 29.

52. Peter M. Shane, "The Trickle-Down Supreme Court," *Washington Monthly,* Dec. 14, 2022, https://washingtonmonthly.com/2022/12/14/the-trickle-down-supreme-court/.

53. *Dobbs v. Jackson Women's Health Organization,* 142 S. Ct. 2228 (2022).

54. *Kennedy v. Bremerton School District,* 597 U.S. __ (2022).

55. *New York State Rifle & Pistol Association, Inc. v. Bruen,* 597 U.S. __ (2022).

56. *Students for Fair Admissions v. Harvard; Students for Fair Admissions v. University of North Carolina* (2023).

57. See, e.g., Frank B. Cross, "Originalism: The Forgotten Years," *Constitutional Commentary* 28, no. 1 (2012), https://scholarship.law.umn.edu/concomm/347.

58. *Plessy v. Ferguson,* 163 U.S. 537, 551 (1896), overruled by *Brown v. Bd. of Ed. of Topeka, Shawnee Cnty., Kan.,* 347 U.S. 483 (1954).

59. Brief for Appellants in Nos. 1, 2, and 4 and for Respondents in No. 10 on Reargument, *Brown v. Bd. of Educ. of Topeka,* 347 U.S. 483 (1954).

60. *Id.*

61. Brief for Appellants in Nos. 1, 2, and 4 and for Respondents in No. 10 on Reargument at 43, *Brown v. Bd. of Educ. of Topeka,* 347 U.S. 483 (1954).

62. Brief for the State of Kansas on Reargument at 15, *Brown v. Bd. of Educ. of Topeka,* 347 U.S. 483 (1954).

63. Brief for the State of Kansas on Reargument at 48, *Brown v. Bd. of Educ. of Topeka,* 347 U.S. 483 (1954).

64. Supplemental Brief for the United States on Reargument, *Brown v. Bd. of Educ. of Topeka,* 347 U.S. 483 (1954).

65. *Id.*

66. See, e.g., Guyora Binder, "Did the Slaves Author the Thirteenth Amendment? An Essay in Redemptive History," *Yale Journal of Law and the Humanities* 5 (1993): 471, 474 ("Whether constitutional authors should or even can retain authority over the interpretation of their products remains controversial. But as long as consultation of "framers' original intent" remains an important convention in constitutional interpretation, a misattribution of the Thirteenth Amendment dispossesses the slaves of their share of influence over the future meaning given emancipation").

67. See, e.g., Gregory Ablavsky and W. Tanner Allread, "We the (Native) People? How Indigenous Peoples Debated the U.S. Constitution,"

Columbia Law Review 123 (2023): 243, 248. ("Nonetheless, though we know quite a bit about how marginalized groups were talked *about* in the period's constitutional discourse, we know little about what they said; they are presented as objects, not creators, of constitutional ideas. This absence has come to be interpreted as evidence of silence rather than, more accurately, of silencing.")

68. *Brown v. Bd. of Ed. of Topeka, Shawnee Cnty., Kan.,* 347 U.S. 483, 492–93 (1954), supplemented sub nom. *Brown v. Bd. of Educ. of Topeka, Kan.,* 349 U.S. 294 (1955).

69. See, e.g., Barbara J. Flagg, "'And Grace Will Lead Me Home': The Case for Judicial Race Activism," *Alabama Civil Rights and Civil Liberties Law Review* 4 (2013): 103, 126 ("[. . .] the opinion in *Brown v. Board of Education* is written entirely in the language of non-subordination: To separate them from others of similar age and qualifications solely because of their race generates a feeling of inferiority as to their status in the community that may affect their hearts and minds in a way unlikely ever to be undone"). See also Michael J. Klarman, "An Interpretive History of Modern Equal Protection," *Michigan Law Review* 90 (1991): 213, 253. ("To strike down public school segregation in *Brown,* therefore, required the Justices consciously to burst asunder the shackles of original intent.")

70. See, e.g., Andrew Glass, "Southern Manifesto Introduced March 12, 1956," *Politico,* March 12, 2009, www.politico.com/story/2009/03/southern-manifesto-introduced-march-12-1956-019897.

71. See, e.g., Justin Driver, "Supremacies and the Southern Manifesto," *Texas Law Review* 92 (2014): 1053, 1063.

72. See, e.g., Reva B. Siegel, "The History of History and Tradition: The Roots of Dobbs's Method (and Originalism) in the Defense of Segregation," *Yale Law Journal Forum* 133 (2023): 99, 107 (showing "how originalism and *Dobbs*'s history-and-tradition method grew out of resistance to *Brown* and backlash to decisions of the Warren and Burger Courts").

73. For a thorough discussion of legal elites' role in legitimizing racial animus and conservatives' political opposition to *Brown v. Board,* see Calvin TerBeek, "'Clocks Must Always Be Turned Back': Brown v. Board of Education and the Racial Origins of Constitutional Originalism," *American Political Science Review* 115, no. 3 (2021).

74. Robert H. Bork, "Neutral Principles and Some First Amendment Problems," *Indiana Law Journal* 47, no. 1 (1971), www.repository.law.indiana.edu/ilj/vol47/iss1/1.

75. William N. Eskridge, Jr., "Destabilizing Due Process and Evolutive Equal Protection," *UCLA Law Review* 47 (2000): 1183, 1188.

76. Supra note 80 at 17.

77. See, e.g., Edward Walsh and Al Kamen, "Senators Question Bork's

Consistency," *Washington Post,* Sept. 17, 1987, www.washingtonpost
.com/archive/politics/1987/09/17/senators-question-borks-consistency
/219c93e5-a0bd-4ba1-ae6c-d0fbd2a27b54/.

78. *United States v. Valleo,* 596 U.S. __ (2022) (Thomas, J., concurring).
See also Mark Joseph Stern, "Clarence Thomas's Jurisprudence Is Only
Getting More Chaotic," *Slate,* April 22, 2022, https://slate.com/news
-and-politics/2022/04/clarence-thomas-equal-protection-citizenship
-constitutional-rights.html.

79. See Program S0298, *Firing Line* (television program) broadcast
records, Hoover Institution Library and Archives, https://digital
collections.hoover.org/internal/media/dispatcher/82207/full. See also
Mark Joseph Stern, "The Conservative Movement's Favorite Legal
Theory Is Rooted in Racism," *Slate,* April 6, 2021, https://slate.com
/news-and-politics/2021/04/originalism-racist-roots-brown-segregation
.html.

80. Bork, "Neutral Principles."

81. Lewis F. Powell, Jr., "The Memo," *Powell Memorandum: Attack
On American Free Enterprise System,* August 23, 1971, https://
scholarlycommons.law.wlu.edu/powellmemo/1.

82. Fred P. Graham, "Senate Confirms Powell by 89 to 1 for Black's Seat,"
New York Times, Dec. 17, 1971, www.nytimes.com/1971/12/07/archives
/senate-confirms-powell-by-89-to-1-for-blacks-seat-first-southern.html.

83. Attorney General Edwin Meese III, speech before the American Bar
Association, July 9, 1985, https://fedsoc.org/commentary/publications
/the-great-debate-attorney-general-ed-meese-iii-july-9-1985.

84. Edwin Meese III, "The Supreme Court of the United States: Bulwark
of a Limited Constitution," *South Texas Law Review* 27 (1986): 455,
465–66.

85. See, e.g., Paul Baumgardner, "Originalism and the Academy in Exile,"
Law and History Review 37 (2019): 787, 798–804.

86. See, e.g., Michael McCough, "Reagan's Legal Revolution Lives through
Federal Bench Appointments," *Pittsburgh Post-Gazette,* June 8, 2004,
www.post-gazette.com/news/nation/2004/06/08/Reagan-s-legal
-revolution-lives-through-federal-bench-appointments/stories
/200406080141.

87. See, e.g., William J. Haun, "The Philosopher in Action: A Tribute to
the Honorable Edwin Meese III," *Engage,* 2012, https://fedsoc.org
/commentary/publications/the-philosopher-in-action-a-tribute-to-the
-honorable-edwin-meese-iii.

88. See, e.g., Geoffrey Stone and David Strauss, "Book Talk: The Enduring
Constitutional Vision of the Warren Court," American Constitution
Society, Feb. 11, 2020, www.acslaw.org/expertforum/democracy-and
-equality-the-enduring-constitutional-vision-of-the-warren-court-oxford
-university-press-2020/. See also Edwin Meese III, "Putting the Fed-

eral Judiciary Back on the Constitutional Track," *Georgia State University Law Review* 14 (1998): 781, 784–89; Robert Post and Reva Siegel, "Originalism as a Political Practice: The Right's Living Constitution," *Fordham Law Review* 75 (2006): 545, 555.

89. See, e.g., Richard Primus, "Is Theocracy Our Politics?," *Columbia Law Review* 116 (2016): 44, 50. ("Modern originalism arose largely as a critique of landmark twentieth-century decisions, from *Brown* to *Reynolds* to *Miranda* to *Roe,* all of which were said to betray original meanings.") See also Dawn E. Johnsen, "Ronald Reagan and the Rehnquist Court on Congressional Power: Presidential Influences on Constitutional Change," *Indiana Law Review* 78 (2003): 363.

90. See, e.g., Akhil Reed Amar, "The Supreme Court, 1999 Term—Foreword: The Document and the Doctrine," *Harvard Law Review* 114 (2000): 26, 38 ("Twentieth-century judges generally underenforced the document-supported rights of blacks and women while overenforcing various nondocumentarian claims of rich and powerful interests").

91. Nikolas Bowie, "The Contemporary Debate over Supreme Court Reform: Origins and Perspectives," Presidential Commission on the Supreme Court of the United States Testimony, June 30, 2021.

92. See, e.g., Erwin Chemerinsky, *The Case Against the Supreme Court* (New York: Penguin, 2014).

93. See, e.g., Keeangah Yahmatta-Taylor, "The Case for Ending the Supreme Court as We Know It," *The New Yorker,* Sept. 25, 2020, www .newyorker.com/news/our-columnists/the-case-for-ending-the-supreme -court-as-we-know-it.

94. Dawn Johnsen, "Justice Brennan: Legacy of a Champion," *Michigan Law Review* 111 (2013): 1151.

95. See, e.g., Madiba Dennie, "The Justices Have No Robes," Brennan Center, Sept. 14, 2021, www.brennancenter.org/our-work/analysis-opinion /justices-have-no-robes; Michael Waldman, *The Supermajority: How the Supreme Court Divided America* (New York: Simon & Schuster, 2023).

96. See, e.g., Marcia Coyle, " 'Restless and Newly Constituted Court': Sotomayor Scorches Conservative Majority for Narrowing Claims Against Law Enforcement," *National Law Journal,* June 8, 2022, www.law .com/nationallawjournal/2022/06/08/restless-and-newly-constituted -court-sotomayor-scorches-conservative-majority-for-narrowing -claims-against-law-enforcement/.

97. See, e.g., Madiba Dennie, "SCOTUS Rulings Last Term Show What to Look for Next," Brennan Center for Justice, Sept. 28, 2022, www .brennancenter.org/our-work/analysis-opinion/scotus-rulings-last-term -show-what-look-next.

98. U.S. Const. pmbl.

99. U.S. Const. Art. IV, Sec. 4.

100. Declaration of Independence (US 1776).

101. William J. Brennan, Jr., "The Constitution of the United States: Contemporary Ratification," *South Texas Law Review* 27 (1986): 433.

102. Tobin Harshaw, "Kennedy, Bork, and the Politics of Judicial Destruction," *New York Times,* Aug. 28, 2009, https://archive.nytimes.com /opinionator.blogs.nytimes.com/2009/08/28/weekend-opinionator -kennedy-bork-and-the-politics-of-judicial-destruction/.

103. Ilya Shapiro, "The Original Sin of Robert Bork," Cato Institute, Sept. 9, 2020, www.cato.org/commentary/original-sin-robert-bork.

104. Hearing before the United States Senate Committee on the Judiciary, The Nomination of Elena Kagan to be an Associate Justice of the Supreme Court of the United States, June 28–30 and July 1, 2010, www .govinfo.gov/content/pkg/CHRG-111shrg67622/pdf/CHRG-111shrg 67622.pdf.

105. See, e.g., James C. Ho, "Fair-Weather Originalism: Judges, Umpires, and the Fear of Being Booed," *Texas Review of Law and Politics* 26 (2022): 335 (claiming that "being an originalist just means being faithful to whatever text you're interpreting" and that "if you don't like our Constitution, then of course you won't like originalism").

106. Kristin Bialik, "Growing Share of Americans Say Supreme Court Should Base Its Rulings on What the Constitution Means Today," Pew Research Center, May 11, 2018, www.pewresearch.org/fact-tank /2018/05/11/growing-share-of-americans-say-supreme-court-should -base-its-rulings-on-what-constitution-means-today/.

107. See, e.g., Douglas T. Kendall and James E. Ryan, "Liberal Reading: Taking Back the Constitution," *The New Republic,* Aug. 6, 2007 (advocating for progressive originalism and arguing "To win these debates in the next election, liberals are going to have to borrow from Justice Antonin Scalia and the conservative lexicon").

108. See, e.g., Stephen M. Griffin, "Optimistic Originalism and the Reconstruction Amendments," *Tulane Law Review* 95 (2021): 281.

109. See, e.g., Yasmin Dawood, "Election Law Originalism: The Supreme Court's Elitist Conception of Democracy," *St. Louis University Law Journal* 64 (2020): 632. ("Not only does an originalist orientation discount longstanding precedents, it also privileges the first framing over the second framing, thereby further diluting the influence of the Reconstruction Amendments.") See also Jamal Greene, "Fourteenth Amendment Originalism," *Maryland Law Review* 71 (2012): 978, 979.

110. See, e.g., Praveen Fernandes, Elizabeth B. Wydra, and Mark Joseph Stern, "Launching Originalism Watch and Exploring Progressive Originalism," Constitutional Accountability Center, May 25, 2021, www .theusconstitution.org/blog/launching-originalism-watch-and-exploring -progressive-originalism/.

111. *Allen v. Milligan,* ___ (2023); *Shelby County v. Holder,* 570 U.S. 529 (2013).

112. Transcript of Oral Argument at 57–60, 96, *Allen v. Milligan*, ___ (2023).
113. Transcript of Oral Argument at 58, *Merrill v. Milligan*, ___ (2023).
114. See, e.g., Marjorie Cohn, "Ketanji Brown Jackson Cleverly Turned the Right's Own Judicial Theory Against It," *truthout*, Oct. 17, 2022, https://truthout.org/articles/ketanji-brown-jackson-cleverly-turned -the-rights-own-judicial-theory-against-it/.
115. See, e.g, Transcript of Oral Argument at 64–68, 172–74, *Students for Fair Admissions v. University of North Carolina*, ___ (2023).
116. Cristian Farias, "'Originalism Is Intellectually Indefensible': Eric Foner on the Enduring Myth of the Colorblind Constitution," *Balls and Strikes*, Oct. 28, 2022, https://ballsandstrikes.org/qa/eric-foner -originalism-colorblind-constitution-myth/.
117. See, e.g., Dale Ho, "Dodging a Bullet: McDonald v. City of Chicago and the Limits of Progressive Originalism," *William and Mary Bill of Rights Journal* 19 (2010): 369. ("Although the Fourteenth Amendment is undoubtedly radically egalitarian in spirit, there can be little doubt that the range of substantive protections that it was originally under-stood to afford is more limited than what is protected under current Supreme Court precedent.")
118. "Equal Rights Under the Law, What's Wrong With That?," League of Women Voters, Oct. 28, 2020, www.lwv.org/blog/equal-rights-under -law-whats-wrong.
119. *Bradwell v. State of Illinois*, 83 U.S. 130 (1873).
120. *Bradwell v. State of Illinois*, 83 U.S. 130, 141 (1873).
121. *Reed v. Reed*, 404 U.S. 71 (1971).
122. Lenora M. Lapidus, "The Constitution Protects Women Despite Jus-tice Scalia's Views," American Civil Liberties Union, Jan. 6, 2011, www .aclu.org/news/smart-justice/constitution-protects-women-despite -justice-scalias-views.
123. John Yoo, "Does the Constitution Protect Against Sex Discrimina-tion?," American Enterprise Institute, Jan. 5, 2011, www.aei.org/articles /does-the-constitution-protect-against-sex-discrimination/.
124. Jamal Greene, "How Constitutional Theory Matters," *Ohio State Law Journal* 72 (2011): 1183, 1194.
125. See, e.g., Eric J. Segall, *Originalism as Faith* (Cambridge: Cambridge University Press, 2018), 122–40.
126. Richard L. Hasen, "Antonin Scalia's Disruption of the Supreme Court's Ways Is Here to Stay," *Washington Post*, Feb. 13, 2018, www .washingtonpost.com/news/posteverything/wp/2018/02/13/antonin -scalias-disruption-of-the-supreme-courts-ways-is-here-to-stay/.
127. Doug Kendall and Jim Ryan, "Originalist Sins: The Faux Originalism of Justice Clarence Thomas," *Slate*, Aug. 1, 2007, https://slate.com/news

-and-politics/2007/08/the-faux-originalism-of-justice-clarence-thomas
.html.

128. Reva B. Siegel, "How 'History and Tradition' Perpetuates Inequality:
Dobbs on Abortion's Nineteenth-Century Criminalization," *Houston
Law Review* 60 (2023): 901.

129. Robert Post and Reva Siegel, "Originalism as a Political Practice: The
Right's Living Constitution," *Fordham Law Review* 75 (2006): 545.

130. Mary Wood, "Scalia Defends Originalism as Best Methodology for
Judging Law," University of Virginia School of Law, April 20, 2010,
www.law.virginia.edu/news/201004/scalia-defends-originalism-best
-methodology-judging-law.

131. See, e.g., Lawrence B. Solum, "Originalism Versus Living Constitutionalism: The Conceptual Structure of the Great Debate," *Northwestern
University Law Review* 113 (2019): 1243, 1246.

132. See, e.g., Ethan J. Leib, "The Perpetual Anxiety of Living Constitutionalism," *Constitutional Commentary* 24 (2007): 353, 354–55.

133. Keith E. Whittington, "Originalism: A Critical Introduction," *Fordham
Law Review* 82 (2013): 375, 389.

134. Siegel, "How 'History and Tradition' Perpetuates Inequality," 901, 909.
("Most originalists are unconcerned about this methodological bias—
uncritical of the democratic deficits of the Founders' Constitution and
of the ways in which their own interpretive method in turn exacerbates
those deficits.")

135. James W. Fox, Jr., "Counterpublic Originalism and the Exclusionary
Critique," *Alabama Law Review* 67 (2016): 675, 685.

136. See, e.g., James E. Fleming, "Fidelity to Our Living Constitution," *Tulsa
Law Review* 50 (2015): 449.

137. Thurgood Marshall, "The Constitution's Bicentennial: Commemorating the Wrong Document?," *Vanderbilt Law Review* 40 (1987):
1337.

138. See, e.g., Douglas NeJaime, "Constitutional Change, Courts, and Social
Movements," *Michigan Law Review* 111 (2013): 877; J. M. Balkin and
Sanford Levinson, "The Canons of Constitutional Law," *Harvard Law
Review* 111, no. 4 (1998): 963.

139. Reva B. Siegel, "Text in Contest: Gender and the Constitution from a
Social Movement Perspective," *University of Pennsylvania Law Review* 150 (2001): 297, 344. See also Robert C. Post, "Foreword: Fash-
ioning the Legal Constitution: Culture, Courts, and Law," *Harvard
Law Review* 117 (2003): 4, 41 ("[. . .] as a matter of history and structure constitutional interpretation is possible only because the Court
engages in a continuous dialogue with the constitutional beliefs and values of nonjudicial actors").

140. William N. Eskridge, Jr., "Channeling: Identity-Based Social Move-

ments and Public Law," *University of Pennsylvania Law Review* 150 (2001): 419.

141. Charles A. Reich, "Mr. Justice Black and the Living Constitution," *Harvard Law Review* 76, no. 4 (1963): 735–36.

142. William H. Rehnquist, "The Notion of a Living Constitution," *Texas Law Review* 54 (1976): 693, 698.

143. Nikolas Bowie, "How the Supreme Court Dominates Our Democracy," *Washington Post,* July 16, 2021, www.washingtonpost.com/outlook /2021/07/16/supreme-court-anti-democracy/.

144. Ryan D. Doerfler and Samuel Moyn, "Democratizing the Supreme Court," *California Law Review* 109 (2021): 1703.

145. Corinna Barrett Lain, "Upside-Down Judicial Review," *Georgetown Law Journal* 101 (2012): 113, 116. See also Miriam Seifter, "Countermajoritarian Legislatures," *Columbia Law Review* 121 (2021): 1733, 1734–35. (Observing that the pervasive rhetoric about state legislatures as "the heart of American democracy" is divorced from reality as "state legislatures are typically a state's least majoritarian branch. Often they are outright countermajoritarian institutions.")

146. Madiba Dennie, "Is Court Reform Possible," *Dame,* June 2, 2022, www .damemagazine.com/2022/06/02/is-court-reform-possible/.

147. Joseph Fishkin and William E. Forbath, "How Liberals Should Confront a Right-Wing Supreme Court," *New York Times,* Oct. 17, 2022, www.nytimes.com/2022/10/17/opinion/liberals-supreme-court -constitution.html.

148. Reva B. Siegel, "Memory Games: Dobbs's Originalism as Anti-Democratic Living Constitutionalism—and Some Pathways for Resistance," Aug. 9, 2022.

149. Chemerinsky, *Worse Than Nothing,* 139.

150. Chemerinsky, *Worse Than Nothing.*

151. *Dobbs v. Jackson Women's Health Organization,* 597 U.S. __, (2022).

152. See, e.g., Paul Finkelman, "Frederick Douglass's Constitution: From Garrisonian Abolitionist to Lincoln Republican," *Missouri Law Review* 81 (2016).

153. John Stauffer, *The Black Hearts of Men: Radical Abolitionists and the Transformation of Race* (Cambridge: Harvard University Press, 2002), 164–66.

154. Frederick Douglass, "The Constitution of the United States: Is It Pro-Slavery or Anti-Slavery?," speech delivered in Glasgow, Scotland, on March 26, 1860, reprinted in Philip S. Foner and Yuval Taylor, eds., *Frederick Douglass: Selected Speeches and Writings* (Chicago: Chicago Review Press, 2000). See also Paul Gowder, "Law for Black Radical Liberation," *Boston Review,* June 13, 2022, www.bostonreview.net /articles/law-for-black-radical-liberation/.

155. See, e.g., Madiba Dennie, "The Big Changes Justice Ketanji Brown

Jackson's Presence Could Bring to the Supreme Court," ABC News, Feb. 28, 2022, www.nbcnews.com/think/opinion/ketanji-brown -jackson-only-one-black-woman-her-presence-key-ncna1290096.

156. Madiba Dennie, "The Supreme Court Can't Be Allowed to Have the Last Word on the Fourteenth Amendment," *The New Republic,* Nov. 2, 2022, https://newrepublic.com/article/168447/14th-amendment -inclusive-supreme-court.

157. Kurt T. Lash, ed., *The Reconstruction Amendments: The Essential Documents, Volume 1* (Chicago: University of Chicago Press, 2021), 225.

158. See, e.g., Dorothy E. Roberts, "Foreword: Abolition Constitutionalism," *Harvard Law Review* 133 (2019): 1, 50 ("After the Reconstruction Amendments were enacted, legal historians largely neglected the role that abolitionists played in the constitutional transformation. It is safe to say that the views of the white supremacists who gutted the Thirteenth and Fourteenth Amendments have gained greater prominence than have the views of the slavery abolitionists who inspired the constitutional amendments and of the Radical Republicans who drafted them."); Rebecca E. Zietlow, "The Ideological Origins of the Thirteenth Amendment," *Houston Law Review* 49 (2012): 393, 398 ("These members of the Reconstruction Congress did not amend the Constitution in a vacuum. In debates over the Amendments and the implementing legislation, they invoked the antislavery constitutionalist beliefs that had inspired them and propelled them into office."); David A. J. Richards, *Conscience and the Constitution: History, Theory, and Law of the Reconstruction Amendments* (Princeton: Princeton University Press, 1993); Manisha Sinha, *The Slave's Cause: A History of Abolition* (New Haven: Yale University Press, 2016).

159. *Id.*

160. See, e.g., Brandon Hasbrouck, "Movement Constitutionalism," *Oklahoma Law Review* 75 (2022): 89, 105 (". . . movement constitutionalism requires judges to recognize how the law sustains oppressive institutions grounded in white supremacy and to center the goal of dismantling these systems in their jurisprudence").

161. See, e.g., Malinda L. Seymore, "The Presidency and the Meaning of Citizenship," *Brigham Young University Law Review* (2005): 927 (criticizing the Natural-Born Citizen Clause for wrongfully perpetuating second-class citizenship in the United States and calling for a constitutional amendment).

162. Gabriel Chin, "Why Senator John McCain Cannot be President: Eleven Months and a Hundred Yards Short of Citizenship," *Michigan Law Review First Impressions* 107, no. 1 (2008).

163. 81 Cong. Rec. 7769 (1937).

164. Supra note 176.

165. S. Res. 511, 110th Cong. (2008).

166. Supra note 176 at 15.

167. Adam Liptak, "A Hint of New Life to a McCain Birth Issue," *New York Times,* July 11, 2008, www.nytimes.com/2008/07/11/us/politics /11mccain.html.

168. See, e.g., Andrew Kaczynski, "John McCain: 'I Don't Know' If Cruz Is Eligible for Presidency with Canadian Birth," *Buzzfeed News,* Jan. 6, 2016, www.buzzfeednews.com/article/andrewkaczynski/john-mccain -i-dont-know-if-cruz-is-eligible-for-presidency-w#.krWPEx2P7. (McCain himself distinguished the characteristics of his birth from Cruz's, clarifying that being born on a military base is "different from being born on foreign soil [. . .] I am not a constitutional scholar on that, but I think it's worth looking into.")

169. See, e.g., Christopher W. Schmidt and Matthew T. Bodie, "The Natural-Born Citizen Clause, Popular Constitutionalism, and Ted Cruz's Eligibility Question," *George Washington Law Review Arguendo* 84 (2016): 36, 39.

170. Liz Mineo, "A Question of Citizenship—Legal Scholars Debate Cruz's Eligibility to Serve as President," *The Harvard Gazette,* Feb. 5, 2016, https://news.harvard.edu/gazette/story/2016/02/a-question-of -citizenship/.

171. Eric Posner, "Ted Cruz Is Not Eligible to Be President," *Slate,* Feb. 8, 2016, https://slate.com/news-and-politics/2016/02/trump-is-right-ted -cruz-is-not-eligible-to-be-president.html.

172. Laurence H. Tribe, "Under Ted Cruz's Own Logic, He's Ineligible for the White House," *Boston Globe,* Jan. 11, 2016, www.bostonglobe.com /opinion/2016/01/11/through-ted-cruz-constitutional-looking-glass /zvKE6qpF31q2RsvPO9nGoK/story.html.

173. Mary Brigid McManamon, "Ted Cruz Is Not Eligible to Be President," *Washington Post,* Jan. 12, 2016, www.washingtonpost.com/opinions /ted-cruz-is-not-eligible-to-be-president/2016/01/12/1484a7d0-b7af -11e5-99f3-184bc379b12d_story.html.

174. *United States v. Carolene Products Co.,* 304 U.S. 144, 145–46 (1938).

175. *United States v. Carolene Products Co.,* 304 U.S. 144, 152–53 n.4 (1938).

176. John Hart Ely, *Democracy and Distrust: A Theory of Judicial Review* (Cambridge: Harvard University Press, 1980).

177. See, e.g., Michael C. Dorf, "*Dobbs* Double-Cross: How Justice Alito Misused Pro-Choice Scholars' Work," *Verdict,* July 6, 2022, https:// verdict.justia.com/2022/07/06/dobbs-double-cross-how-justice-alito -misused-pro-choice-scholars-work. See also Lincoln Caplan, "Ruth Bader Ginsburg and Footnote Four," *The New Yorker,* Sept. 13, 2013, www.newyorker.com/news/news-desk/ruth-bader-ginsburg-and -footnote-four.

178. Nicholas O. Stephanopoulos, "The Anti-Carolene Court," *Supreme Court Review* (2019): 111, 116.
179. *Id.*
180. Ely, *Democracy and Distrust.*
181. Ely, *Democracy and Distrust.*
182. Jamelle Bouie, "It Is a Well-Known Truth that Opponents of Democracy Don't Want You to Have Nice Things," *New York Times,* Sept. 13, 2022, www.nytimes.com/2022/09/13/opinion/democracy-inequality -united-states.html.
183. "Order re Privilege of Documents Dated January 4–7, 2021," *John C. Eastman v. Bennie G. Thompson, Select Committee to Investigate the January 6 Attack on the U.S. Capitol, and Chapman University,* March 28, 2022, https://s3.documentcloud.org/documents/21561099 /3-28-22-order-eastman.pdf.
184. See, e.g., "Justice Alito Discusses Faith and Originalism at TAC Town Hall," Thomas Aquinas College, Nov. 9, 2021, www.thomasaquinas .edu/news/justice-alito-discusses-faith-originalism-tac-town-hall.

Chapter 2: Stealing Our Liberties

1. Andy Kroll, Andrea Bernstein, and Ilya Marritz, "We Don't Talk About Leonard: The Man Behind the Right's Supreme Court Supermajority," *ProPublica,* Oct. 11, 2023, www.propublica.org/article/we-dont-talk -about-leonard-leo-supreme-court-supermajority.
2. Charles Sumner, "No Compromise of Human Rights: No Admission in the Constitution of Inequality of Rights, or Disfranchisement on Account of Color," speech of Hon. Charles Sumner, of Massachusetts, on the proposed amendment of the Constitution fixing the basis of representation delivered in the Senate of the United States, March 7, 1866, Washington, D.C., Congressional Globe Office, 1866.
3. *Stanley v. Illinois,* 405 U.S. 645, 649 (1972).
4. *Meyer v. Nebraska,* 262 U.S. 390 (1923).
5. See, e.g., Erwin Chemerinsky, "Substantive Due Process," *Touro Law Review* 15 (1999): 1501.
6. *Daniels v. Williams,* 474 U.S. 327, 331–32 (1986) (internal citations omitted).
7. *Lawrence v. Texas,* 539 U.S. 558, 579 (2003).
8. See, e.g., Douglas NeJaime and Reva Siegel, "Answering the Lochner Objection: Substantive Due Process and the Role of Courts in a Democracy," *New York University Law Review* 96 (2021): 1902, 1908–22.
9. *Timbs v. Indiana,* 139 S. Ct. 682, 692 (2019) (Thomas, J., concurring).
10. Bork, *Tempting of America,* 31.

11. Ely, *Democracy and Distrust,* 18. But see, e.g., B. Jessie Hill, "Big, Bad Roe," *ConLawNOW* 14 (2023): 65, 69–70. ("This sort of breezy seventies-vintage male chauvinism permeates Ely's essay: he describes abortion bans as 'cramp[ing] the life style of an unwilling mother,' and then later labels forced pregnancy and childbirth an 'inconvenience' and an 'annoyance.' To say that Ely fails to grasp what is at stake for people who are forced to carry an unwanted pregnancy to term hardly captures the deep ignorance underlying these passages, not to mention the casual sexism of Ely's language."); Aliza Forman-Rabinovici and Olatunde C. A. Johnson, "Political Equality, Gender, and Democratic Legitimation in Dobbs," *Harvard Journal of Law and Gender* 46 (2023): 81, 85 (problematizing *Dobbs*'s invocation of women's political equality to legitimize its ruling).

12. Jamal Greene, "The Meming of Substantive Due Process," *Constitutional Commentary* 31 (2016): 253, 277.

13. Peter Irons, *A People's History of the Supreme Court: The Men and Women Whose Cases and Decisions Have Shaped Our Constitution,* rev. ed. (New York: Penguin, 2006), 319.

14. *Lochner v. New York,* 198 U.S. 45 (1905). See also Act of May 13, 1897, art. 8, ch. 415, § 110.

15. See, e.g., Paul Kens, "Lochner v. New York: Tradition or Change in Constitutional Law?," *NYU Journal of Law and Liberty* 1, no. 1 (2020).

16. *Lochner v. New York,* 198 U.S. 45, 52–53 (1905).

17. See, e.g., Victoria F. Nourse, "A Tale of Two Lochners: The Untold History of Substantive Due Process and the Idea of Fundamental Rights," *California Law Review* 97 (2009): 751, 792–93.

18. *Lochner v. New York,* 198 U.S. 45, 75 (1905) (Holmes, J., dissenting).

19. *Id.*

20. On the shocking worker conditions, as well as a different history of *Lochner* that interrogates the seemingly noble motivations of the dissenters, see, e.g., David E. Bernstein, "Lochner v. New York: A Centennial Retrospective," *Washington University Law Quarterly* 83 (2005): 1469. See also Paul Kens, "Lochner v. New York," 404.

21. See, e.g., Rebecca L. Brown, "The Art of Reading Lochner," *New York University Journal of Law and Liberty* 1 (2005): 570. See also David A. Strauss, "Why Was Lochner Wrong?," *University of Chicago Law Review* 70 (2003): 373, 374 ("The striking thing about the disapproval of Lochner, though, is that there is no consensus on why it is wrong"); Jamal Greene, "The Anticanon," *Harvard Law Review* 125 (2011): 379.

22. I use the qualifier "most" because Chief Justice Roberts, Justice Thomas, and a handful of others have claimed that *Dred Scott* was the Court's first use of substantive due process—an accusation that Professor Jamal Greene had previously described as "better rhetoric than it is

legal history." See, e.g., *Obergefell v. Hodges,* 576 U.S. 644, 695–96
(2015) (Roberts, J., dissenting); Jamal Greene, "Meming," 253, 271. See
also Hon. Jon O. Newman, "The Birth, Deaths, and Reincarnations of
Substantive Due Process," *University of Hawai'i Law Review* 41
(2018): 1, 4; Hon. J. Harvie Wilkinson III et al., "Showcase Panel IV: An
Examination of Substantive Due Process and Judicial Activism," *Texas
Review of Law and Politics* 17 (2013): 315, 338. Further, while some
scholars argue that substantive due process arose well before *Lochner,*
others contend that it arose well after. Professor Victoria Nourse argues
that the notion of substantive due process as discussed in modern cases
about reproductive rights is traceable to the country's World War II–
era fight against fascism and did not yet exist when *Lochner* was decided. Victoria F. Nourse, "A Tale of Two Lochners: The Untold History
of Substantive Due Process and the Idea of Fundamental Rights," *California Law Review* 97 (2009): 751.

23. Nourse, "A Tale of Two Lochners," 751, 797. (Grounding strong individual rights in the World War II Era rather than the *Lochner* Era and observing "To the charge that substantive due process was a 'momentous
sham,' no one replied that the historical premise of the argument was
incorrect. No one led the battle to reclaim the memories of the greatest
generation, which used the Due Process Clause to make rights of
speech and religion strong against fears of fascism, rights that vast majorities now support. And because no one led that battle, a false history
was left intact to be revived at the end of the century.")

24. NeJaime and Siegel, "Answering the Lochner Objection," 1902, 1939
n. 187.

25. Washington Secretary of State, Legacy Washington, "Elsie Parrish:
Working Class Shero," Ahead of the Curve Profiles, https://www2.sos
.wa.gov/_assets/legacy/aotc/elsie-parrish.pdf.

26. *W. Coast Hotel Co. v. Parrish,* 300 U.S. 379 (1937).

27. *Id.* at 391.

28. *Id.* at 398–99.

29. *W. Coast Hotel Co. v. Parrish,* 300 U.S. 379, 403 (1937) (Sutherland, J.,
dissenting).

30. G. Edward White, "West Coast Hotel's Place in American Constitutional History," *Yale Law Journal Online* 122 (2012): 69, http://
yalelawjournal.org/forum/west-coast-hotels-place-in-american
-constitutional-history.

31. *Wolf v. People of the State of Colo.,* 338 U.S. 25, 27 (1949), overruled
on other grounds by *Mapp v. Ohio,* 367 U.S. 643 (1961).

32. *Poe v. Ullman,* 367 U.S. 497 (1961); *Griswold v. Connecticut,* 381 U.S.
479 (1965); *Eisenstadt v. Baird,* 405 U.S. 438 (1972).

33. *Poe v. Ullman,* 367 U.S. 497, 498–501 (1961).

34. Dudziak, "Just Say No."

35. Brief for Appellants at 19, *Poe v. Ullman,* 367 U.S. 497 (1961).
36. *Id.* at 507–8.
37. *Poe v. Ullman,* 367 U.S. 497, 541 (1961) (Harlan, J., dissenting).
38. *Poe v. Ullman,* 367 U.S. 497, 543 (1961) (Harlan, J., dissenting).
39. Susan C. Wawrose, *Griswold v. Connecticut: Contraception and the Right of Privacy* (New York: Franklin-Watts, 1996), 10; Dudziak, "Just Say No."
40. *Griswold v. Connecticut,* 381 U.S. 479, 482 (1965).
41. *Id.*
42. *Griswold v. Connecticut,* 381 U.S. 479, 484 (1965).
43. *Griswold v. Connecticut,* 381 U.S. 479, 500 (1965) (Harlan, J., concurring).
44. *Griswold v. Connecticut,* 381 U.S. 479, 502–3 (1965) (White, J., concurring).
45. *Griswold v. Connecticut,* 381 U.S. 479, 522 (1965) (Black, J., dissenting).
46. *Griswold v. Connecticut,* 381 U.S. 479, 527 (1965) (Stewart, J., dissenting).
47. *Griswold v. Connecticut,* 381 U.S. 479, 511 (1965) (Black, J., dissenting).
48. *Griswold v. Connecticut,* 381 U.S. 479, 501 (1965) (Harlan, J., concurring).
49. *Griswold v. Connecticut,* 381 U.S. 479, 493 (1965) (internal citations omitted) (Goldberg, J., concurring).
50. *Loving v. Virginia,* 388 U.S. 1 (1967).
51. *Id.* at 3.
52. Brief for Appellee at 5–7, 10–18, *Loving v. Virginia,* 388 U.S. 1 (1967).
53. Brief of the State of North Carolina as Amicus Curiae at 5, *Loving v. Virginia,* 388 U.S. 1 (1967).
54. Brief for Appellants at 29, *Loving v. Virginia,* 388 U.S. 1 (1967).
55. *Id.* at 9–10, 17–22, 27.
56. *Id.* at 15–28.
57. *Id.* at 27–28.
58. *Id.* at 10, 31–32.
59. *Id.* at 38–39.
60. *Loving v. Virginia,* 388 U.S. 1, 9 (1967), quoting *Brown v. Board of Education,* 347 U.S. 483, 489 (1954).
61. *Loving v. Virginia,* 388 U.S. 1, 11 (1967).
62. *Id.* at 12.
63. See, e.g., Dorothy E. Roberts, "Loving v. Virginia as a Civil Rights Decision," *New York Law School Law Review* 59 (2014–2015): 203 (discussing how the judiciary has ignored the real lessons of *Loving* and its civil rights aims) ("Rather than link invidious racial classifications to political subordination as the *Loving* Court did, subsequent Court opinions have wrongly relied on *Loving* to do just the opposite. *Loving* has

been misused to support a colorblind approach to the Fourteenth Amendment that treats the government's use of race to eliminate the contemporary vestiges of Jim Crow as equally contemptible as the Jim Crow classifications designed to enforce white rule."). See also James E. Fleming, *Constructing Basic Liberties: A Defense of Substantive Due Process* (Chicago: University of Chicago Press, 2022) (describing the role of substantive due process in protecting both liberty and equality).

64. Steven G. Calabresi and Andrea Matthews, "Originalism and Loving v. Virginia," *Brigham Young University Law Review* (2012): 1393, 1426.

65. *Eisenstadt v. Baird,* 405 U.S. 438, 453 (1972).

66. *Roe v. Wade,* 410 U.S. 113 (1973).

67. *Hardwick v. Bowers,* 760 F.2d 1202 (11th Cir. 1985).

68. *Bowers v. Hardwick,* 478 U.S. 186, 190 (1986).

69. *Id.* at 191–92.

70. *Bowers v. Hardwick,* 478 U.S. 186, 197 (Burger, J., concurring).

71. *Bowers v. Hardwick,* 478 U.S. 186, 199 (Blackmun, J., dissenting) (quoting Justice Holmes).

72. *Michael H. v. Gerald D.,* 491 U.S. 110 (1989).

73. *Michael H. v. Gerald D.,* 491 U.S. 110, 125 (1989).

74. *Michael H. v. Gerald D.,* 491 U.S. 110, 123 n. 2 (1989).

75. See, e.g., Darren Lenard Hutchinson, "Thinly Rooted: Dobbs, Tradition, and Reproductive Justice," *Arizona Law Review* 65 (2023): 385, 395 (discussing *Dobbs*'s erroneous reliance on theory embraced by only two Justices in *Glucksberg*).

76. Howard Schweber, "Seven Days in June: The U.S. Supreme Court and a Constitutional Counterrevolution," *Wisconsin Law,* February 2023, 26, 29.

77. Fleming, *Constructing Basic Liberties,* 31.

78. *Washington v. Glucksberg,* 521 U.S. 702, 720–21 (1997) (internal citations and quotation marks omitted).

79. *Id.* at 722–23 (1997).

80. Supra notes 345–80.

81. See, e.g., Brief for Petitioners at 11–16, 32–40, *Lawrence v. Texas,* 539 U.S. 558.

82. Brief for Respondent at 13, 24–25, *Lawrence v. Texas,* 539 U.S. 558.

83. *Lawrence v. Texas,* 539 U.S. 558, 572 (2003) (quoting *County of Sacramento v. Lewis,* 523 U.S. 833, 857 (1998) (Kennedy, J., concurring)).

84. *Lawrence v. Texas,* 539 U.S. 558, 571 (2003).

85. *Id.* at 572.

86. *Id.* at 578–79.

87. *Obergefell v. Hodges,* 576 U.S. 644, 664 (2015).

88. *Id.* at 681.

89. See, e.g., Kenji Yoshino, "A New Birth of Freedom?: Obergefell v. Hodges," *Harvard Law Review* 129 (2015): 147; William N. Eskridge,

Jr., "The Marriage Equality Cases and Constitutional Theory," *Cato Supreme Court Review* (2015): 111; Peter Nicolas, "Fundamental Rights in a Post-Obergefell World," *Yale Journal of Law and Feminism* 27 (2016): 331.

90. See, e.g., Jack B. Harrison, "At Long Last Marriage," *American University Journal of Gender, Social Policy, and the Law* 24 (2015): 1, 57 ("*Obergefell* leaves gay and lesbian persons in the rather odd position of having their marriage legally protected in every state in the union and at the federal level, while at the same time being denied protections from discrimination in employment, housing, and public accommodations at both the federal level and in the twenty-nine states that do not have statewide protections based on sexual orientation or gender identity"). See also Katherine Franke, *Wedlocked: The Perils of Marriage Equality* (New York: NYU Press, 2015) (discussing the paradox experienced by emancipated slaves where "being *freed* was not the same thing as being *free*" in relation to the benefits and burdens of marriage equality and how they affect queer Americans' fight for full citizenship).

91. See, e.g., Laurence H. Tribe, "Equal Dignity: Speaking Its Name," *Harvard Law Review Forum* 129 (2015): 16, 28 (arguing that *Obergefell* teaches "that the deeper purposes of neither equal protection nor due process could be satisfied if only *negative* liberty—the liberty 'to engage in intimate association without criminal liability'—was entitled to constitutional protection"); *Juliana v. United States,* 217 F. Supp. 3d 1224, 1250 (D. Or. 2016), *rev'd and remanded,* 947 F.3d 1159 (9th Cir. 2020) (invoking *Obergefell* in finding that plaintiffs adequately alleged a violation of their fundamental right to a climate system capable of sustaining human life—a necessary condition to exercising all other rights); Ben A. McJunkin, "The Negative Right to Shelter," *California Law Review* 111 (2023): 127, 181–92 (invoking *Obergefell* in its argument for recognizing an essential right to shelter oneself without government interference); Robert J. Smith and Zoë Robinson, "Constitutional Liberty and the Progression of Punishment," *Cornell Law Review* 102 (2017): 413, 479 ("When executing people with marked functional impairments or the demonstrated capacity to change becomes the rule, not the exception, an *Obergefell*-esque concern over equal dignity emerges to cast further doubt on the retributive necessity of the capital punishment enterprise as a whole").

92. See, e.g., *Obergefell v. Hodges,* 576 U.S. 644, 687 (2015) (Roberts, J., dissenting) ("Five lawyers have closed the debate and enacted their own vision of marriage as a matter of constitutional law. [. . .] The majority's decision is an act of will, not legal judgment. [. . .] Just who do we think we are?").

93. See, e.g., Darren Lenard Hutchinson, "Undignified: The Supreme Court, Racial Justice, and Dignity Claims," *Florida Law Review* 69

(2017): 1, 53–54 ("The Supreme Court did not decree a right to same-sex marriage rooted in dignity on its own. Instead, the *Obergefell* decision follows decades of social-movement advocacy, legislative and judicial recognition of same-sex marriage in states, presidential policy, international advocacy and support, changes in ideological composition of the federal government, new appointments to the Supreme Court and other federal courts, protection of LGBT rights outside of the marital context in state and federal law, and increasingly favorable public opinion. Some media accounts of *Obergefell* dismiss the substantial social movement work that led to the ruling by claiming that same-sex marriage was achieved rapidly. Marriage equality was not achieved quickly or through a single governmental institution. It was attained after years of multidimensional advocacy and litigation."); Glen Staszewski, "Obergefell and Democracy," *Boston University Law Review* 97 (2017): 31, 63. ("The fact that this claim went from seemingly inconceivable to seemingly inevitable in less than half a century is undoubtedly a testament to the courageous efforts of countless LGBT individuals and couples and the work of the social movements that advocated on their behalf. It is also a testament to the power of reasoned deliberation and the importance of provisionality in a deliberative democracy. [. . .] While this debate was not always conducted in a manner that accords with ideal deliberative theory, and while political opposition and backlash meant that progress was gradual, intermittent, and halting, there can be no doubt that it produced profound social, cultural, and legal change."); Tribe, "Equal Dignity," 16, 23. ("Justice Kennedy's rhetoric of equal dignity, particularly in his series of gay-rights decisions, has always been fundamentally rooted in the importance of fostering dialogue among ordinary citizens and, in a sense, even among the very clauses of the Constitution itself.")

94. Like Justices Breyer, Sotomayor, and Kagan cowrote in dissent after surveying the breadth of the opinion's implications: "Anyway, today's decision, taken on its own, is catastrophic enough." *Dobbs v. Jackson Women's Health Organization,* 142 S. Ct. 2228, 2333 (2022) (J. Breyer, Sotomayor, Kagan, dissenting).

95. *Dobbs v. Jackson Women's Health Organization,* 142 S. Ct. 2228, 2246–47 (2022).

96. *Id.*

97. U.S. Const. Amend. IX.

98. Mitchell Gordon, "Getting to the Bottom of the Ninth: Continuity, Discontinuity, and the Rights Retained by the People," *Indiana Law Review* 50 (2017): 421, 423.

99. *Id.*

100. Brief of Equal Protection Constitutional Law Scholars Serena Mayeri, Melissa Murray, and Reva Siegel as Amici Curiae in Support of Respon-

dents, *Dobbs v. Jackson Women's Health Organization,* 142 S. Ct. 2228 (2022).

101. *Dobbs v. Jackson Women's Health Organization,* 142 S. Ct. 2228, 2246 (2022); *Bray v. Alexandria Women's Health Clinic,* 506 U.S. 263, 273–74 (1993).

102. *Dobbs v. Jackson Women's Health Organization,* 142 S. Ct. 2228, 2245 (2022).

103. *Roe v. Wade,* 410 U.S. 113 (1973); *Planned Parenthood of Se. Pa. v. Casey,* 505 U.S. 833 (1992).

104. *Dobbs v. Jackson Women's Health Organization,* 142 S. Ct. 2228, 2247 (2022).

105. *Id.* at 2242.

106. *Id.* at 2248–2256.

107. *Id.* at 2266–2267, 2272, 2283.

108. *Dobbs v. Jackson Women's Health Organization,* 142 S. Ct. 2228, 2257 (2022).

109. See, e.g., Michele Goodwin, "Distorting the Reconstruction: A Reflection on Dobbs," *Yale Journal of Law and Feminism* 34 (2023): 30; Dorothy E. Roberts, *Killing the Black Body: Race, Reproduction, and the Meaning of Liberty* (New York: Pantheon, 1997), 22–55; Adrienne Davis, "Don't Let Nobody Bother Yo' Principle: The Sexual Economy of American Slavery," in *Sister Circle: Black Women and Work,* ed. Sharon Harley and the Black Women and Work Collective (New Brunswick: Rutgers University Press, 2002), 103–21. See also Federal Writers' Project, *Slave Narratives: A Folk History of Slavery in the United States from Interviews with Former Slaves,* Slave Narrative Project, Vol. 7, Kentucky (Washington, D.C., 1941), www.loc.gov/item/mesn070/. (For instance, a formerly enslaved woman named Mrs. Amelia Jones described the standard practice of a particular slaveowner when separating families: "The day he was to sell the children from their mother he would tell that mother to go to some other place to do some work and in her absence he would sell the children. It was the same when he would sell a man's wife, he also sent him to another job and when he returned his wife would be gone. The master only said 'don't worry you can get another one.'")

110. Emily West and Sian David, "Hidden Voices: Enslaved Women in the Lowcountry and U.S. South—Reproduction and Resistance," Lowcountry Digital History Initiative, https://ldhi.library.cofc.edu/exhibits/show/hidden-voices/resisting-enslavement/reproduction-and-resistance.

111. See, e.g., Pamela D. Bridgewater, "Un/Re/Dis Covering Slave Breeding in Thirteenth Amendment Jurisprudence," *Washington and Lee Race and Ethnic Ancestry Law Journal* 7 (2001): 11, https://scholarlycommons.law.wlu.edu/crsj/vol7/iss1/4.

112. See, e.g., Goodwin, "Distorting the Reconstruction," 30, 34–35. ("Even if the Court's purported methodology—to derive contemporary meaning from history and traditions deeply rooted in the Constitution—was a morally and ethically sustainable approach to judicial review, it fails on its own accord. Instead, the Court siphons race and sex from Reconstruction and the Reconstruction Amendments. [. . .] Despite the Court's claims otherwise, *Dobbs* offers no searching review of history or the present. To the contrary, the Court neglects any mention of the period leading to and inspiring Reconstruction, evading the Reconstruction debates, and never mentions *slavery, involuntary sexual servitude,* or *forced "breeding"*—hard truths that galvanized abolitionist ratifiers of the Reconstruction Amendments.")

113. See, e.g., David H. Gans, "Reproductive Originalism: Why the Fourteenth Amendment's Original Meaning Protects the Right to Abortion," *SMU Law Review Forum* 75 (2022): 191.

114. Michele Goodwin, "Opportunistic Originalism: Dobbs v. Jackson Women's Health Organization," *Supreme Court Review* (2022): 111, 175.

115. Bridgewater, "Un/Re/Dis Covering," 11, 37.

116. Gans, "Reproductive Originalism," 191, 201.

117. See, e.g., Michele Goodwin, "No, Justice Alito, Reproductive Justice Is in the Constitution," *New York Times,* June 26, 2022, www.nytimes .com/2022/06/26/opinion/justice-alito-reproductive-justice -constitution-abortion.html.

118. See generally Goodwin, "Opportunistic Originalism."

119. *Dred Scott v. Sandford,* 60 U.S. 393, 405 (1857).

120. *Dred Scott,* 60 U.S. at 410 (1857).

121. See, e.g., Brief of American Historical Association and Organization of American Historians as Amici Curiae in Support of Respondents at 18–30, *Dobbs v. Jackson Women's Health Organization,* 142 S. Ct. 2228 (2022); Michele Goodwin, "The Racist History of Abortion and Midwifery Bans," American Civil Liberties Union, July 1, 2020, www .aclu.org/news/racial-justice/the-racist-history-of-abortion-and -midwifery-bans; Alejandra Caraballo, Cynthia Conti-Cook, Yveka Pierre, Michelle McGrath, and Hillary Aarons, "Extradition in Post-Roe America," *CUNY Law Review* (2023): 1, 6–7. ("As other scholars have explained, the newly professionalized practitioners of medicine—primarily men—led the efforts to criminalize abortion care. Chief among these physicians was Horatio Storer, a racist and misogynist who led the American Medical Association's ('AMA') crusade to criminalize abortion. Storer also sought to force white Protestant women to birth babies as a response to an increase in the immigrant population, asking if 'civilization' would be 'filled by our own children or by those of aliens' and 'upon their loins depends the future destiny of this nation.' Storer

was not alone; other white male physicians joined him under the banner of the AMA to monopolize abortion and obstetrics, and keep women out of the profession. This campaign of professional self-interest capitalized on misogyny, racism, and xenophobia to persuade the public and politicians that abortion should be criminalized.")

122. See, e.g., "Action by a Wife Against Her Husband for a Tort to the Person," *Yale Law Journal* 23 (1914): 613, 614; Diane Klein, "Their Slavery Was Her Freedom: Racism and the Beginning of the End of Coverture," *Duquesne Law Review* 59 (2021): 106.

123. See, e.g., Danielle L. McGuire, *At the Dark End of the Street: Black Women, Rape, and Resistance—a New History of the Civil Rights Movement from Rosa Parks to the Rise of Black Power* (New York: Knopf, 2010); Dorothy E. Roberts, *Torn Apart: How the Child Welfare System Destroys Black Families—and How Abolition Can Build a Safer World* (New York: Basic, 2022); Roberts, *Killing the Black Body*.

124. *Lawrence v. Texas,* 539 U.S. 558, 586 (2003).

125. Michael Waldman, *The Second Amendment: A Biography* (New York: Simon & Schuster, 2014); Carol Anderson, *The Second: Race and Guns in a Fatally Unequal America* (New York: Bloomsbury, 2021).

126. For a comprehensive account of the movement that reshaped the country's understanding of the Second Amendment, including the NRA literally redacting the "well-regulated militia" line from the Amendment's text as plastered on the wall in their offices, see Waldman, *Second Amendment*.

127. "Ethics of Deceased Organ Donor Recovery," Organ Procurement and Transplantation Network, U.S. Department of Health and Human Services, Dec. 2016, https://optn.transplant.hrsa.gov/professionals /by-topic/ethical-considerations/ethics-of-deceased-organ-donor -recovery/.

128. *Dobbs v. Jackson Women's Health Organization,* 142 S. Ct. 2228, 2325 (2022) (Breyer, Sotomayor, Kagan, J., dissenting).

129. *Planned Parenthood of Southeastern Pa. v. Casey,* 505 U.S. 833 (1992).

130. See, e.g., Sam Levin, "An Alabama Woman Was Imprisoned for 'Endangering' Her Fetus. She Gave Birth in a Jail Shower," *The Guardian,* Oct. 13, 2023, www.theguardian.com/us-news/2023/oct/13/alabama -pregnant-woman-jail-lawsuit (discussing the criminalization of pregnant people, including a woman who was arrested for allegedly exposing her fetus to drugs; she wasn't pregnant).

131. See, e.g., Munira Z. Gunja, Evan D. Gumas, and Reginald D. Williams II, "The U.S. Maternal Mortality Crisis Continues to Worsen: An International Comparison," *To the Point* (blog), Commonwealth Fund, Dec. 1, 2022, https://doi.org/10.26099/8vem-fc65.

132. E. A. Howell, "Reducing Disparities in Severe Maternal Morbidity and Mortality," *Clinical Obstetrics and Gynecology* 61, no. 2 (2018): 387–99, doi: 10.1097/GRF.0000000000000349. PMID: 29346121; PMCID: PMC5915910.

133. "Advancing New Standards in Reproductive Health," *The Turnaway Study,* www.ansirh.org/research/ongoing/turnaway-study.

134. Corinne Rocca, "Debunking the 'Abortion Regret' Narrative: Data Shows Women Feel Relief, Not Regret," *Salon,* Jan. 12, 2020, www .salon.com/2020/01/12/debunking-the-abortion-regret-narrative-our -data-shows-women-feel-relief-not-regret/.

135. See, e.g., Amy Roeder, "America Is Failing Its Black Mothers," *Harvard Public Health,* Winter 2019, www.hsph.harvard.edu/magazine /magazine_article/america-is-failing-its-black-mothers/; Bria Peacock, M.D., "A Black Abortion Provider's Perspective on Post-Roe America," *New England Journal of Medicine,* June 23, 2022.

136. Sherajum Monira Farin et al., "The Impact of Legal Abortion on Maternal Mortality," *American Economic Journal: Economic Policy,* forthcoming.

137. See, e.g., Devin Dwyer, "After Roe Ruling, Is 'Stare Decisis' Dead? How the Supreme Court's View of Precedent Is Evolving," ABC News, June 24, 2022, https://abcnews.go.com/Politics/roe-ruling-stare -decisis-dead-supreme-court-view/story?id=84997047; Sara Rosenbaum, Katie Keith, and Timothy S. Jost, "The United States Supreme Court Ends the Constitutional Right to Abortion," *To the Point* (blog), June 27, 2022, Commonwealth Fund, https://doi.org/10.26099/t080 -cg68.

138. See, e.g., *Dobbs v. Jackson Women's Health Organization,* 142 S. Ct. 2228, 2240, 2243, 2258, 2261 (2022).

139. See, e.g., Gallup Abortion Poll, https://news.gallup.com/poll/1576 /abortion.aspx (indicating that in May 2022, 85 percent of Americans believed abortion should be legal and only 13 percent of Americans said they thought abortion should be illegal in all circumstances); supra notes 348–446; Joerg Dreweke, "Contraception Is Not Abortion: The Strategic Campaign of Antiabortion Groups to Persuade the Public Otherwise," *Guttmacher Policy Review* 17, no. 4 (Fall 2014), www .guttmacher.org/gpr/2014/12/contraception-not-abortion-strategic -campaign-antiabortion-groups-persuade-public.

140. *Dobbs v. Jackson Women's Health Organization,* 142 S. Ct. 2228, 2301 (2022) (Thomas, J., concurring).

141. Brief of Texas Right to Life as Amicus Curiae in Support of Petitioners at 22–23, *Dobbs v. Jackson Women's Health Organization,* 142 S. Ct. 2228 (2022).

142. See, e.g., Katelyn Burns, "Transphobes are targeting cis people now. That

should be a wakeup call," *Xtra,* May 26, 2023, https://xtramagazine
.com/power/politics/transphobes-targeting-cis-people-251610; Mary
Ziegler, "Fresh Fallout from the Supreme Court's *Dobbs* Ruling Just
Hit Trans People," *Slate,* July 19, 2023, https://slate.com/news-and
-politics/2023/07/supreme-court-dobbs-ruling-trans-backlash.html.

143. *Dobbs v. Jackson Women's Health Organization,* 142 S. Ct. 2228,
2301–2 (2022) (Thomas, J., concurring); U.S. Const. Amend. XIV.

144. *Slaughterhouse Cases,* 83 U.S. 36 (1873).

145. See, e.g., Dale E. Ho, "Dodging a Bullet: McDonald v. City of Chicago
and the Limits of Progressive Originalism," *William & Mary Bill of
Rights Journal* 19 (2010): 369.

146. *Dobbs v. Jackson Women's Health Organization,* 142 S. Ct. 2228, 2302
(2022) (emphasis in original).

147. *Dobbs v. Jackson Women's Health Organization,* 142 S. Ct. 2228,
2248 n.22 (2022); *Corfield v. Coryell,* 6 F. Cas. 546, 551 (C.C.E.D. Pa.
1823).

148. *Dobbs v. Jackson Women's Health Organization,* 142 S. Ct. 2228, 2302
(2022) (Thomas, J., concurring).

149. See, e.g., William E. Forbath, "The New Deal Constitution in Exile,"
Duke Law Journal 51 (2001): 165, 171 (examining "the history of the
liberal Constitution in exile," including advocacy invoking and in support of positive rights).

150. Robin West, "Rights, Capabilities, and the Good Society," *Fordham
Law Review* 69 (2001): 1901, 1908.

151. See, e.g., Goodwin Liu, "Education, Equality, and National Citizenship," *Yale Law Journal* 116 (2006): 330, 337–38. ("The concept of
positive rights, while disfavored in Supreme Court doctrine, has never
been far from the core ideals of the nation's transformative moments. It
was part of the ideology of emancipation and Reconstruction. It ani-
mated the New Deal constitutional vision and President Franklin Roosevelt's call for a 'Second Bill of Rights.' And it found brief expression in
the fundamental rights strand of equal protection doctrine during the
Great Society. Moreover, as Cass Sunstein and David Currie have observed, positive rights to government assistance inhere in a variety of
traditionally 'negative' constitutional protections, although this reality
is obscured by baseline 'assumptions about . . . the natural or desirable
functions of government.' Neither the text nor the history of the Constitution forecloses a reading of its broad guarantees to encompass positive rights, and the experiences of other nations suggest that the
existence of such rights is compatible with constitutionalism. [. . .] As a
growing body of scholarship suggests, however, it is a mistake to equate
the adjudicated Constitution with the full meaning of the Constitution
itself.")

152. Mari J. Matsuda, "This Is (Not) Who We Are: Korematsu, Constitutional Interpretation, and National Identity," *Yale Law Journal Forum* 128 (2019): 657, 674.

Chapter 3: Stealing Our Elections

1. See, e.g., Errin Whack, "Who Was Edmund Pettus?," *Smithsonian,* March 7, 2015, www.smithsonianmag.com/history/who-was-edmund -pettus-180954501/.
2. See, e.g., "Marching for the Vote," United States Civil Rights Trail, https://civilrightstrail.com/experience/marching-for-the-right-to-vote/. See also "Bloody Sunday: Civil Rights Activists Brutally Attacked in Selma," Equal Justice Initiative, https://calendar.eji.org/racial-injustice /mar/07; "History of the Edmund Pettus Bridge," The John Lewis Bridge Project, https://johnlewisbridge.com/history-of-the-edmund -pettus-bridge/.
3. See, e.g., "Rep. John Lewis: 'Your Vote Is Precious, Almost Sacred,'" PBS, Sept. 6, 2012, www.pbs.org/newshour/show/rep-john-lewis-your -vote-is-precious-almost-sacred.
4. See, e.g., "Voting Laws Roundup: February 2023," Brennan Center for Justice, www.brennancenter.org/our-work/research-reports/voting -laws-roundup-february-2023, last updated Feb. 27, 2023.
5. See, e.g., Kevin Morris, "The Impact of Voter Suppression on Communities of Color," Brennan Center for Justice, Jan. 10, 2022, www .brennancenter.org/our-work/research-reports/impact-voter -suppression-communities-color. See also Hearing on Voting in America: The Potential for Polling Place Quality and Restrictions on Opportunities to Vote to Interfere with Free and Fair Access to the Ballot, Before the H. Comm. on House Administration, Subcomm. on Elections, 117th Cong. (2021) (Testimony of Kevin Morris, Researcher, Brennan Center for Justice).
6. Charles Blow, "Welcome to Jim Crow 2.0," *New York Times,* July 14, 2021, www.nytimes.com/2021/07/14/opinion/jim-crow-voter -suppression.html ("America is having a déjà vu moment, reliving in real time a horrendous history of more than a century ago, and it is impossible to understand how Democrats in Washington don't see that").
7. See, e.g., Hearing on Voting in America: A National Perspective on the Right to Vote, Jurisdictional Boundaries, and Redistricting, Before the H. Comm. on House Administration, Subcomm. on Elections, 117th Cong. (2021) (Testimony of Michael Waldman, President, Brennan Center for Justice).
8. Rev. Dr. William J. Barber tweeted, "Yes, these voter suppression bills

target Black people, but we cannot call this 'Jim Crow 2.0,' because this also effects [*sic*] Latinx, native, and poor white people. This is 'James Crow, Esquire.' See https://twitter.com/revdrbarber /status/1493664557780410375, Feb. 15, 2022, 2:12 p.m.

9. See, e.g., Kimberley A. Strassel, "Corporate America's 'Big Lie,'" *Wall Street Journal,* April 1, 2021, www.wsj.com/video/series/potomac -watch-strassel/wsj-opinion-corporate-americas-big-lie/CE6CFE84 -CFA4-4433-810E-9AF86F1B70CF ("Referring to the situation in Georgia today as Jim Crow 2.0 lacks any factual basis, especially when looking at recent history or other states").

10. Jamelle Bouie, "If It's Not Jim Crow, What Is It?," *New York Times,* April 6, 2021, www.nytimes.com/2021/04/06/opinion/georgia-voting -law.html. (Analyzing whether Georgia's notorious 2021 election law was a return to Jim Crow, Bouie wrote, "It is true that the 'yes' argument of President Biden and other Democrats overstates similarities and greatly understates key differences—chief among them the violence that undergirded the Jim Crow racial order. But the 'no' argument of conservatives and Republicans asks us to ignore context and extend good faith to lawmakers who overhauled their state's election laws because their party lost an election.")

11. "Segregation in America," Equal Justice Initiatives, 2018, https:// segregationinamerica.eji.org/report/massive-resistance.html.

12. See, e.g., Susan Smith-Richardson and Lauren Burke, "In the 1950s, Rather Than Integrate Some Public Schools, Virginia Closed Them," *The Guardian,* Nov. 27, 2021, www.theguardian.com/world/2021 /nov/27/integration-public-schools-massive-resistance-virginia -1950s.

13. See, e.g., "An Assessment of Minority Voting Rights Access in the United States: 2018 Statutory Enforcement Report," U.S. Commission on Civil Rights, 279–80, www.usccr.gov/files/pubs/2018/Minority _Voting_Access_2018.pdf. See also Ashoka Mukpo, "The Battle Over Voting Rights in America Is Red-Hot. Here's What Has Changed Since 2010," American Civil Liberties Union, Oct. 31, 2018, www.aclu.org /issues/voting-rights/voting-rights-2010.

14. "Voting Laws Roundup: December 2021," Brennan Center for Justice, www.brennancenter.org/our-work/research-reports/voting-laws -roundup-december-2021 (last updated Jan. 12, 2022); "Voting Laws Roundup: December 2022," Brennan Center for Justice, Dec. 19, 2022, www.brennancenter.org/our-work/research-reports/voting-laws -roundup-december-2022.

15. Reid Wilson, "Arizona Bill Would Allow Legislature to Overturn Election Results," *The Hill,* Jan. 27, 2022, https://thehill.com/homenews /state-watch/591597-arizona-bill-would-allow-legislature-to-overturn -election-results/.

16. Boris Bazhanov, *The Memoirs of Stalin's Former Secretary* (1992).

17. Karen Yourish, Larry Buchanan, and Denise Lu, "The 147 Republicans Who Voted to Overturn Election Results," *New York Times,* www .nytimes.com/interactive/2021/01/07/us/elections/electoral-college -biden-objectors.html (last updated Jan. 7, 2021); 117th Congress Second Session House Report 117–663, Final Report of the Select Committee to Investigate the January 6th Attack on the United States Capitol, Dec. 22, 2022, www.govinfo.gov/content/pkg/GPO-J6 -REPORT/pdf/GPO-J6-REPORT.pdf.

18. *Id.*

19. Sarah Hauer, "Paul Ryan Claims the U.S. Is the 'Oldest Democracy' in the World. Is He Right?," *Politifact,* July 11, 2016, www.politifact.com /factchecks/2016/jul/11/paul-ryan/paul-ryan-claims-us-oldest-democracy -world-he-righ/.

20. "Milestone Documents: Voting Rights Act (1965)," National Archives, www.archives.gov/milestone-documents/voting-rights-act (page last reviewed Feb. 8, 2022).

21. See, e.g., Maureen A. Edobor, "Reconstruction's Last Monument: Judicial Erosion of the Fifteenth Amendment and Section 2 of the Voting Rights Act, and a Proposal for a Constitutional Amendment," Dec. 31, 2022 ("History counsels us that formidable enforcement of the Fifteenth Amendment's promises did not exist until the passage of the Voting Rights Act of 1965").

22. Carl Hulse, "By a Vote of 98–0, Senate Approves 25-Year Extension of Voting Rights Act," *New York Times,* July 21, 2006, www.nytimes .com/2006/07/21/washington/21vote.html.

23. James Blacksher and Lani Guinier, "Free at Last: Rejecting Equal Sovereignty and Restoring the Constitutional Right to Vote: Shelby County v. Holder," *Harvard Law and Policy Review* 8 (2014): 39.

24. Guy-Uriel E. Charles and Luis Fuentes-Fohwer, "The Voting Rights Act in Winter: The Death of a Superstatute," *Iowa Law Review* 100 (2015): 1391.

25. See, e.g., *Shelby Cnty., Ala. v. Holder,* 570 U.S. 529 (2013), *Abbott v. Perez,* 138 S. Ct. 2305 (2018), *Rucho v. Common Cause,* 139 S. Ct. 2484 (2019), *Brnovich v. Democratic Nat'l Comm.,* 141 S. Ct. 2321 (2021).

26. "Global State of Democracy 2022: Forging Social Contracts in a Time of Discontent," International Institute for Democracy and Electoral Assistance, 2022, https://idea.int/democracytracker/gsod-report-2022. See also "Authoritarian Threat Index," Protect Democracy, https:// protectdemocracy.org/threat-index/? (last updated Feb. 20, 2023).

27. "Few Think Our Democracy Is Working Well These Days," Associated Press-NORC Center for Public Affairs Research, Oct. 19, 2022, https://apnorc.org/projects/few-think-our-democracy-is-working-well -these-days/.

28. Complaint at 20, *Shelby Cnty., Ala. v. Holder,* 811 F. Supp. 2d 424 (D.D.C. 2011) (No. 10-0651).

29. Voting Rights Act of 1965, Pub. L. No. 89-110, 79 Stat. 437, as amended, 52 U.S.C. § 10301 *et seq.*

30. *Shelby Cnty., Ala. v. Holder,* 811 F. Supp. 2d 424, 431 (D.D.C. 2011).

31. Complaint at 19–20, *Shelby Cnty., Ala. v. Holder,* 811 F. Supp. 2d 424 (D.D.C. 2011) (No. 10-0651).

32. Brief of Veterans of the Mississippi Civil Rights Movement as Amicus Curiae in Support of Respondents and Intervenor-Respondents at 3, *Shelby Cnty., Ala. v. Holder,* 570 U.S. 529 (2013) (internal citations omitted), quoting *The Federalist,* No. 45. See also David Kow, "An 'Equal Sovereignty' Principle Born in Northwest Austin, Texas, Raised in Shelby County, Alabama," *Journal of Race, Gender, and Ethnicity* 7, no. 1 (2015) (discussing *Shelby County* placing a premium on "deference to equal state sovereignty over equal protection of individuals").

33. U.S. Const. Amend. X.

34. See, e.g., U.S. Const. Art. I, § 4, cl. 1; U.S. Const. Amend. XV.

35. U.S. Const. Art. IV.

36. *Dred Scott v. Sandford,* 60 U.S. 393 (1857). See also Blacksher and Guinier, "Free at Last"; Akhil Amar, "The Lawfulness of Section 5— and Thus of Section 5," *Harvard Law Review Forum* 126 (2013): 109.

37. *Dred Scott v. Sandford,* 60 U.S. 393, 417–18 (1857).

38. *Dred Scott v. Sandford,* 60 U.S. 393, 416 (1857).

39. *Nw. Austin Mun. Util. Dist. No. One v. Holder,* 557 U.S. 193, 203 (2009).

40. See, e.g., Randy E. Barnett and Lawrence B. Solum, "Originalism After Dobbs, Bruen, and Kennedy: The Role of History and Tradition," *Northwestern University Law Review* 118 (2023): 433.

41. *Pollard v. Hagan,* 44 U.S. 212, 228–29 (1845) ("Alabama is therefore entitled to the sovereignty and jurisdiction over all the territory within her limits, subject to the common law, to the same extent that Georgia possessed it before she ceded it to the United States. To maintain any other doctrine, is to deny that Alabama has been admitted into the union on an equal footing with the original states, the constitution, laws, and compact, to the contrary notwithstanding."); *Texas v. White,* 74 U.S. 700, 725 (1868) ("The union between Texas and the other States was as complete, as perpetual, and as indissoluble as the union between the original States").

42. See, e.g., Eric Biber, "The Price of Admission: Causes, Effects, and Patterns of Conditions Imposed on States Entering the Union," *American Journal of Legal History* 46 (2004): 119. See also David Kow, "An 'Equal Sovereignty' Principle" (discussing unequal sovereignty among the states even under the equal footing doctrine).

43. *Nw. Austin Mun. Util. Dist. No. One v. Holder,* 557 U.S. 193, 203 (2009).

44. *Nw. Austin Mun. Util. Dist. No. One v. Holder,* 557 U.S. 193, 228 (2009) (Thomas, J., dissenting in part).

45. *Shelby Cnty., Ala. v. Holder,* 811 F. Supp. 2d 424, 428 (D.D.C. 2011).

46. *Id.*

47. *Shelby Cnty., Ala. v. Holder,* 811 F. Supp. 2d 424, 503 (D.D.C. 2011).

48. *Shelby Cnty., Ala. v. Holder,* 811 F. Supp. 2d 424, 442–43 (D.D.C. 2011); Complaint, *United States v. The City of Calera, AL,* No. CV-08-BE-1982-S, (N.D. Ala. 2008); Consent Decree, *United States v. The City of Calera, AL,* No. CV-08-BE-1982-S, (N.D. Ala., Oct. 29, 2008).

49. *Id.*

50. Brief of the Plaintiff at 14, *South Carolina v. Katzenbach,* 383 U.S. 301 (1966).

51. *South Carolina v. Katzenbach,* 383 U.S. 301, 328–29 (1966).

52. See, e.g., Joseph Fishkin, "The Dignity of the South," *Yale Law Journal* 123 (2013): 175, http://yalelawjournal.org/forum/the-dignity-of-the-south. See also Jon Greenbaum, Alan Martinson, and Sonia Gill, "Shelby County v. Holder: When the Rational Becomes Irrational," *Howard Law Journal* 57, no. 3 (2014): 846.

53. *Shelby Cnty., Ala. v. Holder,* 811 F. Supp. 2d 424, 498 (D.D.C. 2011).

54. *Shelby Cnty., Ala. v. Holder,* 811 F. Supp. 2d 424, 508 (D.D.C. 2011).

55. See, e.g., Josh Chafetz, "The New Judicial Power Grab," *St. Louis University Law Journal* 67 (2023): 635.

56. *Id.* See also Mark A. Lemley, "The Imperial Supreme Court," *Harvard Law Review Forum* 136 (2022): 97.

57. See, e.g., Rebecca E. Zietlow, "Rights of Belonging for Women," *Indiana Journal of Law & Social Equality* 1, no. 1 (2013), University of Toledo Legal Studies Research Paper No. 2013-16, Available at SSRN: https://ssrn.com/abstract=2314451.

58. Rebecca E. Zietlow, "The Judicial Restraint of the Warren Court (and Why It Matters)," *Ohio State Law Journal* 69, no. 2 (2008). See also Nikolas Bowie and Daphna Renan, "The Separation-of-Powers Counterrevolution," *Yale Law Journal* 131 (2022): 2020.

59. *Shelby Cnty., Ala. v. Holder,* 679 F.3d 848, 860 (D.C. Cir. 2012).

60. *Shelby Cnty., Ala. v. Holder,* 679 F.3d 848, 873 (D.C. Cir. 2012).

61. *Shelby Cnty., Ala. v. Holder,* 679 F.3d 848, 884 (D.C. Cir. 2012).

62. *Shelby Cnty., Ala. v. Holder,* 570 U.S. 529, 535 (2013).

63. Leah M. Litman, "Inventing Equal Sovereignty," *Michigan Law Review* 114 (2016): 1207, 1242–53.

64. *South Carolina v. Katzenbach,* 383 U.S. 301, 328–29 (1966).

65. *Shelby Cnty., Ala. v. Holder,* 570 U.S. 529, 580 (2013) (Ginsburg, J., dissenting).

66. H.R. Rep. 109-478, 21 (2006).
67. See, e.g., "An Assessment of Minority Voting Rights Access in the United States: 2018 Statutory Enforcement Report," U.S. Commission on Civil Rights, 39, www.usccr.gov/files/pubs/2018/Minority_Voting _Access_2018.pdf.
68. *Shelby Cnty., Ala. v. Holder,* 570 U.S. 529, 548 (2013).
69. *Shelby Cnty., Ala. v. Holder,* 570 U.S. 529, 557 (2013) (Thomas, J., concurring).
70. *Shelby Cnty., Ala. v. Holder,* 570 U.S. 529, 559 (2013) (Thomas, J., concurring).
71. *Shelby Cnty., Ala. v. Holder,* 570 U.S. 529, 588-90 (2013) (Ginsburg, J., dissenting).
72. U.S. Const. Art. I, Sec. 4. See also Franita Tolson, Reinventing Sovereignty? Federalism as a Constraint on the Voting Rights Act," *Vanderbilt Law Review* 65 (2012): 1195, 1256. ("The Roberts Court makes an error by viewing Congress's power to pass section 5 as limited to Congress's remedial authority under the Fifteenth Amendment and ignoring that the Elections Clause gives Congress broad authority over state electoral schemes more generally. As the sovereign authority, Congress has significant room to craft a regulatory regime that achieves the goals and values that are the aims of the policy.")
73. For reference, the majority opinion was authored by Chief Justice John Roberts and signed on to by Justices Scalia, Kennedy, Thomas, and Alito. Do with that information what you will.
74. Kevin Morris, "Patterns in the Introduction and Passage of Restrictive Voting Bills are Best Explained by Race," Brennan Center for Justice, Aug. 3, 2022, www.brennancenter.org/our-work/research-reports /patterns-introduction-and-passage-restrictive-voting-bills-are-best.
75. Charles and Fuentes-Fohwer, "Voting Rights Act in Winter," 1391; Vann Newkirk II, "How *Shelby County v. Holder* Broke America," *The Atlantic,* July 10, 2018, www.theatlantic.com/politics/archive/2018/07 /how-shelby-county-broke-america/564707/.
76. See, e.g., "An Assessment of Minority Voting Rights Access in the United States: 2018 Statutory Enforcement Report," U.S. Commission on Civil Rights, 60, www.usccr.gov/files/pubs/2018/Minority_Voting _Access_2018.pdf.
77. *Id.*
78. Kevin Morris, Peter Miller, and Coryn Grange, "Racial Turnout Gap Grew in Jurisdictions Previously Covered by the Voting Rights Act," Brennan Center for Justice, Aug. 20, 2021, www.brennancenter.org/our -work/research-reports/racial-turnout-gap-grew-jurisdictions-previously -covered-voting-rights.
79. See, e.g., *Brnovich v. Democratic Nat'l Comm.,* 141 S. Ct. 2321, 2355 (2021) ("The election laws passed in *Shelby County*'s wake 'may have

negated many of the gains made under preclearance.'") (Kagan, J., dissenting, n. 3).

80. *City of Mobile v. Bolden,* 446 U.S. 55, 104 (1980).

81. *Thornburg v. Gingles,* 478 U.S. 30, 35 (1986).

82. 52 U.S.C. § 10301.

83. Memorandum from John Roberts to Attorney General, Dec. 22, 1981, www.archives.gov/files/news/john-roberts/accession-60-88-0498/030 -black-binder1/folder030.pdf. See also Ari Berman, "Inside John Roberts' Decades-Long Crusade Against the Voting Rights Act," *Politico,* Aug. 10, 2015, www.politico.com/magazine/story/2015/08/john -roberts-voting-rights-act-121222/.

84. Memorandum from John Roberts to Attorney General, Jan. 26, 1982, www.archives.gov/files/news/john-roberts/accession-60-88-0498/030 -black-binder1/folder030.pdf.

85. *N. Carolina State Conf. of NAACP v. McCrory,* 831 F.3d 204, 214 (4th Cir. 2016).

86. Hearing on Protecting a Precious, Almost Sacred Right: The John R. Lewis Voting Rights Advancement Act, Before the Senate Judiciary Committee, 117th Cong. (2021) (Testimony of Kristen Clarke, Assistant Attorney General, Civil Rights Division, U.S. Department of Justice), www.judiciary.senate.gov/imo/media/doc/Clarke%20Testimony1.pdf.

87. Ariz. Rev. Stat. Ann. §§16-122, 16-135, 16-584I, 16-452(C); National Conference of State Legislatures, Provisional Ballots Report, www.ncsl .org/elections-and-campaigns/provisional-ballots#statesuse (last updated Nov. 4, 2022).

88. Ariz. Rev. Stat. Ann. §§ 16-1005(H)—(I) (2016).

89. Department of Justice, "Jurisdictions Previously Covered by Section 5," www.justice.gov/crt/jurisdictions-previously-covered-section-5.

90. See, e.g., *Democratic Nat'l Comm. v. Hobbs,* 948 F.3d 989, 1000 (9th Cir. 2020) (quoting expert report of Dr. Jonathan Rodden, which was afforded great weight at the district court).

91. *Democratic Nat'l Comm. v. Reagan,* 329 F. Supp. 3d 824, 856 (D. Ariz.) (2018).

92. See, e.g., *Democratic Nat'l Comm. v. Reagan,* 329 F. Supp. 3d 824, 857–58, 871–72 (D. Ariz.) (2018).

93. *Democratic Nat'l Comm. v. Reagan,* 904 F.3d 686, 732 (9th Cir. 2018), quoted in *Democratic Nat'l Comm. v. Hobbs,* 948 F.3d 989 (9th Cir. 2020).

94. Arizona Voter Registration Form, Box 23, https://azsos.gov/sites /default/files/voter_registration_form.pdf.

95. Brief of Navajo Nation as Amicus Curiae in Support of Respondents at 16–17, *Brnovich v. Democratic National Committee,* 141 S. Ct. 2321 (2021).

96. *Id*. See also Sue Halpern, "The Political Attack on the Native American

Vote," *The New Yorker,* Nov. 4, 2022, www.newyorker.com/news /dispatch/the-political-attack-on-the-native-american-vote.

97. See, e.g., Jen Fifield/Votebeat, "Republicans Helped Arizona Champion Voting by Mail. Now They Want It Gone," *AZ Mirror,* June 13, 2022, www.azmirror.com/2022/06/13/republicans-helped-arizona-champion -voting-by-mail-now-they-want-it-gone/.

98. See, e.g., Matthew Hendley, "Viral Video of 'Ballot Stuffing' in Phoenix Shows a Perfectly Legal Practice," *Phoenix New Times,* Oct. 23, 2014, www.phoenixnewtimes.com/news/viral-video-of-ballot-stuffing-in -phoenix-shows-a-perfectly-legal-practice-6647259; brief of Mi Familia Vota, Arizona Center for Empowerment, Chispa Arizona, and League of Women Voters of Arizona as Amici Curiae in Support of Respon-dents at 7–10, *Brnovich v. Democratic National Committee,* 141 S. Ct. 2321 (2021).

99. *Id.*

100. Howard Fischer, "Ducey Signs Bill to Make Ballot Harvesting a Felony," *Arizona Capitol Times,* March 9, 2016, https://azcapitoltimes.com /news/2016/03/09/senate-passes-bill-outlawing-early-ballot-collection/.

101. See, e.g., Caroline Sullivan, " 'The Goal Is to Confuse': How Arizona's Ballot Collection Ban Harms Voters," *Democracy Docket,* March 17, 2023, www.democracydocket.com/analysis/the-goal-is-to-confuse -how-arizonas-ballot-collection-ban-harms-voters/; Andrew Oxford, "People Impersonating Election Officials Are Knocking on Doors in Yavapai County, Sheriff Warns," *AZ Central,* June 14, 2021, www .azcentral.com/story/news/politics/elections/2021/06/14/yavapai -county-sheriff-warns-imposters-asking-voting-history/7693805002/; Yvonne Wingett Sanchez and Adriana Usero, "Video Offers Rare Glimpse of Police Enforcing Arizona's Election Laws," *Washington Post,* March 9, 2023, www.washingtonpost.com/politics/2023/03/09 /video-arizona-ballot-drop-box-observers/.

102. Sue Halpern, "The Political Attack on the Native American Vote," *The New Yorker,* Nov. 4, 2022, www.newyorker.com/news/dispatch/the -political-attack-on-the-native-american-vote; brief of National Con-gress of American Indians as Amicus Curiae in Support of Respondents at 22–23, *Brnovich v. Democratic National Committee,* 141 S. Ct. 2321 (2021).

103. Brief of Navajo Nation as Amicus Curiae in Support of Respondents at 19–20, *Brnovich v. Democratic National Committee,* 141 S. Ct. 2321 (2021).

104. *Democratic Nat'l Comm. v. Reagan,* 329 F. Supp. 3d 824, 868 (D. Ariz.) (2018).

105. *Democratic Nat'l Comm. v. Reagan,* 329 F. Supp. 3d 824, 882–83 (D. Ariz.) (2018).

106. *Brnovich v. Democratic Nat'l Comm.,* 141 S. Ct. 2321, 2333 (2021).

107. See, e.g., *League of Women Voters of North Carolina v. North Carolina,* 769 F.3d 224, 239 (4th Cir. 2014) ("But the predominance of vote dilution in Section 2 jurisprudence likely stems from the effectiveness of the now-defunct Section 5 preclearance requirements that stopped would-be vote denial from occurring"); Richard L. Hasen, "The Supreme Court's Latest Voting Rights Opinion Is Even Worse Than It Seems," *Slate,* July 8, 2021, https://slate.com/news-and-politics/2021/07/supreme-court-sam-alito-brnovich-angry.html.

108. See, e.g., Dale E. Ho, "Building an Umbrella in a Rainstorm: The New Vote Denial Litigation Since Shelby County," *Yale Law Journal Forum* 127 (2018): 799, 802 (describing how all five courts of appeal which had considered Section 2 liability cases had "(at least nominally) embraced the same two-part standard").

109. See, e.g., Doni Gewirtzman, "Lower Court Constitutionalism: Circuit Court Discretion in a Complex Adaptive System," *American University Law Review* 61 (2012): 457.

110. *Brnovich v. Democratic Nat'l Comm.,* 141 S. Ct. 2321, 2337 (2021).

111. David D. Daniels III, "The Black Church Has Been Getting 'Souls to the Polls' for More Than 60 Years," *Urban Edge,* Kinder Institute for Urban Research, Rice University, Oct. 30, 2020, https://kinder.rice.edu/urbanedge/black-church-has-been-getting-souls-polls-more-60-years.

112. M. C. Herron and D. A. Smith, "Race, Party, and the Consequences of Restricting Early Voting in Florida in the 2012 General Election," *Political Research Quarterly* 67, no. 3 (2014): 646–65, https://doi.org/10.1177/1065912914524831.

113. *Brnovich v. Democratic Nat'l Comm.,* 141 S. Ct. 2321, 2339 (2021).

114. Brief of Senate Staffers and Other Leading Participants in the 1982 Amendments to the Voting Rights Act as Amici Curiae in Support of Respondents at 1, 6, *Brnovich v. Democratic Nat'l Comm.,* 141 S. Ct. 2321 (2021).

115. Brief of Senate Staffers and Other Leading Participants in the 1982 Amendments to the Voting Rights Act as Amici Curiae in Support of Respondents at 8, *Brnovich v. Democratic Nat'l Comm.,* 141 S. Ct. 2321 (2021).

116. *Brnovich v. Democratic Nat'l Comm.,* 141 S. Ct. 2321, 2363 (2021) (Kagan, J., dissenting).

117. *Shelby Cnty., Ala. v. Holder,* 570 U.S. 529, 557 (2013).

118. *Brnovich v. Democratic Nat'l Comm.,* 141 S. Ct. 2321, 2339–40 (2021).

119. See, e.g., Anthony J. Gaughan, "Illiberal Democracy: The Toxic Mix of Fake News, Hyperpolarization, and Partisan Election Administration," *Duke Journal of Constitutional Law and Public Policy* 12 (2017): 57, 101 ("Time and again, allegations of widespread fraud have been dis-

proved by academic studies, government investigations, and court cases"). Even the conservative Heritage Foundation has only found 1,422 proven instances of voter fraud out of billions of ballots cast over nearly fifty years, amounting to about 0.001 percent of total ballots (one percent of one percent). "Election Fraud Database Tops 1,400 Cases," Heritage Foundation, Jan. 18, 2023, www.heritage.org/voter fraud.

120. David Litt, "Claims of 'Voter Fraud' Have a Long History in America. And They Are False," *The Guardian,* Dec. 4, 2020, www.theguardian .com/commentisfree/2020/dec/04/trump-voter-fraud-america-false.

121. "When Women Lost the Vote: A Revolutionary Story, 1776–1807," Museum of the American Revolution, www.amrevmuseum.org/virtual exhibits/when-women-lost-the-vote-a-revolutionary-story.

122. *Brnovich v. Democratic Nat'l Comm.,* 141 S. Ct. 2321, 2362 (2021) (Kagan, J., dissenting).

123. *Brnovich v. Democratic Nat'l Comm.,* 141 S. Ct. 2321, 2366 (2021) (Kagan, J., dissenting).

124. *City of Mobile, Ala. v. Bolden,* 446 U.S. 55, 60 (1980).

125. *Arkansas State Conference NAACP v. Arkansas Board of Apportionment,* 2023 WL 8011300, 8th Cir. (Ark.), Nov. 20, 2023.

126. *Brnovich v. Democratic Nat'l Comm.,* 141 S. Ct. 2321, 2361 (2021) (Kagan, J., dissenting).

127. Julia Kirschenbaum and Michael Li, "Gerrymandering Explained," Brennan Center for Justice, Aug. 10, 2021, www.brennancenter.org /our-work/research-reports/gerrymandering-explained.

128. The word "gerrymandering" itself is a portmanteau coined in 1812. Then-Governor of Massachusetts Elbridge *Gerry* approved a congressional map with weirdly shaped districts designed to entrench a party's power, including a district that a newspaper observed looked like a sala-*mander.* Elmer Cummings Griffith, *The Rise and Development of the Gerrymander* (Chicago: Scott, Foresman, and Co., 1907), 16–20.

129. Kirschenbaum and Li, "Gerrymandering Explained."

130. Yurij Rudensky and Annie Lo, "A Better Way to Draw Districts," Brennan Center for Justice, Dec. 12, 2019, www.brennancenter.org/our -work/policy-solutions/better-way-draw-districts.

131. *Benisek v. Lamone,* 348 F. Supp. 3d 493, 502 (D. Md. 2018).

132. *Common Cause v. Rucho,* 318 F. Supp. 3d 777, 808 (M.D.N.C. 2018).

133. *Rucho v. Common Cause,* 139 S. Ct. 2484 (2019).

134. See, e.g., *Baker v. Carr,* 369 U.S. 186, 217 (1962).

135. *Davis v. Bandemer,* 478 U.S. 109 (1986).

136. *Davis v. Bandemer,* 478 U.S. 109, 123 (1986). ("Disposition of this question does not involve us in a matter more properly decided by a co-equal branch of our Government. There is no risk of foreign or domestic disturbance, and in light of our cases since *Baker* we are not

persuaded that there are no judicially discernible and manageable standards by which political gerrymander cases are to be decided.")

137. *Rucho v. Common Cause*, 139 S. Ct. 2484, 2496 (2019).

138. *Rucho v. Common Cause*, 139 S. Ct. 2484, 2497 (2019).

139. See, e.g., *Baker v. Carr*, 369 U.S. 186 (1962), *Reynolds v. Sims*, 377 U.S. 533 (1964).

140. *Rucho v. Common Cause*, 139 S. Ct. 2484, 2499 (2019).

141. *Id.* at 2506.

142. Travis Crum, "Reconstructing Racially Polarized Voting," *Duke Law Journal* 70 (2020): 261–331.

143. Brief of Lawyers' Committee for Civil Rights Under Law as Amicus Curiae in Support of Appellees at 8, *Rucho v. Common Cause*, 139 S. Ct. 2484 (2019).

144. *Davis v. Bandemer*, 478 U.S. 109, 123 (1986). ("The mere fact, however, that we may not now similarly perceive a likely arithmetic presumption in the instant context does not compel a conclusion that the claims presented here are nonjusticiable. The one person, one vote principle had not yet been developed when *Baker* was decided.")

145. *Rucho v. Common Cause*, 139 S. Ct. 2484, 2509 (2019).

146. *Rucho v. Common Cause*, 139 S. Ct. 2484, 2512 (2019). ("To its credit, the majority does not frame that point [that gerrymanders have always been with us] as an originalist constitutional argument. After all (as the majority rightly notes), racial and residential gerrymanders were also once with us, but the Court has done something about that fact. . . . The majority's idea instead seems to be that if we have lived with partisan gerrymanders so long, we will survive.") (Kagan, J., dissenting) (internal citations omitted.)

147. Guy-Uriel Charles and Luis E. Fuentes-Rohwer, "Dirty Thinking About Law and Democracy in Rucho v. Common Cause," American Constitution Society, Sept. 4, 2019, www.acslaw.org/analysis/acs-supreme-court -review/dirty-thinking-about-law-and-democracy-in-rucho-v-common -cause/#_ftnref21.

148. See, e.g., Edward B. Foley, "Originalism and Election Law (or, The Difference between Reynolds and Benisek)," *Election Law Blog*, March 21, 2018, https://electionlawblog.org/?p=98255. See also Ilya Somin, "Originalism and the 'One Person, One Vote' Principle," *Washington Post*, March 31, 2016, www.washingtonpost.com/news/volokh -conspiracy/wp/2016/03/31/originalism-and-the-one-person-one-vote -principle/; Earl M. Maltz, "Inconvenient Truth: Originalism, Democratic Theory, and the Reapportionment Cases," *Mississippi Law Journal* 86 (2017): 1.

149. *Rucho v. Common Cause*, 139 S. Ct. 2484, 2523 (2019) (Kagan, J., dissenting).

150. John O. McGinnis, "Silent Originalism and the Reweighting of Prece-

dent," *Law and Liberty,* Aug. 22, 2019, https://lawliberty.org/silent
-originalism-and-the-reweighting-of-precedent/.
151. See, e.g., *Reynolds v. Sims,* 377 U.S. 533, 561–62 (1964).
152. See, e.g., *Dunn v. Blumstein,* 405 U.S. 330, 336 (1972).
153. *Gray v. Sanders,* 372 U.S. 368, 380 (1963).
154. See, e.g., Justice William J. Brennan, Jr., "The Constitution of the
United States: Contemporary Ratification," address before the Georgetown University Text and Teaching Symposium, Oct. 12, 1985. But see
Brett Kavanaugh, "From the Bench: The Constitutional Statesmanship
of Chief Justice William Rehnquist," Walter Berns Constitution Day
Lecture, Sept. 18, 2017. ("It is sometimes said that the Constitution is a
document of majestic generalities. I view it differently. As I see it, the
Constitution is primarily a document of majestic specificity, and those
specific words have meaning.")
155. *Vieth v. Jubelirer,* 541 U.S. 267, 314 (2004) (Kennedy, J., concurring).
156. *Gill v. Whitford,* 138 S. Ct. 1916, 1939 (2018) (Kagan, J., concurring).
157. See, e.g., *Elrod v. Burns,* 427 U.S. 347, 357 (1976).
158. *Arizona Free Enter. Club's Freedom Club PAC v. Bennett,* 564 U.S.
721, 741 (2011).
159. See, e.g., Guy-Uriel Charles, "Racial Identity, Electoral Structures, and
the First Amendment Right of Association," *California Law Review*
91 (2003): 1209; Daniel P. Tokaji, "Voting Is Association," *Florida State
University Law Review* 43 (2017): 763; Daniel Tokaji, "Symposium:
A Path through the Thicket—the First Amendment Right of Association," *SCOTUSblog,* Aug. 10, 2017, www.scotusblog.com/2017/08
/symposium-path-thicket-first-amendment-right-association/; Bertrall
Ross, "Partisan Gerrymandering, the First Amendment, and the Political Outsider," *Columbia Law Review* 118 (2018): 2187.
160. *Gill v. Whitford,* 138 S. Ct. 1916, 1941 (2018).
161. *Rucho v. Common Cause,* 139 S. Ct. 2484, 2513 (2019).
162. Declaration of Independence (1776).
163. Kirschenbaum and Li, "Gerrymandering Explained."
164. *Wesberry v. Sanders,* 376 U.S. 1, 6 (1964).
165. *Allen v. Milligan,* 143 S. Ct. 1487 (2023).
166. *Singleton v. Merrill,* 582 F. Supp. 3d 924 (N.D. Ala. 2022).
167. *Merrill v. Milligan,* 142 S. Ct. 879 (2022).
168. See, e.g., *Merrill v. Milligan,* 142 S. Ct. 879, 889 (2022) (Kagan, J., dissenting). ("Today's decision is one more in a disconcertingly long line of
cases in which this Court uses its shadow docket to signal or make
changes in the law, without anything approaching full briefing and argument. Here, the District Court applied established legal principles to
an extensive evidentiary record. Its reasoning was careful—indeed,
exhaustive—and justified in every respect. To reverse that decision re-

quires upsetting the way Section 2 plaintiffs have for decades—and in line with our caselaw—proved vote-dilution claims. [. . .] And most of all, it does a disservice to Black Alabamians who under that precedent have had their electoral power diminished—in violation of a law this Court once knew to buttress all of American democracy."); Madiba K. Dennie, "Supreme Court Shocks Nation by Remembering Racial Gerrymandering Is Still Presently Illegal Under Voting Rights Act," *Balls and Strikes,* June 10, 2023, https://ballsandstrikes.org/scotus/john -roberts-shocks-the-nation-by-doing-the-bare-minimum-remembering -racial-gerrymandering-is-still-very-much-illegal-under-voting-rights -act/.

169. *Allen v. Milligan,* 143 S. Ct. 1487, 1524 (2023) (Thomas, J., dissenting).
170. Kira Lerner, "Alabama Republicans Refuse to Create Second Majority -Black District," *The Guardian,* Aug. 14, 2023, www.theguardian.com /us-news/2023/aug/14/alabama-republican-majority-black-district -update-supreme-court; "What's Happening with Alabama's Redistrict- ing Post-Milligan?," League of Women Voters, December 5, 2023, https://www.lwv.org/blog/whats-happening-alabamas-redistricting -post-milligan.
171. *Chisom v. Roemer,* 501 U.S. 380, 403 (1991) (internal citations omitted).

Chapter 4: Stealing the Census

1. U.S. Const. Art. I, § 2.
2. "U.S. Census Connections: A Resource Guide—History of the U.S. Cen- sus," Library of Congress, https://guides.loc.gov/census-connections /census-history.
3. "2020 Census: A More Complete Lessons Learned Process for Cost and Schedule Would Help the Next Decennial," GAO-23-105819, U.S. Governmental Accountability Office, March 2023, www.gao.gov/assets /gao-23-105819.pdf; "2020 Census Operational Plan: A New Design for the 21st Century," version 5.0, U.S. Census Bureau, Jan. 2022, www2 .census.gov/programs-surveys/decennial/2020/program-management /planning-docs/2020-oper-plan5-and-memo.pdf.
4. Margo Anderson, "The Census and the Federal Statistical System: His- torical Perspectives," *Annals of the American Academy of Political and Social Science* 631 (2010): 152, 154.
5. *The Federalist,* No. 54 (James Madison).
6. "The Currency of Our Data: A Critical Input Into Federal Funding," U.S. Census Bureau, June 14, 2023, www.census.gov/library/fact -sheets/2023/adcom/federal-funding-distribution.html.
7. Madiba Dennie, Kelly Percival, and Yurij Rudensky, "The 2020 Census

Population and Apportionment Data, Explained," Brennan Center for Justice, April 26, 2021, www.brennancenter.org/our-work/research-reports/2020-census-population-and-apportionment-data-explained.

8. "Community Resilience Estimates," U.S. Census Bureau, May 30, 2023, www.census.gov/programs-surveys/community-resilience-estimates.html.

9. U.S. Const. Art. I, Sec. 2, Cl. 3.

10. See, e.g., Native American Rights Fund, "Counting All Persons in the U.S. Census," Nov. 21, 2020, https://narf.org/trump-v-newyork/; brief of National Congress of American Indians as Amicus Curiae in Support of Appellees at 5–6, *Trump v. New York,* 141 S. Ct. 530 (2020); Dan Bouk, *Democracy's Data: The Hidden Stories in the U.S. Census and How to Read Them* (New York: Farrar, Straus & Giroux, 2022), 146 ("The inclusion of the phrase 'Indians not taxed' might be taken as a recognition of the sovereignty of Native American nations, even as that sovereignty was frequently transgressed").

11. James P. Collins, "Native Americans in the Census, 1860–1890," *Prologue* 38, no. 2 (Summer 2006), www.archives.gov/publications/prologue/2006/summer/indian-census.html.

12. William Seltzer and Margo Anderson, "The Darker Side of Numbers: The Role of Population Data Systems in Human Rights Abuses," *Social Research* 68 (2001): 481.

13. See, e.g., Janai Nelson, "Counting Change: Ensuring an Inclusive Census for Communities of Color," *Columbia Law Review* 119 (2019): 1399, 1409–11.

14. Margo J. Anderson, *The American Census: A Social History* (New Haven: Yale University Press, 1990), 75–76.

15. U.S. Const. Amend. XIV, § 2.

16. U.S. Const. Amend. XIV, § 2.

17. U.S. Const. Amend. XIV, § 2.

18. See, e.g., Ethan Herenstein and Yurij Rudensky, "The Penalty Clause and the Fourteenth Amendment's Consistency on Universal Representation," *New York University Law Review* 96 (2021): 1021.

19. See, e.g., Gary Y. Okihiro, ed., *Encyclopedia of Japanese American Internment* (New York: Bloomsbury Publishing, 2013), 32–35; Public proclamation No. 4, March 27, 1942; American Civil Liberties Union of Northern California Records—Case Files, 1934–1993—Korematsu, Fred, 1942–1946—California Courts 1942–1944, MS-3580_1385; California Historical Society.

20. U.S. Congress, Commission on Wartime Relocation and Internment of Civilians, "Personal Justice Denied: Report of the Commission on Wartime Relocation and Internment of Civilians," 66 (1982).

21. National Archives, "Executive Order 9066: Resulting in Japanese-American Incarceration (1942)," www.archives.gov/milestone

-documents/executive-order-9066; "Japanese Americans in World War II and the Census," "Power and the People: The U.S. Census and Who Counts," exhibit, Berkeley Library, University of California, https://exhibits.lib.berkeley.edu/spotlight/census/feature/japanese -americans-in-world-war-ii-and-the-census.

22. John DeWitt, *Japanese Evacuation from the West Coast, 1942: Final Report* (Washington, D.C.: U.S. Government Printing Office, 1943), https://archive.org/details/japaneseevacuati00dewi/page/n5/mode/2up; see also Margo Anderson, "The Census and the Japanese 'Internment': Apology and Policy in Statistical Practice," *Social Research* 87 no. 4 (2020): 789–812.

23. *Korematsu v. United States,* 323 U.S. 214 (1944). See also Todd C. Peppers, "Justice Hugo L. Black, His Chambers Staff, and the Ku Klux Klan Controversy of 1937," Supreme Court Historical Society, April 27, 2021, https://supremecourthistory.org/scotus-scoops/justice-hugo-black-ku -klux-klan-controversy-1937/.

24. Kathryn M. Stanchi, "The Rhetoric of Racism in the United States Supreme Court," *Boston College Law Review* 62 (2021): 1251, 1253.

25. *Korematsu v. United States,* 323 U.S. 214, 242 (1944) (Murphy, J., dissenting).

26. See, e.g., Anderson, "Census and the Japanese 'Internment.' "

27. *Id.* See also Lynette Clemetson, "Homeland Security Given Data on Arab-Americans," *New York Times,* July 30, 2004, www.nytimes .com/2004/07/30/us/homeland-security-given-data-on-arab-americans .html.

28. Jessica Taylor, "Trump Calls for 'Total and Complete Shutdown of Muslims Entering' U.S.," NPR, Dec. 7, 2015, www.npr.org/2015/12/07 /458836388/trump-calls-for-total-and-complete-shutdown-of-muslims -entering-u-s.

29. Brief of Karen Korematsu, Jay Hirabayashi, Holly Yasui, The Fred T. Korematsu Center for Law and Equality, Civil Rights Organizations, and National Bar Associations of Color as Amici Curiae in Support of Respondents at 20–21, *Trump v. Hawaii,* 138 S. Ct. 2392 (2018).

30. *Trump v. Hawaii,* 138 S. Ct. 2392, 2423 (2018).

31. Michael F. Leonen, "Etiquette for Activists," *Yes,* May 21, 2004, www .yesmagazine.org/issue/hope-conspiracy/2004/05/21/etiquette-for -activists (describing hearing Murri artist and activist Lilla Watson say "If you have come to help me, I don't need your help. But if you have come because your liberation is tied to mine, come let us work together").

32. James Baldwin, "An Open Letter to My Sister, Miss Angela Davis," *New York Review of Books,* Nov. 19, 1970, www.nybooks.com /articles/1971/01/07/an-open-letter-to-my-sister-miss-angela-davis/.

33. Anderson, "Census and the Japanese 'Internment.'" See also Clemetson, "Homeland Security Given Data on Arab-Americans."
34. Michael Wines, "Deceased G.O.P. Strategist's Hard Drives Reveal New Details on the Census Citizenship Question," *New York Times,* May 30, 2019, www.nytimes.com/2019/05/30/us/census-citizenship-question-hofeller.html.
35. David Daley, "The Secret Files of the Master of Modern Republican Gerrymandering," *The New Yorker,* Sept. 6, 2019, www.newyorker.com/news/news-desk/the-secret-files-of-the-master-of-modern-republican-gerrymandering.
36. New York Immigration Coalition Plaintiffs' Motion for an Order to Show Cause in *New York v. Department of Commerce,* 18-CV-2921, Exhibit D, "The Use of Citizen Voting Age Population in Redistricting" available at www.commoncause.org/wp-content/uploads/2019/05/2015-Hofeller-Study.pdf (hereinafter "Hofeller Study").
37. Edwin Flores, "A Quarter of All U.S. Children Are Latino, U.S. Census Study Finds," ABC News, June 2, 2023, www.nbcnews.com/news/latino/quarter-children-us-are-latino-us-census-study-finds-rcna87253.
38. See, e.g., Jowei Chen and Nicholas O. Stephanopoulos, "Democracy's Denominator," *California Law Review* 109 (2021): 1019, 1022 ("To reiterate, we find a significant decline in the volume of minority opportunity districts, and a smaller drop in the volume of Democratic districts, when districts equalize CVAP rather than total population").
39. Hofeller Study at 8–9.
40. Text of Dec. 2017 DOJ Letter to Census, Contributed by Justin Elliott (ProPublica), www.documentcloud.org/documents/4340651-Text-of-Dec-2017-DOJ-letter-to-Census.
41. Sam Levine, "'An Embarrassment': Trump's Justice Department Goes Quiet on Voting Rights," *The Guardian,* June 23, 2020, www.theguardian.com/us-news/2020/jun/23/us-justice-department-voting-rights-2020-election.
42. See, e.g., Brief of the Leadership Conference on Civil and Human Rights, the Brennan Center for Justice at NYU School of Law, and Civil Society Organizations as Amici Curiae in Support of Respondents, *Department of Commerce v. New York,* 139 S. Ct. 2551 (2019); Brief of NAACP Legal Defense and Educational Fund, Inc. of Amicus Curiae in Support of Respondents, *Department of Commerce v. New York,* 139 S. Ct. 2551 (2019); Brief of National Asian Pacific American Bar Association, Asian American Legal Defense and Education Fund et al. as Amici Curiae in Support of Respondents, *Department of Commerce v. New York,* 139 S. Ct. 2551 (2019).
43. See, e.g., *New York v. Department of Commerce,* 351 F. Supp. 3d 502, 565–71 (S.D.N.Y. 2019).
44. Commerce Secretary Wilbur Ross's Memo on 2020 Census Citizen-

ship Question, Contributed by Hansi Lo Wang (NPR), www.document
cloud.org/documents/4426785-commerce2018-03-26-2#document
/p4/a2012969.

45. *Department of Commerce v. New York,* 139 S. Ct. 2551 (2019).

46. 5 U.S.C. § 706.

47. Hansi Lo Wang, "Jeff Sessions Told DOJ Not to Discuss Citizenship
Question Alternative," NPR, Oct. 27, 2018, www.npr.org/2018/10/27
/661270003/jeff-sessions-told-doj-not-to-discuss-citizenship-question
-alternatives; Hansi Lo Wang, "How the 2020 Census Citizenship
Question Ended Up in Court," NPR, Nov. 4, 2018, www.npr.org
/2018/11/04/661932989/how-the-2020-census-citizenship-question
-ended-up-in-court.

48. *New York v. Department of Commerce,* 351 F. Supp. 3d 502, 516
(S.D.N.Y.) (2019).

49. See, e.g., Kelly Percival, "What the Blockbuster Documents Uncovered
This Week Mean for the Census Citizenship Case at the Supreme
Court," Brennan Center for Justice, www.brennancenter.org/our-work
/analysis-opinion/what-blockbuster-documents-uncovered-week-mean
-census-citizenship-case; Jacqueline Thomsen, "Supreme Court Set to
Deliver Ruling on Census Citizenship Question," *The Hill,* June 23,
2019, https://thehill.com/regulation/court-battles/449869-supreme
-court-set-to-deliver-ruling-on-census-citizenship-question/.

50. Robert L. Tsai, "Equality Is a Brokered Idea," *George Washington Law
Review Arguendo* 88 (2020): 1, 9.

51. *Department of Commerce v. New York,* 139 S. Ct. 2551, 2575 (2019)
(quoting *United States v. Stanchich,* 550 F.2d 1294, 1300 [CA2 1977]
[Friendly, J.]).

52. *Department of Commerce v. New York,* 139 S. Ct. 2551, 2575 (2019).

53. *Department of Commerce v. New York,* 139 S. Ct. 2551, 2575 (2019).

54. Adam Liptak, "Supreme Court Leaves Census Question on Citizenship
in Doubt," *New York Times,* June 27, 2019, www.nytimes.com
/2019/06/27/us/politics/census-citizenship-question-supreme-court
.html; Kelly Percival and Brianna Cea, "Four Takeaways from the Supreme Court's Census Citizenship Question Ruling," Brennan Center
for Justice, July 1, 2019, www.brennancenter.org/our-work/analysis
-opinion/four-takeaways-supreme-courts-census-citizenship-question
-ruling.

55. *Department of Commerce v. New York,* 139 S. Ct. 2551, 2576 (2019).

56. See, e.g., Michael J. Klarman, "Foreword: The Degradation of American
Democracy—and the Court," *Harvard Law Review* 134 (2020):
1, 264 (warning that "Plenty of younger Republican politicians with
equally autocratic instincts but a lot more intelligence, discipline, and
political skill are waiting in the wings and taking notes"); see also Richard L. Hasen, "The Supreme Court's Pro-Partisanship Turn," *George-*

town Law Journal Online 109 (2020): 50, 67–70 (describing Roberts leaving a "door open for animus laundering" in *Department of Commerce v. New York*).

57. Exec. Order No. 13,880, 84 Fed. Reg. 33,821, July 16, 2019, www .govinfo.gov/content/pkg/FR-2019-07-16/pdf/FR-2019-07-16.pdf.

58. Presidential Memorandum, 85 Fed. Reg. 44,679, July 23, 2020, www .govinfo.gov/content/pkg/FR-2020-07-23/pdf/2020-16216.pdf.

59. Miriam Jordan, "New Findings Detail Trump Plan to Use Census for Partisan Gain," *New York Times,* July 20, 2022, https://www.nytimes .com/2022/07/20/us/census-citizenship-question-oversight.html.

60. See, e.g., U.S. House of Representatives Committee on Oversight and Reform, Investigation of Census Citizenship Question Memorandum, July 20, 2022, https://oversightdemocrats.house.gov/sites/democrats .oversight.house.gov/files/2022.07.20%20COR%20Census%20 Memorandum.pdf.

61. *Id*.

62. Hearing on Counting Every Person: Safeguarding the 2020 Census Against the Trump Administration's Unconstitutional Attacks, Before the H. Comm. on Oversight and Reform, 116th Cong. (2020).

63. Hearing on Counting Every Person: Safeguarding the 2020 Census Against the Trump Administration's Unconstitutional Attacks, Before the H. Comm. on Oversight and Reform, 116th Cong. (2020) (Testimony of Vincent Barabba, Former Director, Census Bureau (1973–1976 and 1979–1981); Testimony of Kenneth Prewitt, Former Director, Census Bureau (1998–2001); Testimony of Robert M. Groves, Former Director, Census Bureau (2009–2012); Testimony of John H. Thompson, Former Director, Census Bureau (2013–2017).

64. Hearing on Counting Every Person: Safeguarding the 2020 Census Against the Trump Administration's Unconstitutional Attacks, Before the H. Comm. on Oversight and Reform, 116th Cong. (2020) (Testimony of John Eastman, Henry Salvatori Professor of Law and Community Service Director, Center for Constitutional Jurisprudence, Dale E. Fowler School of Law, Chapman University, and Senior Fellow, Claremont Institute).

65. Charlie Savage and Adam Goldman, "The Trump Jan. 6 Indictment, Annotated," *New York Times,* Aug. 1, 2023, www.nytimes.com/interactive /2023/08/01/us/politics/trump-jan-6-indictment-2020-election -annotated.html; John Eastman, "January 6 Scenario Memorandum," CNN, Jan. 2020, https://cdn.cnn.com/cnn/2021/images/09/20/eastman .memo.pdf. See also "'We the People' Does Not Include Foreign Nationals"—Testimony of Dr. John C. Eastman before the United States House of Representatives Committee on Oversight and Reform, Hearing on "Counting Every Person: Safeguarding the 2020 Census Against the Trump Administration's Unconstitutional Attacks," July 20,

2020, https://docs.house.gov/meetings/GO/GO00/20200729/110948
/HHRG-116-GO00-Wstate-EastmanJ-20200729.pdf.

66. *Id.*

67. See, e.g., U.S. Census Bureau, 1860 Census: Population of the United States at vi–vii, xi, xv–xvi (Gov't Printing Office, 1864); *City of San Jose, California v. Trump,* 497 F. Supp. 3d 680, 693 (N.D. Cal. 2020) ("For example, escaped slaves who were unlawfully present in northern states were counted in the 1860 Census as part of the apportionment base in those northern states").

68. Cong. Globe, 39th Cong., 1st Sess. 141 (1866).

69. Cong. Globe, 39th Cong., 1st Sess. 359 (1866). (Over 150 years ago, Rep. Conkling of New York stated on the House floor, "It has been insisted that 'citizens of the United States' and not 'persons' should be the basis of representation and apportionment. These words were in the amendment as I originally drew it and introduced it, but my own judgment was that it should be 'persons,' and to this the committee assented. There are several answers to the argument in favor of 'citizens' rather than 'persons.' The present Constitution is, and always was, opposed to this suggestion. 'Persons,' and not 'citizens,' have always constituted the basis.")

70. See, e.g., Brief of National Congress of American Indians as Amicus Curiae in Support of Appellees, *Trump v. New York,* 141 S. Ct. 530, 536 (2020).

71. *Yick Wo v. Hopkins,* 118 U.S. 356, 369 (1886).

72. *Plyler v. Doe,* 457 U.S. 202, 221–22 (1982).

73. See, e.g., *Plyler v. Doe,* 457 U.S. 202, 210 (1982).

74. See, e.g., Brief of the United States House of Representatives as Amicus Curiae in Support of Appellees, *Trump v. New York,* 141 S. Ct. 530 (2020) (discussing the Executive Branch's consistent recognition that apportionment must be based on total population"); *City of San Jose v. Trump,* 497 F. Supp. 3d 680, 723–29 (N.D. Cal. 2020) (discussing Congress's and the Executive Branch's consistently interpreting the Constitution as requiring the inclusion of all of a state's residents in the apportionment base, including undocumented residents).

75. *New York v. Trump,* 485 F. Supp. 3d 422, 435 (S.D.N.Y. 2020).

76. *Trump v. New York,* 141 S. Ct. 530, 541 (2020) (Breyer, J., dissenting).

77. Exec. Order No. 13,986, 86 Fed. Reg. 7015, Jan. 20, 2021, www.govinfo .gov/content/pkg/FR-2021-01-25/pdf/2021-01755.pdf.

78. See, e.g., Brief of Ilya Somin and Sanford Levinson as Amicus Curiae in Support of Appellees, *Trump v. New York,* 141 S. Ct. 530 (2020).

79. Complaint, *Alabama v. U.S. Dept. of Commerce,* Civil Action No.: 2:18-CV-00772-RDP, May 21, 2018.

80. *Id.*

81. *Dred Scott v. Sandford,* 60 U.S. 393, 411 (1857).

82. Cong. Globe, 39th Cong., 1st Sess. 705 (1866).

83. Jennifer M. Chacón, *The Inside-Out Constitution: Department of Commerce v. New York,* 2019 Sup. Ct. Rev. 231, 235 (2019).

84. See, e.g., Ming Hsu Chen, "The Political (Mis)representation of Immigrants in the Census," *New York University Law Review* 96 (2021): 901.

85. See, e.g., Stephanie Mencimer, "The Craziest Thing About This Supreme Court Case Isn't That One Plaintiff Believes Unicorns Are Real," *Mother Jones,* Dec. 4, 2015, www.motherjones.com/politics/2015/12 /evenwel-abbott-supreme-court-redistricting/; Sue Evenwel, "The Islamization of America?," *Mount Pleasant Daily Tribune,* March 13, 2011.

86. *Id.* See also Stephanie Mencimer, "Meet the Brains Behind the Effort to Get the Supreme Court to Rethink Civil Rights," *Mother Jones,* March/April 2016, www.motherjones.com/politics/2016/04/edward -blum-supreme-court-affirmative-action-civil-rights/; Jon Booth, "While You're Busy Mocking Abigail Fisher, the Powerful Racist Forces Behind Her Are Getting a Pass," *In These Times,* June 27, 2016, https:// inthesetimes.com/article/abigail-fisher-affirmative-action-supreme -court-project-fair-representation; Anemona Hartocollis, "He Took On the Voting Rights Act and Won. Now He's Taking On Harvard," *New York Times,* Nov. 19, 2017, www.nytimes.com/2017/11/19/us/affirmative -action-lawsuits.html; Jean Guerrero, "Affirmative Action Challenges Aren't about Ending Discrimination. Their Goal Is White Supremacy," *Los Angeles Times,* Nov. 21, 2022, www.latimes.com/opinion/story /2022-11-21/affirmative-action-racism-supreme-court-white -supremacists.

87. *Evenwel v. Abbott,* 578 U.S. 54, 64 (2016).

88. See, e.g., *Evenwel v. Abbott,* 578 U.S. 54, 74 (2016).

89. See, e.g., Domenico Montanaro, "Poll: Despite Record Turnout, 80 Million Americans Didn't Vote. Here's Why," *NPR Morning Edition,* NPR, Dec. 15, 2020, www.npr.org/2020/12/15/945031391/poll-despite -record-turnout-80-million-americans-didnt-vote-heres-why.

90. Hearing on Counting Every Person: Safeguarding the 2020 Census Against the Trump Administration's Unconstitutional Attacks, Before the H. Comm. on Oversight and Reform, 116th Cong. (2020).

91. See, e.g., Anderson, *American Census,* 4, 14–16.

92. Library of Congress, "History of the U.S. Census," https://guides.loc .gov/census-connections/census-history.

93. "2020 Census Innovation," U.S. Census Bureau, Dec. 12, 2019, www .census.gov/newsroom/press-kits/2019/2020-census-innovation.html.

94. See, e.g., "2020 Census Integrated Communications Plan Final Report," U.S. Census Bureau, May 27, 2021, 26–27, https://www2.census

.gov/programs-surveys/decennial/2020/program-management
/planning-docs/integrated-communications-plan-final-report.pdf.

95. Ron Jarmin, "Counting Everyone Once, Only Once, and in the Right
Place," U.S. Census Bureau, Nov. 5, 2018, www.census.gov/newsroom
/blogs/director/2018/11/counting_everyoneon.html.

96. *Id.*

97. "Census Bureau Releases Estimates of Undercount and Overcount in
the 2020 Census," U.S. Census Bureau, March 10, 2022, www.census
.gov/newsroom/press-releases/2022/2020-census-estimates-of-under
count-and-overcount.html.

98. *Id.*

99. *Id.*

100. Eric Jensen, "Census Bureau Expands Focus on Improving Data for
Young Children," U.S. Census Bureau, March 10, 2022, www.census
.gov/library/stories/2022/03/despite-efforts-census-undercount-of
-young-children-persists.html.

101. See, e.g., Linda A. Jacobsen, "How Accurate Was the 2020 Census—and
Why Should You Care?," Population Reference Bureau, Feb. 10, 2023,
www.prb.org/resources/how-accurate-was-the-2020-census-and-why
-should-you-care/.

102. "Census Bureau Releases Estimates of Undercount and Overcount
in the 2020 Census," U.S. Census Bureau, March 10, 2022, www
.census.gov/newsroom/press-releases/2022/2020-census-estimates
-of-undercount-and-overcount.html.

103. "2020 Census Undercounts in Six States, Overcounts in Eight," America Counts Staff, U.S. Census Bureau, May 19, 2022, www.census.gov
/library/stories/2022/05/2020-census-undercount-overcount-rates
-by-state.html; "Census Bureau Releases Results of Post-Enumeration
Survey for Puerto Rico From 2020 Census," U.S. Census Bureau,
Aug. 12, 2022, www.census.gov/newsroom/press-releases/2022/2020
-post-enumeration-survey-results-puerto-rico.html.

104. Tommy Wright and Joyce Farmer, "A Bibliography of Selected Statistical Methods and Development Related to Census 2000," Statistical
Research Report Series No. RR 2000/02, U.S. Census Bureau Statistical Research Division, Aug. 10, 2000, www.census.gov/history/pdf
/Wright.pdf.

105. *Id.* at iv.

106. "A Census That Mirrors America: Interim Report," National Academies
of Sciences, Engineering, and Medicine, National Academies Press,
Washington, D.C., 1993, https://doi.org/10.17226/2234.

107. 13 U.S.C. § 195.

108. *Dep't of Commerce v. U.S. House of Representatives,* 525 U.S. 316
(1999).

109. *Dep't of Commerce v. U.S. House of Representatives,* 525 U.S. 316, 343–44 (1999).
110. *Id.* at 344–49 (Scalia, J., concurring).
111. *Id.* at 346 (Scalia, J., concurring).
112. *Id.* at 346–47 (Scalia, J., concurring).
113. *Id.* at 348 (Scalia, J., concurring).
114. *Dep't of Commerce v. U.S. House of Representatives,* 525 U.S. 316, 362–64 (1999) (Stevens, J., dissenting).
115. Todd R. Williams, Statistical Research Report Series No. RR98/07, "Imputing Person Age for the 2000 Census Short Form: A Model-Based Approach," Statistical Research Division, U.S. Bureau of the Census, Dec. 17, 1998, www.census.gov/content/dam/Census/library /working-papers/1998/adrm/rr98-07.pdf; "Data Editing and Imputation," U.S. Census Bureau, Aug. 18, 2022, www.census.gov/programs -surveys/sipp/methodology/data-editing-and-imputation.html.
116. *Utah v. Evans,* 536 U.S. 452, 457 (2002).
117. See, e.g., *Utah v. Evans,* 536 U.S. 452, 465–70 (2002).
118. *Id.* at 473–79.
119. *Id.* at 478–79.
120. *Id.* at 503 (Thomas, J., dissenting).
121. *Id.* at 509 (Thomas, J., dissenting).
122. *Id.* at 500–503 (Thomas, J., dissenting).
123. See, e.g., Thomas Wolf, Brianna Cea, Kelly Percival, Madiba Dennie, and Clara Fong, "Improving the Census: Legal and Policy Reforms for a More Accurate, Equitable, and Legitimate Count," Brennan Center for Justice, Sept. 13, 2022, www.brennancenter.org/our-work/policy -solutions/improving-census.
124. Siegel, "How 'History and Tradition' Perpetuates Inequality," 901, 911.

Chapter 5: Taking It All Back

1. Baumgardner, "Originalism and the Academy in Exile," 787, 794.
2. See, e.g., David S. Cohen, Greer Donley, and Rachel Rebouché, "Re-thinking Strategy After Dobbs," *Stanford Law Review Online* 75 (2022): 1, 7; Jack M. Balkin, "From Off the Wall to On the Wall: How the Mandate Challenge Went Mainstream," *The Atlantic,* June 4, 2012, http://perma.cc/6ZGC-SU79.
3. Frank Crosby, ed., *Life of Abraham Lincoln, sixteenth president of the United States. Containing his early history and political career; to-gether with the speeches, messages, proclamations and other official documents illustrative of his eventful administration* (Philadelphia: John E. Potter, 1865), 435, https://quod.lib.umich.edu/l/lincoln2/ack 7441.0001.001/437.

4. *Students for Fair Admissions, Inc. v. President & Fellows of Harvard Coll.*, 143 S. Ct. 2141, 2263 (2023) (Sotomayor, J., dissenting).

5. See generally work by scholars including Bruce Ackerman, Jack Balkin, Robert Cover, William Eskridge, Lani Guinier, Michael Klarman, Larry Kramer, Sanford Levinson, Robert Post, and Reva Siegel, the influence of which permeates this book and extends beyond any one endnote.

6. Douglas NeJaime, "Constitutional Change, Courts, and Social Movements," *Michigan Law Review* 111 (2013): 877, 881.

7. *Gayle v. Browder*, 352 U.S. 903 (1956); Martin Luther King, Jr., *Stride toward Freedom: The Montgomery Story* (Boston: Beacon Press, 2010), 29 (discussing the "nearly fifty thousand people, tired people who had come to see that it is ultimately more honorable to walk the streets in dignity than to ride the buses in humiliation").

8. "Roadmap to Victory," Freedom to Marry, http://www.freedomtomarry .org/pages/Roadmap-to-Victory; Evan Wolfson, "'Love is Love' and Other Stories: The Role of Narrative in Winning the Freedom to Marry," *The Forge*, July 22, 2020, https://forgeorganizing.org/article /love-love-and-other-stories-role-narrative-winning-freedom-marry.

9. *Lawrence v. Texas*, 539 U.S. 558 (2003).

10. *Lawrence v. Texas*, 539 U.S. 558, 571–72 (2003).

11. *Kitchen v. Herbert*, 961 F. Supp. 2d 1181, 1203 (D. Utah 2013), aff'd, 755 F.3d 1193 (10th Cir. 2014).

12. *Bowers v. Hardwick*, 478 U.S. 186, 190–91, 195–96 (1986).

13. Letter, Billy Gobitas to Minersville, Pennsylvania, school directors, explaining why the young Jehovah's Witness refused to salute the American flag. November 5, 1935. Manuscript/Mixed Material. Retrieved from the Library of Congress, www.loc.gov/item/mcc.016/.

14. *Minersville Sch. Dist. v. Gobitis*, 310 U.S. 586, 592 (1940).

15. Brad Snyder, "Frankfurter and Popular Constitutionalism," *U.C. Davis Law Review* 47 (2013): 343, 373–74 (describing Justice Frankfurter's involvement in the war mobilization effort); Robert L. Tsai, "Reconsidering Gobitis: An Exercise in Presidential Leadership," *Washington University Law Review* 86 (2008): 363, 381–83 (discussing presidential rhetoric around national unity and cohesiveness on the eve of World War II and how it influenced the Court).

16. *Minersville Sch. Dist. v. Gobitis*, 310 U.S. 586, 595–96 (1940).

17. *Minersville Sch. Dist. v. Gobitis*, 310 U.S. 586, 601, 604 (1940) (Stone, J., dissenting).

18. *Minersville Sch. Dist. v. Gobitis*, 310 U.S. 586, 600 (1940).

19. Justin Driver, "The Supreme Court as Bad Teacher," *University of Pennsylvania Law Review* 169 (2021): 1365, 1408–1409.

20. *Id*.

21. See, e.g., *West Virginia State Bd. of Educ. v. Barnette*, 319 U.S. 624, 630 (1943).

22. Neal Devins and Louis Fisher, *The Democratic Constitution,* 2nd ed. (New York: Oxford University Press, 2015), 206; Snyder, "Frankfurter and Popular Constitutionalism," 343, 375.
23. Irons, *People's History of the Supreme Court,* rev. ed., 431.
24. Devins and Fisher, *Democratic Constitution,* 2nd ed., 207.
25. *Barnette v. W. Virginia State Bd. of Educ.,* 47 F. Supp. 251, 252–53 (S.D.W. Va. 1942). ("Ordinarily we would feel constrained to follow an unreversed decision of the Supreme Court of the United States, whether we agreed with it or not. [. . .] The developments with respect to the *Gobitis* case, however, are such that we do not feel that it is incumbent upon us to accept it as binding authority. Of the seven justices now members of the Supreme Court who participated in that decision, four have given public expression to the view that it is unsound. [. . .] Under such circumstances and believing, as we do, that the flag salute here required is violative of religious liberty when required of persons holding the religious views of plaintiffs, we feel that we would be recreant to our duty as judges, if through a blind following of a decision which the Supreme Court itself has thus impaired as an authority, we should deny protection to rights which we regard as among the most sacred of those protected by constitutional guaranties.")
26. Tsai, "Reconsidering Gobitis," 363, 406.
27. *Id.* at 403.
28. Franklin D. Roosevelt, "The Four Freedoms," State of the Union Address, Jan. 6, 1941.
29. Victor W. Rotnem and F. G. Folsom, "Recent Restrictions upon Religious Liberty," *American Political Science Review* 36, no. 6 (1942): 1053–68, https://doi.org/10.2307/1949065.
30. Noah Feldman, *Scorpions: The Battles and Triumphs of FDR's Great Supreme Court Justices* (New York: Twelve, 2010), 228 ("To liberals, tolerance, not saluting, had become the American form of patriotism").
31. *West Virginia State Bd. of Educ. v. Barnette,* 319 U.S. 624, 635 (1943).
32. Devins and Fisher, *Democratic Constitution,* 2nd ed., 208.
33. *West Virginia State Bd. of Educ. v. Barnette,* 319 U.S. 624, 634–35 (1943).
34. Tsai, "Reconsidering Gobitis," 363, 433.
35. *Bowers v. Hardwick,* 478 U.S. 186, 213–14 (1986) (Blackmun, J., dissenting).
36. Lani Guinier and Gerald Torres, "Changing the Wind: Notes toward a Demosprudence of Law and Social Movements," *Yale Law Journal* 123 (2014): 2740, 2752.
37. See, e.g., "Judicial Selection: An Interactive Map," Brennan Center for Justice, www.brennancenter.org/judicial-selection-map (last updated Oct. 11, 2022).
38. See, e.g., Brandon Hasbrouck, "Movement Judges," *New York Univer-*

sity Law Review 97 (2022): 631; Daniel Farbman, "Judicial Solidarity?," *Yale Journal of Law and the Humanities* 33 (2022): 1. For a discussion on keeping elected officials accountable to movements, see Mark Engler and Paul Engler, "Can Movements Keep Politicians from Inevitably Selling Out?," *The Forge*, April 3, 2023, https://forgeorganizing.org /article/can-movements-keep-politicians-inevitably-selling-out.

39. See, e.g., David E. Pozen, "Judicial Elections as Popular Constitutionalism," *Columbia Law Review* 110 (2010): 2047.

40. *Matter of Hawai'i Elec. Light Co., Inc.,* 152 Haw. 352 (2023).

41. *Juliana v. United States,* 217 F. Supp. 3d 1224, 1250 (D. Or. 2016); *Juliana v. United States,* 339 F. Supp. 3d 1062 (D. Or. 2018).

42. *Juliana v. United States,* 947 F.3d 1159, 1166, 1171 (9th Cir. 2020).

43. *Juliana v. United States,* 947 F.3d 1159, 1175 (9th Cir. 2020) (Staton, J., dissenting).

44. See, e.g., Glenn E. Martin, "Those Closest to the Problem Are Closest to the Solution," *The Appeal,* Sept. 22, 2017, https://theappeal.org /those-closest-to-the-problem-are-closest-to-the-solution-555e 04317b79/; Srilatha Batliwala, "All About Movements: Why Building Movements Creates Deeper Change," Creating Resources for Empowerment in Action, https://creaworld.org/wp-content/uploads/2020/12 /All-About-Movements_Web.pdf.

45. See, e.g., Patricia J. Williams, "Alchemical Notes: Reconstructing Ideals from Deconstructed Rights," *Harvard Civil Rights–Civil Liberties Law Review* 22 (1987): 401.

46. See, e.g., Archibald Cox, "Strikes, Picketing, and the Constitution," *Vanderbilt Law Review* 4 (1951): 574; James Gray Pope, "Labor's Constitution of Freedom," *Yale Law Journal* 106 (1997): 941; James Gray Pope, Ed Bruno, and Peter Kellman, "The Right to Strike," *Boston Review,* May 17, 2017, www.bostonreview.net/forum/james-gray-pope-ed -bruno-peter-kellman-right-strike/; Kate Andrias, "Peril and Possibility: Strikes, Rights, and Legal Change in the Age of Trump," *Berkeley Journal of Employment and Labor Law* 40 (2019): 135.

47. Andrias, "Peril and Possibility," 135.

48. *Id.* See also Diana S. Reddy, "'There Is No Such Thing as an Illegal Strike': Reconceptualizing the Strike in Law and Political Economy," *Yale Law Journal Forum* 130 (2021): 421.

49. See, e.g., Emily Bazelon, "The Surprising Places Where Abortion Rights Are on the Ballot, and Winning," *New York Times,* Sept. 12, 2023, www.nytimes.com/2023/09/12/magazine/abortion-laws-states .html; Grace Panetta, "The 19th Explains: What to Know About Ohio Issue 1," *The 19th,* Oct. 16, 2023, https://19thnews.org/2023/10/ohio -issue-1-what-to-know-abortion-amendment-november/.

50. See, e.g., Paul Butler, "In Defense of Jury Nullification," *Litigation* 31, no. 1 (Fall 2004): 46; Dinesh McCoy, Eli Hadley, and Rachel Foran,

"Voting 'Not Guilty': A Toolkit on Jury Nullification," *Beyond Criminal Courts,* July 2022, https://beyondcourts.org/en/act/voting-not-guilty -toolkit-jury-nullification.

51. A word of caution: those advocates were just engaging in general education, so the prosecutions were unsuccessful. However, if they were trying to influence a particular juror assigned to a particular case, it would be a different story. *Id.* See also Janet Oravetz, "Colorado Supreme Court Sides with 2 Men Accused of Jury Tampering," KUSA Channel 9 (Denver), Sept. 24, 2019, www.9news.com/article/news/local/colorado -supreme-court-jury-tampering-ruling/73-5e6ad145-4c86-4265-8433 -d4f3712cbc81.

52. See, e.g., McCoy, Hadley, and Foran, "Voting 'Not Guilty.' "

53. See, e.g., John Ruch, "Major Human Rights, Press Freedom Groups Condemn RICO Charges against 'Cop City' Activists," *Saporta Report,* Sept. 28, 2023, https://saportareport.com/major-human-rights-press -freedom-groups-condemn-rico-charges-against-cop-city-activists /sections/reports/johnruch/.

54. See, e.g., Madiba Dennie and Jackie Fielding, "Miscarriage of Justice: The Danger of Laws Criminalizing Pregnancy Outcomes," *Ms.,* Nov. 9, 2021, https://msmagazine.com/2021/11/09/miscarriage-criminalizing -pregnancy-outcomes-unconstitutional-abortion-ban/; Robert Baldwin III, "Losing a Pregnancy Could Land You in Jail in Post-Roe America," July 3, 2022, https://www.npr.org/2022/07/03/1109015302/abortion -prosecuting-pregnancy-loss.

55. Butler, "In Defense of Jury Nullification," 46, 47.

56. Renee Winkler, "Camden 28 Testimony Again Fills Courtroom," *Courier-Post* (Cherry Hill, N.J.), May 5, 2002.

57. Donald Jansen, "17 of Camden 28 Found Not Guilty," *New York Times,* May 21, 1973, www.nytimes.com/1973/05/21/archives/17-of-camden -28-found-not-guilty-admitted-draftoffice-raidboth.html.

58. "The Story," *The Camden 28,* http://www.camden28.org/master .html?http://www.camden28.org/thestory.htm.

59. Renee Winkler, "Camden 28 Testimony Again Fills Courtroom," *Courier-Post* (Cherry Hill, N.J.), May 5, 2002.

60. See, e.g., "Excerpt: From the Trial of the Camden 28, Good: Sending Boys to Die for Tin, Rubber, and Oil," *POV,* http://archive.pov.org /camden28/excerpt-from-the-trial/8/.

61. See, e.g., "Excerpt: From the Trial of the Camden 28, Zinn: Civil Disobedience and Democracy," *POV,* http://archive.pov.org/camden28 /excerpt-from-the-trial/5/.

62. See, e.g., "Excerpt: From the Trial of the Camden 28, Introduction," *POV,* http://archive.pov.org/camden28/excerpt-from-the-trial/.

63. Jansen, "17 of Camden 28 Found Not Guilty."

64. Renee Winkler, "Camden 28 Testimony Again Fills Courtroom," *Courier-Post* (Cherry Hill, N.J.), May 5, 2002.

65. Tsai, "Reconsidering Gobitis," 363.

66. Yvonne Wingett Sanchez and Rob O'Dell, "What Is ALEC? 'The Most Effective Organization' for Conservatives, Says Newt Gingrich," *USA Today,* April 3, 2019, www.usatoday.com/story/news/investigations /2019/04/03/alec-american-legislative-exchange-council-model-bills -republican-conservative-devos-gingrich/3162357002/.

67. "Chapter 16: The Albany Movement," Martin Luther King, Jr. Research and Education Institute, Stanford University, https://kinginstitute .stanford.edu/publications/autobiography-martin-luther-king-jr /chapter-16-albany-movement.

68. See, e.g., Madiba Dennie, "Supreme Court Expansion Is About More Than Avenging Merrick Garland," *Balls and Strikes,* Dec. 13, 2021, https://ballsandstrikes.org/court-reform/supreme-court-reform -garland-vengeance/.

69. See, e.g., Laura Krugman Ray, "Justice Brennan and the Jurisprudence of Dissent," *Temple Law Review* 61 (1988): 307.

70. See, e.g., Justice William J. Brennan, Jr., "In Defense of Dissents," *Hastings Law Journal* 37 (1986): 427, 430; Diane P. Wood, "When to Hold, When to Fold, and When to Reshuffle: The Art of Decisionmaking on a Multi-Member Court," *California Law Review* 100 (2012): 1445; compare the shift from *Evans v. Newton,* 382 U.S. 296 (1966) to *Evans v. Abney,* 396 U.S. 435 (1970).

71. Orit Gan, "I Dissent: Justice Ginsburg's Profound Dissents," *Rutgers University Law Review* 74 (2022): 1037.

72. See, e.g., James Romoser, "John Roberts Is the Chief. But It's Clarence Thomas's Court," *SCOTUSblog,* Oct. 2, 2022, www.scotusblog.com /2022/10/john-roberts-is-the-chief-but-its-clarence-thomass-court/.

73. Robert L. Tsai, "Supreme Court Precedent and the Politics of Repudiation," in *Law's Infamy: Understanding the Canon of Bad Law,* ed. Austin Sarat, Lawrence Douglas, and Martha Merrill Umphrey (New York: NYU Press, 2021).

74. See, e.g., Todd E. Pettys, "Judging Hypocrisy," *Emory Law Journal* 70 (2020): 251, 278.

INDEX

Rucho and, 143
substantive due process and, 99
use of law to diffuse power, 60

Jackson, Andrew, 196
Jackson, Ketanji Brown, 31–32, 34
Jackson, Robert, 194
Jefferson, Thomas, 5
Jim Crow 2.0, 102–3, 248n10
Jones, Amelia, 242n109
judiciary
development of pipeline for
future appointees, 211–12
duty of, to ensure democracy
works for marginalized
people, 47–48
Federalist Society and, 50
importance of states', 197–99
as instrument for change, 24
living constitutionalism
unrestrained, 38–40
originalism and restraint of, 28
partisan gerrymandering as
political issue beyond, 137, 138
power grab by, 67
power of, 217–18
responsibility of, 142
Juliana v. United States (2020),
198–99
jury duty, 203
jury nullification, 203–7, 272n51

Kagan, Elena
Brnovich and, 133
Dobbs and, 241n94
First Amendment and voting,
145
Gill and, 145, 146
progressive originalism and, 30
Rucho and, 141, 146
Katzenbach, South Carolina v.,
112–13, 115
Kavanaugh, Brett, 148, 258n254
Kendall, Doug, 35

Kennedy, Anthony
census use of sampling and,
179–80, 181
consensual gay sex and, 55, 82
First Amendment and voting,
144
on growing awareness of gay
rights, 190
Shelby and, 252n73
Kennedy, Ted, 28–29
*Kennedy v. Bremerton School
District,* 216
King, Martin Luther, Jr., 212
Korematsu v. United States (1944),
155–56

Law for Black Lives, 211
"law office history" methodology, 7
Lawrence v. Texas (2003), 16, 57,
81–83, 92
Lawyers' Committee for Civil Rights
Under Law, 140–41
legal interpretative method,
elements of, 4
Lemley, Mark, 114
Leo, Leonard, 52
Lewis, John, 101
liberal originalism, 30, 31–32, 38
Lincoln, Abraham, 186–87
living constitutionalism
as American tradition, 41–42
discrimination and, 36–37,
231n134
unrestrained judiciary and,
38–40
Lochner v. New York (1905), 57–60,
65, 67, 237n23
Loving v. Virginia, 16, 68–73, 80,
238n63

Madison, James, 151
marginalized people. *See also* gay
rights; race; voting rights
Barnette and, 194–95

Blum and, 174
effects of, 117–19
"equal sovereignty" and, 108–9,
115, 121
NAMUDNO and, 111–12, 113,
115
Supreme Court decision, 115–17,
252n73
Tenth Amendment and, 109
Siegel, Reva
on backward- and forward-
looking interpretation, 183
Constitution's inability to be
fixed and uninterpretable, 38,
231n139
Dobbs as example of living
constitutionalism, 40
on modern substantive due
process cases, 60
originalists' use of history, 35
Sims, Reynolds v. (1964), 142
socialism and *Lochner*, 58–59
social movements
appeals to Constitution in
advocacy of, 199–200
ballot initiatives enhancing
democracy, 202–3
Equal Protection Clause and, 38
role of, in changing Supreme
Court decisions, 188–90,
192–95, 196
role of attorneys in, 208–12
tactics of, 207–8
"trigger laws" enhancing
democracy, 201–2
Sotomayor, Sonia, 27, 187, 216,
241n94
South Carolina v. Katzenbach,
112–13, 115
Southern Manifesto, 22, 103
Sparkman, John, 44
state legislatures, 17, 232n145
Stephanopoulos, Nicholas, 47–48
Stewart, Potter, 67

Stone, Harlan, 194
Storer, Horatio, 243n121
*Students for Fair Admissions
[SFFA] v. University of
North Carolina [UNC],* 32,
34, 174
*Students for Fair Admissions v.
Harvard College,* 174
Sumner, Charles, 53, 89, 235n2
Sunstein, Cass, 246n151
Supreme Court
apportionment for elections
precedents, 170, 265n74
conservative supermajority on,
26, 27
history of failure to protect rights
of marginalized people, 26,
228n90
importance of dissents, 215–16
opinions of, as definitive
statements of law, 188
as product and source of
antidemocracy, 39
reputation of legitimacy of, 209,
213
role of laypeople in decisions,
187–96, 270n25

Tenth Amendment, 108, 109
Third Amendment, 66
Thirteenth Amendment, 6,
200–201
Thomas, Clarence
Allen and, 148
Brnovich and, 133, 134
census use of sampling and,
179–80, 181
as choosing specific point in
history to support argument,
10–11
desire to end substantive due
process, 96
Dobbs and, 16, 85
effect of dissents by, 216

ABOUT THE AUTHOR

MADIBA K. DENNIE is the deputy editor and senior contributor at the critical legal commentary website *Balls and Strikes* and the co-director of the Democracy Committee of the New Jersey Reparations Council. Her work as an attorney, columnist, and professor focuses on fostering an equitable multiracial democracy. In her previous role as a counsel at the Brennan Center for Justice, she provided legal and policy analysis regarding a range of democracy issues including the census, the courts, and attempts to disempower communities of color. Her legal and political commentary has been featured in *The Atlantic, The Washington Post, The New Republic,* and elsewhere. She has been interviewed on-air about race, gender, and the law on outlets including the BBC and MSNBC. She has taught at Western Washington University and NYU School of Law. Dennie earned her law degree from Columbia Law School and her undergraduate degree from Princeton University. *The Originalism Trap* is her first book.

madibadennie.com
X: @AudreLawdAMercy